5/12

Obama at the Crossroads

OBAMA AT THE CROSSROADS

Politics, Markets, and the Battle for America's Future

Edited by

LAWRENCE R. JACOBS
AND
DESMOND KING

OXFORD
UNIVERSITY PRESS

Oxford University Press, Inc., publishes works that further
Oxford University's objective of excellence
in research, scholarship, and education.

Oxford   New York
Auckland   Cape Town   Dares Salaam   Hong Kong   Karachi
KualaLumpur   Madrid   Melbourne   Mexico City   Nairobi
NewDelhi   Shanghai   Taipei   Toronto

With offices in
Argentina   Austria   Brazil   Chile   Czech Republic   France   Greece
Guatemala   Hungary   Italy   Japan   Poland   Portugal   Singapore
SouthKorea   Switzerland   Thailand   Turkey   Ukraine   Vietnam

Copyright © 2012 by Oxford University Press

Published by Oxford University Press, Inc.
198 Madison Avenue, New York, New York 10016

www.oup.com

Oxford is a registered trademark of Oxford University Press

Library of Congress Cataloging-in-Publication Data
Obama at the crossroads : politics, markets, and the battle for America's future / edited by
Lawrence R. Jacobs and Desmond S. King.
     p.   cm.
Includes bibliographical references and index.
ISBN 978-0-19-984536-1 (hbk. : acid-free paper) — ISBN 978-0-19-984538-5 (pbk. : acid-free paper)
1. United States—Politics and government—2009– 2. Obama, Barack—Political and social views.
3. United States—Economic policy—2009– 4. United States—Social policy—1993– 5. Financial crises—United
States—History—21st century. 6. Health care reform—United States—History—21st century.
7. Race—Political aspects—United States—History—21st century. 8. United States—Foreign relations—2009–
9. Political leadership—United States—History—21st century. 10. Progressivism (United States politics)—
History—21st century. I. Jacobs, Lawrence R. II. King, Desmond S.
E907.O215   2012
973.932092—dc23   2011032009

Table of Contents

PART IV: *Obama's Critical Juncture*

Acknowledgments

THIS VOLUME ORIGINATED as the second conference at Nuffield College, Oxford, devoted to bringing a political economy approach to understanding American politics. Even before the 2008 financial crises that saw long-time Wall Street banks like Lehman Brothers fail and unemployment soar, it was apparent that the American economy and political system were stretching sustainability, pervaded with contradictions and tensions. Making sense of these cross-pressures within the miasma of deepening partisan polarization and sharp electoral shifts requires a broader perspective than the typical approach to scholarly analysis of American politics—one that is common in Europe and in the study of comparative politics. Filling this gap is the purpose of the Nuffield series.

The first Nuffield conference in May 2008 focused on America's unsustainable state, bringing together a group of American and European scholars to identify and explain the growing instability of the intermeshed systems of U.S. politics and economics. The conference produced *The Unsustainable American State* in 2009 (Oxford University Press).

The present volume originated from the second Nuffield conference on American political economy, which occurred in March 2010 and focused on the Obama presidency. Where much analysis of the Obama presidency has been preoccupied with his personality (dithering and lacking conviction) or with important narrow questions related to changing party strategy and rules within Congress, *Obama at the Crossroads* offers a sustained analysis of Obama within America's political economic system.

The Nuffield series has been generously supported by the Mellon Trust Fund of Nuffield College, and we wish to thank this source for enabling valuable and unique intellectual collaborations and the resulting published volumes. The Rothermere American Institute at the University of Oxford generously hosted a public lecture by E. J. Dionne Jr. as part of the conference, for which we thank its director, Dr. Nigel Bowles. We also acknowledge support from the Hubert H. Humphrey School and Department of Political Science at the University of Minnesota and the Walter F. and Joan Mondale Chair for Political Studies.

The Oxford conference on Obama benefited greatly from a range of participants who acted as discussants and respondents to paper sessions. We are immensely grateful to these colleagues and wish to thank them for their valuable contributions: Joel Aberbach, Nancy Bermeo, Nadia Hilliard, Godfrey Hodgson, Christopher Hood, Jeffrey Isaac, Kimberley Johnson, Robin D.G. Kelley, Robert Kuttner, Patrick Le Gales, Robert Lieberman, James Purnell, Gwendolyn Sasse, Adam Sheingate, Marc Stears, Sven Steinmo, Helen Thompson, and Laurence Whitehead.

We have been fortunate that OUP's senior social science editor in New York, Dave McBride, has supported this intellectual endeavor, making decisive differences to this and the previous volume. We are very grateful to Dave for his intellectual support and editorial guidance, and to Niko Pfund, President of OUP New York, for his encouragement of the project. Alexandra Dauler and Caelyn Cobb, Dave's colleagues at OUP, have done an excellent job in putting the manuscript into production and print.

Contributors

Daniel Carpenter is Freed Professor of American Government and Director of the Center for American Political Studies at Harvard University. His publications include *The Forging of Bureaucratic Autonomy: Reputations, Networks and Policy Innovation in Executive Agencies 1862–1928* (2001) which won APSA's Kammerer Prize and IPSA's Charles Levine Prize, and *Reputation and Power: Organizational Image and Pharmaceutical Regulation at the FDA* (2010), which recently received a rare four-star rating from the *British Medical Journal*.

E. J. Dionne Jr. is an influential columnist on the *Washington Post*, having previously worked for the *New York Times*, and a commentator on American politics. He was a Rhodes Scholar at Balliol College, Oxford. He is University Professor at Georgetown University and a senior fellow at Brookings Institution. His publications include *Why Americans Hate Politics* (1991) and *They Only Look Dead: Why Progressives Will Dominate the Next Political Era* (1996). His numerous awards include the APSA's Carey McWilliams Award in 1996.

Lawrence R. Jacobs is the Walter F. and Joan Mondale Chair for Political Studies and Director of the Center for the Study of Politics and Governance in the Hubert H. Humphrey School and Department of Political Science at the University of Minnesota. Dr. Jacobs co-edits the *Chicago Series in American Politics* for the University of Chicago Press. His recent publications include *Health Care Reform and American Politics* (with Theda Skocpol, 2010); *Class War? What Americans Really Think about Economic Inequality* (with Ben Page, 2009); *Talking Together: Public Deliberation in America and the Search for Community* (with Fay Lomax Cook and Michael Delli Carpini, 2009), and *The Unsustainable American State* (co-edited with Desmond King, 2009).

Desmond King is Andrew W. Mellon Professor of American Government at the University of Oxford, and Fellow of Nuffield and St. John's Colleges, Oxford. He is a Fellow of the British Academy. His publications include *Actively Seeking Work? The Politics of Unemployment and Welfare in the US and Britain* (1995); *In the Name of Liberalism: Illiberal Social Policy in Britain and the US* (1999); *Democratization in America* (co-edited 2009); *The Unsustainable American State* (co-edited with Lawrence Jacobs, 1999); and *Still a House Divided: Race and Politics in Obama's America* (with Rogers M. Smith, 2011).

Suzanne Mettler is the Clinton Rossiter Professor of American Institutions in the Government Department at Cornell University. Her most recent book is *The Submerged State: How Invisible Government Policies Undermine American Democracy* (2011). Her previous books include *Dividing Citizens: Gender and Federalism in New Deal Public Policy* (1998), and *Soldiers to Citizens: The G.I. Bill and the Making of the Greatest Generation* (2005), both of which won APSA's Kammerer Prize.

Leo Panitch is Canada Research Chair in Comparative Political Economy at York University, Toronto. He is the co-editor of *The Socialist Register* and the author of numerous papers and books, including *Social Democracy and Industrial Militancy* (1976); *Working Class Politics in Crisis* (1986); *The End of Parliamentary Socialism* (1997); *Renewing Socialism* (2008); *American Empire and the Political Economy of Global Finance* (co-editor, 2009); and *In and Out of Crisis* (2010).

Rogers M. Smith is the Christopher H. Browne Distinguished Professor of Political Science at the University of Pennsylvania and Chair of the Executive Committee for the Penn Program on Democracy, Citizenship and Constitutionalism. He is a Fellow of the American Academy of Arts and Sciences and of the American Academy of Political and Social Science. His publications include *Civic Ideals* (1997); *The Unsteady March* (with Philip A. Klinkner, 1999); *Stories of Peoplehood* (2003); and *Still a House Divided: Race and Politics in Obama's America* (with Desmond King, 2011).

Obama at the Crossroads

PART I

Obama at the Crossroads

1

Varieties of Obamaism

STRUCTURE, AGENCY, AND THE OBAMA PRESIDENCY

Lawrence R. Jacobs and Desmond King[1]

BARACK OBAMA'S PRESIDENCY is marked by startling contrasts that both define the politics during his term in office and underscore the need for a more integrated approach to analyzing presidential leadership. With the largest popular vote in two decades and the largest Democratic victory margin since Lyndon Johnson's in 1964, Obama's election in 2008 smashed the race barrier and inspired majorities of voters to believe in the possibility of change that would remedy the country's economic problems while soothing the long-standing and bitter partisan divide. The high hopes surrounding Obama's election boosted his approval to stratospheric levels of 60 percent or higher during his first months in office and were realized in the passage of historic reforms of health care and higher education. These reforms have reshaped policy and politics in these areas—both substantially extending government responsibilities and provoking a furious backlash that has propelled unprecedented legal and legislative efforts to repeal health reform. But these accomplishments and breakthroughs also coincided with President Obama's failure to deliver on a new, post-partisan politics, to enact far-reaching legislation on labor, immigration, and energy, or to recast foreign policy toward the Middle East and global climate change. The striking contrasts between historic accomplishment and abject failure are also accompanied by more ambiguous cases. None stands out more than the strained effort to reform America's financial system: the scope of change is unprecedented since the New Deal, but the final legislation was substantially watered down and falls short of the restructuring that the administration proposed and that many experts recommend to prevent future system breakdowns.[2]

The remarkable range of policy change during Obama's first two years—from landmark breakthroughs to ambiguous or failed efforts—was compounded by the historic Democratic losses in November 2010. Much of Obama's ambitious agenda was stopped and the administration was thrust on the defensive to forestall Republican efforts to roll back earlier accomplishments. Even as partisan divisions defined the second half of Obama's first term in office, there were politically momentous splits within each party and, especially, among Republican legislators as their leaders attempted to strike deals with Democrats on the budget, the debt, and other issues that both satisfied insurgent Tea Party movement supporters and risked alienating swing voters who will determine the 2012 elections.

Fluctuating policy outcomes characterize all presidencies. But Obama's record stands out among modern presidents because of the wide range between landmark legislation on health reform and historic but compromised legislation to unfulfilled promises and deadlock or legislative retreats in the divided government that took form after the November 2010 elections. Obamaism, then, is a complex phenomenon, characterized by wide variations in success, political circumstances, and policy areas.

Commentary on presidents is normally extensive, as their decisions and personal style and behavior draw intense scrutiny. But interest in Obama appears to exceed even these high levels, owing to his unique significance for America's racial orders, the enormous range of outcomes associated with his administration, and the extraordinary partisan and intra-partisan divisions. The magnitude of Obama commentary has not, however, produced much analysis that goes beyond simplistic, often personalistic or insular, observations.

Obama at the Crossroads reveals the deeper, systemic structures that define the Obama presidency and the range of political and policy dynamics that have characterized it. Eschewing a personalistic approach, this volume brings together a diverse collection of original analyses of the political economy of the state—the political, economic, and institutional structures that defined both the opportunities and the constraints facing Obama and tested his political skills. The apparatus of the state inherited by Obama is bureaucratically complex and resource-rich in many respects, but enmeshed in an institutionally convoluted latticework of competing structures and dependent on the private market economy to sustain employment, to finance programs that generate public support, and to staff key policy-making operations, including regulatory oversight.

Obama at the Crossroads is a sharp correction against the personalistic accounts of the Obama presidency in favor of a structured agency approach. This volume analyzes the Obama presidency by drawing on political economy frameworks that are well-established within the study of comparative politics. To this end, we outline the structural context that constrains his actions in ways obscured by the all-too-common privileging of personal traits and specify President Obama's relative skill in identifying vulnerabilities, designing suitably targeted policies, and building the support to enact them.

I. The Limits of Personalism

Popular commentary attributes Obama's accomplishments and setbacks to his personality and that of his senior advisors, including Rahm Emanuel, his former chief of staff who left Washington to become mayor of Chicago. Echoing the broad frustration of many supporters of Obama's reform agenda in the weeks following the victory of Scott Brown in the Massachusetts race for the U.S. Senate seat of the late Ted Kennedy in early 2010, Mike Lux (a former Clinton White House staffer) blamed Obama's "passivity" and "lack of leadership on pulling everyone together" for the failure to move health reform. Liberal *New York Times* columnist Paul Krugman regularly chastises Obama for "not enough audacity" owing to his insufficient tenacity or naïve belief in the possibilities for "'post-partisan' . . . common ground where none exists."[3] The persistent result, Krugman suggests, has been "policies that are far too weak" and "cautious," stemming from Obama's failure "to exploit his early opportunities" and his "strong mandate . . . to take bold action" after his election. Other observers criticize Obama and his aides for failing to engage in a "radical rethink" of existing political economic arrangements and, in particular, of the "busted" model of the free market.[4] Indicative of a general criticism, Joseph Stiglitz disapproves of Obama's deferential approach to finance reform because it "muddle[s] through" instead of breaking up big banks, heavily regulating derivatives, and suffocating the securitization of mortgages.[5]

Beyond criticizing his allegedly cautious personality, commentators have repeatedly focused on Obama's failure to perform what one Senate aide called a "major sales job."[6] Other Washingtonians have yearned for "more toughness" and the ability to "dominat[e] the room."[7]

The personalistic account is alluring. The press chronicles in minute detail the travails and whims of the President and White House staff. It is hard to resist drawing what intuitively seems like reasonable connections between, say, an aloof professorial president and the maddeningly slow, meandering trajectory of health reform through months of backroom squabbling and last minute negotiations and agreements.

But personality is not a solid foundation for a persuasive explanation of presidential impact and the shortfalls or accomplishments of Obama's presidency. Modern presidents have brought divergent individual traits to their jobs and yet they have routinely failed to enact much of their agendas. Preeminent policy goals of Bill Clinton (health reform) and George W. Bush (Social Security privatization) met the same fate, though these presidents' personalities vary widely. And presidents like Jimmy Carter—whose personality traits have been criticized as ill-suited for effective leadership—enjoyed comparable or stronger success in Congress than presidents lauded for their personal knack for leadership—from Lyndon Johnson to Ronald Reagan.[8] Indeed, a personalistic account provides little leverage for explaining the *disparities* in Obama's record— for example, why he succeeded legislatively in restructuring health care and higher education, failed in other areas, and often accommodated stakeholders.

Decades of rigorous research find that *impersonal, structural* forces offer the most compelling explanations for presidential impact.[9] Quantitative research that compares legislative success and presidential personality finds no overall relationship.[10] In his magisterial qualitative and historical study, Stephen Skowronek reveals that institutional dynamics and ideological commitments structure presidential choice and success in ways that trump the personal predilections of individual presidents.[11] Research findings point to the predominant influence on presidential legislative success of the ideological and partisan composition of Congress, entrenched interests, identities, and institutional design, and a constitutional order that invites multiple and competing lines of authority. The political system's close interrelationship—through lobbying, campaign contributions, and shared personnel—with corporate business, organized labor, and other major stakeholders are fundamental elements of the political order within which presidents operate.

The widespread presumption, then, that Obama's personal traits or leadership style account for the obstacles to his policy proposals is questioned by a generation of scholarship on the presidency. Indeed, the presumption is not simply problematic analytically, but practically as well. This misdiagnosis of the source of presidential weakness may, paradoxically, induce policy failure by distracting the White House from strategies and tactics where presidents can make a difference. Following a meeting with Obama shortly after Senator Brown's win, one Democratic senator lamented the White House's delusion that a presidential sales pitch will pass health reform—"Just declaring that he's still for it doesn't mean that it comes off life support."[12] Although Obama's re-engagement after the Brown victory (such as the televised day-long seminar on health care) did contribute to restarting reform, the senator's comment points to the overriding importance of ideological and partisan coalitions in Congress, organizational combat, institutional roadblocks, and anticipated voter reactions. Presidential sales pitches go only so far.

Yet if presidential personality and leadership style come up short as primary explanations for presidential success and failure, this does not render them irrelevant. There is no need to accept the false choice between volition and structure—between explanations that reduce politics to personality and those that focus alone on system imperatives and contradictions.

The most satisfying explanations lie at the intersection of agency and structure—what we describe as *structured agency*. Presidents have opportunities to lead, but not under circumstances they choose or control. Circumstances both restrict the parameters of presidential impact and highlight the significance of presidential skill in accurately identifying and exploiting opportunities. Indeed, Obama himself talks about walking this tightrope—exercising "ruthless pragmatism" in seizing opportunities for reform while accepting the limits and seeking to "bridge that gap between the status quo and what we know we have to do for our future."[13]

The extraordinary economic and political circumstances under which Obama took office as well as the dramatic disparity between his administration's successes and failures underscore the need to synthesize the study of presidency with the analysis of political economy, American political development, and comparative policy analysis.[14] A structured agency approach focuses on the intermeshing of government policy making with differentially organized interests; the relative advantages or disadvantages that different institutional settings provide to different organized groups; and the ways in which substantive policy decisions both reflect and shape political struggles.

Structural constraints and differences in organizational power do not literally prohibit Obama, or any president, from taking initiatives—say, nationalizing the banks—but they do create two significant barriers to dramatic policy change: (1) a political environment in which members of Congress, independent regulatory bodies, and officials in his administration (especially in the Department of Treasury) can reject, stymie, or sabotage policies that threaten key relationships (such as sources of campaign contributions or future employment); and (2) an economic environment in which private firms and their customers could respond to policy proposals with inaction (such as refusing to invest) or unwelcome actions like shifting capital out of the United States, as happened in Latin America during its debt crisis and in France after the election of Socialist Francois Mitterrand as president. Obama's presidency can thus be viewed as a delicate dance to formulate policies that navigate these barriers and blunt conflicts with established economic/political relationships.

The President adapted to the contradictory opportunities and constraints by relying on selective accommodation to pursue far-reaching change. More than acclaim, this approach has generated dueling frustrations. On the one hand, liberals and progressives steam that Obama's policy proposals are too tepid and too easily stymied by stakeholders, which Lawrence Jacobs traces in Chapter 7 to a Progressive Era moralistic and teleological understanding of U.S. history. On the other hand, conservatives fume at Obama's temerity in challenging (at times successfully, if incompletely) the basic market-deferring precepts of American political economy as exemplified by health care reform, which imposed new regulations on private insurers and new taxes on the affluent by raising existing taxes and by creating a new capital gains tax.[15]

In short, the structured agency perspective integrates two critical components of social science analysis. First, it situates Obama's initiatives within the existing political economic structure of organizational combat, institutions, and policy, and probes how these factors shape options and choices. Second, it scrutinizes Obama's strategic and tactical decisions both to mobilize coalitions that are targeted at points of political economic vulnerability as well as to use his expressive powers to manage the political narrative, to control expectations, and to frame challenges to the existing power structure in ways that sustain and broaden support.

A *political economy perspective* offers distinct contributions to analyzing the Obama presidency and especially his domestic policies.

The first contribution is to recalibrate expectations of presidential leadership and, in particular, Obama's capacity for change. The initial expectation that Obama would transform America—which he himself encouraged in his 2008 campaign, as have most presidential candidates over the years—needs to be refocused on the opportunities and constraints within the existing U.S. political economy. This shifts attention from Obama as a kind of secular messiah to the strategic challenge of seizing opportunities within existing institutional and economic structures and instituting changes that instigate future developmental paths in desired directions. For example, President Obama tailored his initial economic stimulus package in 2009 to the votes he could win in Congress in the face of nearly uniform Republican opposition and potentially crippling divisions within Democratic ranks; the result was both far greater ($787 billion) than initially proposed by his campaign ($50 billion) but smaller than many independent economists deemed necessary as the scale of America's 2008 recession unfolded.

The second contribution is to broaden our understanding of presidential action and inaction and its significance. Research in political economy, American political development, and comparative public policy finds that distinctive national constellations of institutions, policy, and economic practices generate "varieties of capitalism" and wide differences among capitalistic countries in the timing and nature of government policies and how they interact with individuals and markets. These traditions of analysis study the content of public policies (instead of treating them, for instance, as dichotomous variables based on whether or not they legislatively succeed), with a particular focus on the degree to which policy change reflects or restructures established political and economic relationships.[16] This approach sheds light on sources of inaction and *stasis*. Stalemate on candidate Obama's agenda for reform of labor and climate change, for example, has often been chalked up to Obama's leadership failings. Yet neglected in these accounts are the organizational advantages of stakeholders and institutional rules (such as the Senate filibuster) that favor defenders of the existing political/economic status quo and disadvantage reformers and the less well-established.[17]

II. Obama's Presidency and Structured Agency

As candidate and president, Obama targeted the overhaul of American political economy as a primary objective. Not long after his inauguration, he maintained that "we can't just look at things in the aggregate . . . [W]e want to make sure that prosperity is spread across the spectrum of regions, and occupations and genders and races. . . . to make sure that everybody has got opportunity" to "find good employment and see their incomes rise."[18] The President targeted reforms in health care, education (both secondary and higher), and energy as decisive for expanding opportunities. He also sought to restructure finance and "change . . . [the] situation where corporate profits in the finance sector were such a heavy part of our overall profitability over the last decade." In particular, Obama proposed substantial reforms that entailed an "updating of the regulatory regimes comparable to what we did in the 1930s. . . . [in order to] inhibit some of the massive leveraging and the massive risk-taking that has become so common."[19]

How has Obama done and what accounts for his variable success? The analytic challenge is both to situate Obama's actions (and inactions) within America's political economic regime and to assess his success and failure in identifying and exploiting opportunities within the regime. Has Obama accurately identified vulnerabilities or openings within the regime of financial capitalism? If so, has he been able to build the coalitions and support to establish policies that achieve his aims partially in the short term and more robustly over time? How has he responded to the midterm elections that confronted him with a Republican majority in the House and diminished Democratic majority in the Senate?

Three features of American political economy condition Obama's initiatives, generating both constraints and opportunities for his presidency.

Politics and Private Markets

The economic and political circumstances that greeted Obama at his inauguration created opportunities for his presidency. The profound disruption of the economy and of political/economic relationships jarred received wisdom, eroding in the short term at least the position of financial and corporate interests and relationships and opening up space for economic and social welfare reform. As White House Chief of Staff Rahm Emanuel famously observed at the outset of Obama's presidency, "You never want a serious *crisis* to go to waste." In health care financing and delivery, cost escalations for business and government and the unraveling of employer health insurance coverage and rising rates of un-insurance, which the Great Recession accelerated, unsettled the stakeholder community and created political and fiscal pressure for change. On finance reform, Congressman Barney Frank, chair of the House Financial Services Committee, declared that the financial and economic crises had created a "new political consensus" to shift from "light-touch regulation" to stricter financial regulation.[20]

The crises turned out, however, not to be as destabilizing as Emanuel or Frank assumed. The opposition from stakeholders in the finance sector and elsewhere remained intense, well-organized, and skilled at exploiting its institutional connections and advantages. In addition, the responses to the crises—from the 2009 stimulus package to the financial rescue passed under Bush but popularly blamed on Obama—were judged by Americans as ineffectual and subservient to Wall Street and fueled an intense backlash that contributed to the 2010 Republican gains.

The reforms of health care and higher education highlight the openings for change, but Obama's efforts on finance, immigration, and labor, as well as the public backlash and Republican resurgence, point to three durable barriers that slowed and watered-down reforms or stopped them in their tracks.

Where's the Class War?

One of the most striking features of recent American politics is the absence of a sustained and organized backlash against rising inequality by the broad public or the working and middle classes.[21] The Tea Party meetings around the country tap the public rage against "big government" and big banks, but the movement has failed to articulate a coherent vision of class politics and remains programmatically inchoate. Fury against government and the conviction by a quarter of Tea Party supporters that violence is justified (according to an April 2010 *New York Times* survey)[22] mixes with acknowledgment by 62 percent that Medicare and Social Security are worth their expenses; majorities both oppose Obama's policies and report differences with the Republican Party; 52 percent report that too much is made of problems facing blacks, while 65 percent report that Obama's policies treat blacks and whites equally; and nearly three-quarters complain of favoritism for rich and poor, though a profile of Tea Party supporters finds that they enjoy more wealth, education, and personal economic well-being than the average American. The Republican Party both benefited from the Tea Party's surge of midterm support and suffered from the defections in congressional votes of its legislative allies, compelling GOP leaders to embrace more draconian policies (especially on budgets) at the risk of alienating swing voters.[23] The burgeoning Occupy Wall St movement is a potentially significant left riposte about America's income inequalities, whose actions may influence the 2012 presidential debates.

In other affluent democracies, conflict on class lines is more clearly drawn and institutionalized in high levels of unionization and laws and practices that routinize collective bargaining; effective political parties that are directly aligned with employees and their interests; and parliamentary coalitions that enact responsive policies.[24] As Walter Korpi and Joakim Palme argue, economic and social welfare policies are the "outcomes of, and arenas for, conflict between class-related socio-economic interest groups."[25]

The proportion of American employees who are unionized and covered by collective bargaining agreements is low compared to the levels found in other affluent democracies.[26] The comparative lack of unionization in the United States reflects and contributes to politically consequential features of American politics. American employees have traditionally not defined their interests in class terms, and there is no political party and governing coalition that directly and consistently represents labor within government as in Europe, leading to complaints that American unions are stuck in a "barren marriage" with the Democratic Party.[27] Unions not only lack institutional muscle but have also become the target for budget-cutters and Republicans: with more union members working in the public than the private sector, republican governors—led by Wisconsin's Scott Walker and Ohio's John Kasich—took aim at public sector unions in 2011.

In contrast, business has improved its organizational advantage since the 1970s to shape Washington's agenda both to devote sustained attention to issues of importance as well as to discourage discussion of others.[28] Individual firms and coalitions of firms in Washington have proliferated in number, size, and resources as have associations—namely, the U.S. Chamber of Commerce, the National Association of Manufacturers, and others. The Chamber has expanded its financial and organizational advantages by claiming to have built a grassroots following of 6 million new members spread across 22 states. Business groups seek to influence policy both through active lobbying during session and by influencing who is elected through campaign contributions in the hopes of securing a favorable audience for their views.

With labor shrinking and under fire and business influence on the rise, President Obama has lacked an encompassing organization to build support and legislative votes for his initiatives. The result is an imbalance between the unorganized and diffuse support of beneficiaries, on the one hand, and the intense, well-organized opposition of stakeholders, on the other hand. In health reform, the administration chose to accept its vulnerability and to strike deals with doctors, hospitals, and pharmaceutical companies that split the stakeholder opposition. In finance, the imbalance in organized pressure produced new regulations to revive (not restructure) Wall Street, sweetheart rescues for mammoth investment firms, and dithering on the foreclosures that are threatening millions of everyday Americans.

Our central point is to caution against the alluring but simplistic formulation that attributes the defeat or severe watering down of the administration's initiatives to the lack of personal tenacity on the part of Obama and his advisors. In truth, administration reform efforts were delayed or defeated in large part because their opponents were far better organized, funded, and programmatically coherent. The resurgence of Republicans in the 2010 midterm elections augmented the baseline organizational imbalance in American politics.

It's Who You Know

The U.S. Constitution promises an independent and representative democracy in which government officials would, according to James Madison in *Federalist Paper* 51, "best discern the true interest of their country, and whose patriotism and love of justice will be least likely to sacrifice it to temporary or partial considerations." Madison's vision of a representative democracy devoted to the "public good" was complemented by Alexander Hamilton's devotion to building a working "system of administration" that was "steady" and organizationally capable of fending off an "artful cabal [that] . . . would be able to distract and to enervate the whole system of administration [and to introduce] . . . a spirit of habitual feebleness and dilatoriness."[29]

In reality, a substantial number of government officials held high-paying corporate positions before returning to government. The public harbors intense doubt whether these officials serve the "true interests of their country" and "public good" or whether they are members of "artful cabals" that promote the "temporary or partial considerations" of certain private business. Seventy-eight percent of the February 2010 *New York Times* and CBS poll indicated that "government is pretty much run by a few big interests looking out for themselves" instead of benefiting all, and less than a fifth indicated that they trust the government in Washington always or even most of the time.[30] To the public and many political observers, the U.S. government and its officials are an "instrument" or tool of the leading economic powers within finance capitalism.[31]

The interchangeability of personnel from business and government is glaring in finance. The "revolving door" between Washington and Wall Street starkly illustrates Hamilton's fear of an "artful cabal" that used its government positions to distract, enervate, and enfeeble effective administration to serve private interests. The motivation of Washington's Wall Street transplants may be overt, or they may be implicit in their understanding of what will "work." As Stiglitz explains, the "mindsets" of government officials who work on Wall Street are "shaped by [the] people [they] associate with [so they come] to think that what's good for Wall Street is good for America," even though their policies contain "deeply obvious flaws."[32]

Former IMF chief economist Simon Johnson sounded the alarms about the "channel of influence [that has created] . . . the flow of individuals between Wall Street and Washington" and the "easy access of leading financiers to the highest U.S. government officials." The "Wall Street–Washington Corridor" has "interw[oven] the career tracks" of former Federal Reserve President Alan Greenspan as well as the top echelons of the Department of Treasury, from former Secretaries Robert Rubin and Henry Paulson, and incumbent Secretary Timothy Geithner to Geithner's current chief of staff (former Goldman Sachs's lobbyist) and senior advisor (former Citigroup chief economist).[33] Drawing on his IMF experience battling corruption in Russia and less well-developed countries, Johnson sharply criticizes the "quiet coup" by "America's Oligarchs"—a takeover carried off not by rifles but by the "confluence of campaign finance, personal connections, and ideology."[34]

Money pervades the business of government lobbying and contributions to campaign funding. The November 2010 midterm elections showcased an even larger role of money in the wake of the Supreme Court's January 2010 decision, *Citizens United v. FEC*, which allowed corporations, labor unions, and trade associations to devote unrestricted and increasingly unreported independent expenditures on candidate advertisements.

For all of the significant and growing presence of money in American politics, the profound point is that the most visible form of corruption—bribery—is not necessary in Washington. The revolving door between government and business—along with other enduring features of the U.S. political economy—ensures that business and its interests are often present or represented within government without literally paying bribes or knocking on doors.[35] In drafting the Obama administration's legislative proposals on finance reform, senior officials (namely, Geithner and Summers) often anticipated the reactions of Wall Street based on their previous close working relationships and understanding of its "mind-set" (Suskind 2011).

Although business does exert disproportionate influence, there are countervailing factors. Disagreement between stakeholders can offset even the best-placed industries. Wall Street's efforts, for instance, have been countered by aggrieved commercial banks and "Main Street" businesses, as well as by Democratic and some Republican members of Congress and President Obama, who face outcry from voters that sustained its intensity from the bailouts through the 2010 elections. Even the "pro-business" Republican Party ran and elected candidates that were hostile to policies (like the rescue of Wall Street or TARP) that were supported by the U.S. Chamber of Commerce and other business groups.

The counter-pressure reflects the fracturing of American economy and politics based on distinct (often geographically based) cleavages between different industries (service vs. manufacturing) and regions and divergent ideologies (including libertarian Republican legislators who philosophically opposed funding and tax exemptions for their Party's business base).[36] In addition, business influence is also offset by incomplete or inaccurate information, as well as by uncertainty and risk. After all, the winners in the battle for lowering capital requirements and deregulating finance and repealing the Glass-Steagall Act gutted the rules that had protected them from unleashing a crisis that terminated some of the earlier "winners" (Lehman Brothers stands out).

Yet, despite the limits on the stakeholder influence in American finance, the preeminent firms and pressure groups do impact policy. Part of their success is keeping the most threatening options (such as nationalization) off the agenda of sustained government attention. Even after financial institution reform was harshly scrubbed to exclude threatening issues or policy options, the watered-down proposals faced continued intense pressure for further accommodation or outright defeat. Wall Street firms, commercial banks, and insurers have spent millions to oppose reform, to seek friendly amendments, and, where legislation has been passed, to achieve favorable implementation by, for instance, loosening the availability of the bailout funds to commercial banks and insurers and by weakening the independence and power of the consumer protection agency. Senate Leader Dick Durbin candidly acknowledged that the track record of the finance industry as "major contributors . . . is a major factor in the decision making process in Washington."[37] This influence is not partisan: financial sector donors contribute generously to both the Republicans and the Democrats.

Living with Structure

Focusing on the Wall Street–Washington revolving door directs our attention to individuals and, specifically, the personnel who work in both domains. Names like Rubin, Paulson, and Geithner put a face on the overlapping workforce for government and American finance. Beyond this interweaving of personnel, however, the dominant political economic relationships shape government policy by determining the conditions and structures that define what seems rational and feasible to government officials who have no direct ties to the providers and funders in finance, health care, and other arenas. After all, Washington is dependent on the success of business to generate revenues, to create or maintain the public or private sector jobs that voters expect, and to sustain desired services.[38] The reform of health care, for instance, was premised on sustaining and, indeed, handsomely rewarding private medical providers, suppliers, and payers with billions in profitable new business and subsidies (Jacobs and Skocpol 2010; Hacker 2002).

In the financial sector, the dependence of businesses and ordinary Americans on credit constrains the administration and the Democratic Party. Even if they favor taking more aggressive measures against this sector, they are fully aware of their reliance on private firms to resume their business of extending credit in order to renew consumer purchases and reignite the economy. In a telling analysis, two seasoned financial reporters express frustration with Wall Street's success in imposing an "enormous barrier to reform" but conclude by stressing its structural hold on Washington—"Realistically, there is only so much that can be done to fix the problem."[39]

Resurgent Republicans accentuated the logic of private markets that pervaded even Obama's reformist efforts. Republicans, in particular, pressed for cutting government spending and repealing health and finance reform, which were forcing unwelcome changes on businesses, even as Democrats had rejected policies that threatened true "government takeovers" (such as single-payer health financing and bank nationalization).

In short, the opportunities and constraints on Obama's presidency reflect not simply his personal predilections but the mediated structural pressure of private markets. The institutional self-interest of Washington generates pressures both to create and to sustain conditions for the continuation of private markets and to avoid policies that may unsettle markets or lead to an exodus of capital in a fluid international market.

Institutions Matter

Government institutions themselves form an environment that shapes how private interests and lawmakers size up relative power and define interests and whether new policies emerge or are delayed and blocked.[40] The administration's decisions over policy and its track record in pursuing them and then defending them against Republican repeal attempts have been informed by three critical features of the American political system that we review below.

A Legacy of Hapless Administrative Capacity

National administrative capacity affects the ability of presidents to pursue their agendas as well as to win the confidence of administration officials, legislators, and "opinion makers."[41] The nature, extent, and form of the government administration have been a long-standing fulcrum of intense political conflict.

Proposals to create a national health insurance exchange and a public option were defeated by well-organized interests and their advocates within Congress in a policy arena where provision and financing among the non-elderly is privately controlled.[42] Whether the government could be trusted to control costs and work within the budgetary projections of the Congressional Budget Office was a flashpoint within the Democratic Party during the 2009–2010 debate and between the parties—including the period after the inauguration of Republicans to the 112th Congress in January 2011.

The federal government's role and administrative capacity within the financial sector is a long-standing source of conflict. The financial crises stemmed, in part, from the ineffectiveness of America's administrative system to tame the "tyranny of the short term"—as conservative jurist Richard Posner explains in his critique of the financial crisis—and to guide self-interested behavior toward "enlightened self-interest."[43] The system failed to supervise the securitization of mortgages (as exemplified by the failure of the SEC to regulate credit default swap trading), to insist on reasonable capital requirements for trades, or to take necessary steps to check the drive of bankers, insurers, and others to reap massive short-term returns to them. Gillian Tett, a *Financial Times* journalist, reports that the "story of the great credit boom and bust is . . . a story of how an entire financial *system* went wrong" owing to nonexistent or ineffectual regulation and oversight.[44]

America's 2008–2009 financial crises confirm a broader and well-known theme in American political development—the administrative state's generally porous, easily penetrated boundaries; its consistent (though not uniform) lack of independent expertise to assess and respond to the behavior of markets and individuals; and multiple and competing lines of authority that stymie even necessary intervention.[45] Indeed, the low confidence of legislators and other policy makers in American public administration has fueled their tendency to create multiple and competing bodies with redundancies and checks. The flip side, though, is that pressure groups exploit this plethora of options to "venue shop" for the friendliest government forum or to play them off against each other. The financial industry searched for a sponsor and protector in the regulatory bazaar of the Treasury Department, Federal Reserve, Federal Deposit Insurance Corporation, Office of the Currency, and the Security and Exchange Commission. For instance, when the states attempted to use consumer protection laws to crack down on predatory lending, the lenders turned to the Comptroller of the Currency to block these efforts.

America's administrative structure is also prone—as generations of research demonstrate—to penetration and influence by pressure groups and parochial interests. If the lobbyists fail to shape agency behavior, they turn to the White House or, if that turns out to be unrewarding, to responsive members of Congress. What seems from afar like inexplicable lapses in administrative competence can often be traced to successful industry interventions into a porous administrative structure. For instance, the "light touch" regulation of Freddie Mac and Fannie Mae has been blamed for their stupendous failure to accurately assess risk and intervene. But a careful retracing of this breakdown finds that it originated in campaign contributions and intense lobbying of both agencies and relevant members of Congress.[46] The continued whittling down of provisions for independent financial consumer protection prompted one consumer advocate to complain that "it's hard for your voice to be heard" when faced with the "money and the resources of the banking industry."[47]

Republicans in the 112th Congress are focusing on exacerbating administrative incapacities. Their most public efforts are directed to denying, reducing, or restricting funding for implementing the new health reform law, enforcing new regulations to slow global climate change that were issued by the Environmental Protection Agency, and other Obama administration initiatives from 2009 and 2010. Republicans used congressional oversight powers to cajole and, on occasion, to attempt to intimidate civil servants into slowing down and resisting Obama administration policies through threatened reductions in budgets and authority and harsh hearings.

Overall, the American administrative state often lacks independent and skilled capacity to monitor and intervene to prevent market breakdowns. Enduring distrust of government, along with political combat, both sustains and extends competing lines of authority, gaps in expertise, and deference to stakeholders.

The Booby-Trapped Road to Lawmaking

The comparative weakness of America's administrative state is compounded by a legislative process that is individualized and diffuse and therefore habitually resistant to presidential efforts to form supportive coalitions, even under the most propitious circumstances. The 112th Congress typifies the normal pattern of divided government when lawmaking is hobbled by the conflict between a president and one or both chambers of Congress that are controlled by the opposing party. The 111th Congress in 2009 and 2010 presented the more uncommon situation of unified government; presidents enjoy more legislative success when their party controls not only the White House but also both chambers in Congress. Nonetheless, as Obama discovered, unified government is no protection against deadlock and delay.[48]

The individualization of Congress poses challenges for presidents and repeatedly put Obama in the awkward situation of facing resistance from his own party in Congress. All members of Congress enjoy "rights" to serve on major committees, as the power of seniority has eroded; enjoy staff support that allows them to develop their personal legislative agenda; and, for their reelection, depend on assembling their own record with money they have raised and a staff they have hired and organized. Although party leaders can provide services to individual legislators, the centrifugal forces of individualization often prevail, with presidents and congressional leaders unable to dictate nomination—the key power in parliamentary systems to discipline legislators who defect from party coalitions.[49]

With neither presidents nor congressional leaders able to control votes by legislators (even under conditions of unified party control), they rely on a more subtle but nonetheless potent power—setting the agenda. In particular, they limit floor votes to bills that enjoy the support of party caucuses. Critics chastised the Obama White House for proposing vague principles of health reform rather than a detailed plan; but the decision reflected its acceptance that the legislative process required time and deference to the leadership to build agreement in committees and caucus meetings before moving reform onto the agenda. Facing an institutionally similar predicament, Republican Speaker John Boehner found newly elected GOP members challenging or even voting against his proposals, joining with Democrats on a few occasions to defeat the leader.

The institutional hurdles of lawmaking do not shape organized interests equally. Rather, they interact with America's market-deferring political economy to the advantage of stakeholders and their allies, who capitalize on multiple veto points that protect the status quo by blocking new government action. Conservative Senate Democrats extracted concessions from health reformers in fall 2009 by threatening to allow the filibuster to continue, producing the so-called Cornhusker Kickback for the state's senator and several policy concessions to Joe Lieberman (including the omission of an extension of Medicare to near retirees). During the 112th Congress, Democratic dependence on House Republicans to pass a budget in 2011 was converted into bargaining advantages, compelling Democrats to accept steep spending cuts.

In addition to favoring the status quo over change, the institutional maze advantages conservatives over reformers seeking to expand social welfare policy generally. Republicans more frequently pass their top legislative priority (tax cuts) by using the budget reconciliation process that requires a simple majority.[50] By comparison, the filibuster requirement of 60 Senate votes in an environment of polarization makes it quite difficult (as Obama discovered) to enact ambitious new social welfare programs; party leaders are unlikely to receive Republican votes and are forced to contend with deep divisions among Democrats. This conservative bias of building legislative coalitions in an environment of intense polarization and institutional booby-traps is broadly consistent with the partisan differences in macroeconomic and tax policies and, of late, the weakening impacts of Democratic presidents in expanding employment and economic growth.[51]

What stands out about Obama's legislative record, then, are not simply the delays, compromises, defeats, and failures—from energy and climate change to financial reform and strengthened labor rights. These are the predictable outcomes of the current legislative process and the networks of vested interests that permeate it. More remarkable and surprising is the intermixing pattern of plain vanilla "delay and deadlock" with success, as epitomized by health reform in 2010.[52]

Despite the usual tendency toward impasse, reforms in 2009 and 2010 passed in the House and in the Senate (with the support of all Democrats and two independents). The polarization of the parties created unusual unity among Democrats at a time when they enjoyed the largest majorities in three decades and intermittent presidential promotion. Nonetheless, the process was slow, close to deadlocked at several junctures, and doomed after Brown's Senate win until the bane of progressives—the reconciliation process—was converted into a mechanism for modifying aspects of the originally enacted Senate legislation in ways that were acceptable to the House.

Obama's Refuge: The Administrative Presidency

As parts of his agenda are delayed or dragged down by the veto-strewn legislative process, Obama has employed—as have presidents for three decades—the institutional prerogatives in his office to bypass Congress. The White House issued more than three dozen executive orders in its first year in order to take unilateral action on a host of issues from restoring regulatory powers over workplace safety and the environment to enhancing the power of employees of government contractors.[53]

Perhaps the most striking domestic example is the Treasury's implementation of funds for the Term Asset-Backed Securities Loan Facility (TALF). Bereft of legislative authorization, the Federal Reserve authorized TALF to make up to $200 billion in loans, of which close to $70 billion were drawn to purchase securities backed by credit cards, student loans, and other assets. Credit protection for TALF came to the Federal Reserve from the Treasury using $20 billion of the TARP funds, thus enabling the Federal Reserve not to increase its credit risk, other than minimally, to participate in the emergency lending program.[54] In addition, the administration created a program to mitigate the mortgage crisis (by enabling borrowers to gain short-term relief from lenders without losing their equity stake) based on the executive branch's authority and without congressional approval. Moreover, shortly after his health care victory, Obama appointed 15 senior nominees by executive authority during Congressional recess. Reviewing the administration's unilateral initiatives, one *New York Times* columnist concluded that the "crises have expanded the power of the executive branch."[55] After the surge of Republican congressional strength following the

2010 elections, Obama accelerated his use of Executive Orders and other types of unilateral actions to circumvent the stalemated legislative process.

Obama's Presidency Within America's Racial Orders

Obama's election as president is a product of and challenge to America's racial orders. Racial inequities and struggles are historically constitutive of U.S. politics, generating competing coalitions of political actors with distinct conceptions of race equity.[56] Competing conceptions of America's racial orders have structured every era of U.S. history—from antebellum battles over slavery and Reconstruction struggles about segregation to today's controversies over whether government policy should include race-conscious measures to address continuing inequities including the disproportionately high levels of foreclosures, unemployment, and other economic woes among African Americans and Latinos.[57]

As Smith and King elaborate in Chapter 5, racial orders are part of the structured context of policy making for any American president, but they uniquely affect Obama, America's first African American in the White House. Obama's election is a culmination of centuries of struggle for racial equity and, yet, his presidency is constrained by the enduring conflict of racial orders. While liberal commentators and activists yearn for Obama to channel Lyndon Johnson's notorious skill in lobbying Congress and to unleash sharp denunciation of his predecessors as had Ronald Reagan, the reality is that Obama is haunted by lingering stereotypes and bias. His advisors have steered him away from actions and rhetoric that could trigger the "angry black man" stereotype, which bubble up in protests.[58] He has resisted pleas from African American leaders to target resources into their communities and into reducing unemployment among blacks. Instead, President Obama pursues universal programs—such as health care insurance rights for all Americans—to provide ameliorations in U.S. society that will assist all disadvantaged citizens.

Republicans in the 112th Congress have also struggled with America's racial order. Even as they attempted to broaden the GOP's appeal to an increasingly diverse electorate, they and their supporters have repeatedly renewed their racially tinged reputation among Americans of color through a series of highly public events—Tea Party supporters sporting racialized images of Obama, draconian proposals for immigration crackdowns, and hearings on "homegrown" terrorists that single out Muslim communities.

III. The Second Presidency

When presidents find their party split and the rival party blocking them on the domestic front, the opportunity to look "presidential" by seeming to take charge abroad with orders to deploy U.S. troops or with the conclusion of historic agreements are enticing. For many years, researchers have debated whether and under what conditions the "two presidencies" thesis holds.[59]

The structured agency approach applies to the "second presidency." Economic and security interests are critical—perhaps overwhelming—considerations in U.S. foreign policy, helping to account for the intervention in the Middle East to protect oil supplies and valued allies.[60] One study found that business (far more than labor and, especially, general public opinion) was the driving influence on U.S. foreign policy.[61] Domestic and international institutions condition how American policy makers understand and pursue U.S. interests. A body of research points to the significant impacts of pressure groups—especially, those of business and organized interests—on Congress in particular, though administration officials are more resistant.[62]

Obama's national security and foreign policy departed from the Bush administration in certain respects (such as increased U.S. troops in Afghanistan), but the continuities are the most striking given the rhetorical emphasis on "change." Despite promises and some initial efforts to shake up U.S. foreign policy, general continuity characterizes Obama's policies toward Israel and Palestinian peace negotiations after the Netanyahu government rebuffed American calls for a cessation of West Bank settlements, authoritarian regimes (from the Middle East to Central and South Asia) that cooperate with U.S. military and security services, and financial and trade relations with China in spite of tough campaign talk about change. Even in areas where Obama did appear to depart on a new policy, some of the most high-profile changes were initiated by the Bush administration, which, for instance, reached agreement on the withdrawal of U.S. troops from Iraq and terminated controversial policies toward terrorist suspects (including torture).

The pattern of Obama abiding by the foreign policy and national security commitments of his predecessor and Bush revising his earlier policy in anticipation of future U.S. policy contradicts one of the defining features of contemporary American politics—polarization. The pattern of different presidents from different political parties adopting similar foreign policies cannot be persuasively explained by personal temperament or other personalistic explanations. Rather, the convergence of Obama with Bush reflects their common responses to interstate competition within stable institutional structures.

Although structured agency rather than personality offer important insights into both domestic and foreign policy during the Obama presidency, this volume concentrates on the national governing process. The two are interrelated, but this volume's explanation of variations in Obama's record is strengthened by focusing on distinctive policies within the shared context of domestic institutions and politics.

Varieties of Obamaism

Avoiding personalist accounts need not lead to one-sided structural interpretations that exclusively focus on economic and state structures and their relationships. Rather, Obama's presidency is defined by structured agency. The constellation of America's entwined economic and political relationships and embedded institutional dynamics conditioned the proposals that Obama developed, as well as their differential outcomes.

Seeking to understand the wide range of Obama's policy outcomes poses enduring questions about the nature of presidential power and the reconstitution of private markets, government, and the individual's relationship to each at a critical historic juncture. The real world of American politics today poses remarkable shifts of historic consequence. It also opens up exceptional opportunities for synthesizing the study of the presidency with political economy, American political development, and comparative public policy.

Notes

1. Text in this chapter is reproduced with permission from Lawrence R. Jacobs and Desmond King, "Varieties of Obamaism: Structure, Agency, and the Obama Presidency," *Perspectives on Politics* 8(3) (August 2010): 793–802.
2. Stiglitz 2010.
3. Krugman 2009a, 2009b.
4. Augar 2009.
5. Stiglitz 2010.
6. Herszenhorn and Stolberg 2010; Weston 2011.
7. Stolberg 2010.
8. Bond and Fleisher 1990; Edwards 2009.
9. Jacobs 2009; Howell 2009.
10. Bond and Fleisher 1990; Edwards 2009.
11. Skowronek 1993.
12. Quoted in Werner 2010.
13. Quoted in Leonhardt 2009.

14. Bartels 2008; Hacker and Pierson 2010; Jacobs and King 2009; Kenworthy 2009; Skowronek 2009.
15. Jacobs and Skocpol, 2010.
16. Esping-Andersen 1990.
17. McCarty 2007.
18. Quoted in Leonhardt 2009, 41.
19. Quoted in Leonhardt 2009, 38.
20. Quoted in Walsh 2009.
21. Page and Jacobs 2009.
22. *New York Times*, April Survey 2010.
23. Skocpol and Williamson 2011
24. Esping-Andersen 1990; Korpi 1983.
25. Korpi and Palme 2003, 425.
26. Visser 2006 and see Silverstein 2009.
27. Katznelson 1981; Davis 1980.
28. Walker, 1991; Hacker and Pierson, 2010.
29. *Federalist Papers* 69, 70, 71.
30. cf. Pew Research Center April 2010 survey of trust.
31. Lindblom 1977; Miliband 1969.
32. Quoted in Becker and Morgenson 2009.
33. Becker and Morgenson 2009; see Morgenson and Story 2010.
34. Johnson 2009; Page and Winters 2009.
35. Kaiser 2009.
36. Trubowitz 1998.
37. Quoted in Schouten, Dilanian, and Kelley 2008.
38. Hacker and Pierson 2010; Lindblom 1977.
39. Einhorn and Lewis 2009.
40. Pierson 1993.
41. Orloff and Skocpol 1984.
42. Hacker 2002.
43. Posner 2009.
44. Tett 2009.
45. Jacobs and King 2009; Johnson 2007; Sheingate 2009; Skowronek 1982.
46. Becker, Labaton, and Stolberg 2008.
47. Chan 2010.
48. Bond and Fleisher 1990.
49. Aldrich 1995.
50. McCarty 2007.
51. Bartels 2008.
52. Burns 1984.
53. Judis 2010; National Archives 2009.
54. Nelson 2011.

55. Cowen 2009.
56. Cohen 2009; King and Smith 2005; Lieberman 2005.
57. Smith and King 2009.
58. Halperin and Heilemann 2010, 206.
59. Wildavsky 1966; Sigelman, 1979
60. Morgenthau 1973.
61. Jacobs and Page 2005.
62. Milner 1997.

References

Aldrich, John. 1995. *Why Parties? The Origin and Transformation of Political Parties in America*. Chicago: University of Chicago Press.

Augar, Philip. 2009. *Chasing Alpha: How Reckless Growth and Unchecked Ambition Ruined the City's Golden Decade*. London: Bodley Head.

Bartels, Larry. 2008. *Unequal Democracy: The Political Economy of the New Gilded Age*. New York: Russell Sage Foundation and Princeton University Press.

Becker, Jo, Stephen Labaton, and Sheryl Gay Stolberg. 2008. "White House Philosophy Stoked Mortgage Bonfire." *New York Times* (December 21).

Becker, Jo, and Gretchen Morgenson. 2009. "Geithner, Member and Overseer of the Finance Club." *New York Times*, April 27.

Black, William, Frank Partnoy, and Eliot Spitzer. 2009. "Show Us the E-Mail." *New York Times*, December 20.

Bond, Jon R., and Richard Fleisher. 1990. *The President in the Legislative Arena*. Chicago: University of Chicago Press.

Burns, James MacGregor. 1984. *The Power to Lead: The Crisis of the American Presidency*. New York: Simon and Schuster.

Canes-Wrone, Brandice, William Howell, and David Lewis. 2009. "Toward a Broader Understanding of Presidential Power." *Journal of Politics* 70 (January): 1–16.

Chan, Sewell. 2010. "In Senate, A Renewed Effort to Reach a Consensus on Financial Regulation." *New York Times*, March 1.

Cohen, Cathy J. 2009. "From Kanye West to Barack Obama: Black Youth, the State and Political Alienation." In *The Unsustainable American State*, eds. Lawrence Jacobs and Desmond King. New York: Oxford University Press.

Cowen, Tyler. 2009. "There's Work to Be Done, but Congress Opts Out." *New York Times*, May 10.

Davis, Mike. 1980. "The Barren Marriage of American Labour and the Democratic Party." *New Left Review* 124 (November–December): 43–50.

Edwards, George C., III. 2009. *The Strategic President: Persuasion and Opportunity in Presidential Leadership*. Princeton: Princeton University Press.

Einhorn, David, and Michael Lewis. 2009. "The End of the Financial World as We Know It." *New York Times*, January 4.

Esping-Andersen, Gosta. 1990. *The Three Worlds of Welfare Capitalism*. Princeton, NJ: Princeton University Press.

Hacker, Jacob. 2002. *The Divided Welfare State: The Battle over Public and Private Social Benefits in the United States*. New York: Cambridge University Press.

Hacker, Jacob S., and Paul Pierson. 2010. *Winner Take All Politics*. New York: Simon Schuster.

Halperin, Mark, and John Heilemann. 2010. *Game Change: Obama and the Clintons, McCain and Palin, and the Race of a Lifetime*. New York: Harper.

Hamilton, Alexander. 1982. *Federalist Papers* No. 69, 70, and 71 in *The Federalist Papers*. New York: Bantam.

Herszenhorn, David, and Sheryl Gay Stolberg. 2010. "Up Next! On Live TV! Battle over . . . Health? *New York Times*, February 21.

Howell, William G. 2009. "Quantitative Approaches to Studying the Presidency." In *The Oxford Handbook of the American Presidency*, eds. George C. Edwards III and William G. Howell. Oxford: Oxford University Press.

Jacobs, Lawrence. 2009. "Building Reliable Theories of the Presidency." *Presidential Studies Quarterly* 39 (December): 771–780.

Jacobs, Lawrence, and Desmond King, eds. 2009. *The Unsustainable American State*. Oxford: Oxford University Press.

Jacobs, Lawrence, and Benjamin I. Page. 2005. "Who Influences U.S. Foreign Policy?" *American Political Science Review* 99 (February): 107–124.

Jacobs, Lawrence and Theda Skocpol. 2010. *Health Care Reform and American Politics*. New York: Oxford University Press.

Johnson, Kimberley. 2007. *Governing the American State*. Princeton: Princeton University Press.

Johnson, Simon. 2009. "The Quiet Coup." *The Atlantic Monthly*, May.

Judis, John. 2010. "The Quiet Revolution." *The New Republic*, February 1.

Kaiser, Robert G. 2009. *So Damned Much Money: The Triumph of Lobbying and the Corrosion of American Government*. New York: Knopf.

Katznelson, Ira. 1981. *City Trenches: Urban Politics and the Patterning of Class in the United States*. New York: Pantheon.

Kenworthy, Lane. 2009. "How Much Do Presidents Influence Income Inequality?" Unpublished manuscript. Department of Sociology, University of Arizona, February 2009.

King, Desmond, and Rogers M. Smith. 2005. "Racial Orders in American Political Development." *American Political Science Review* 99: 75–92.

Konings, Martijn, and Leo Panitch. 2009. "Myths of Neoliberal Deregulation." *New Left Review* 57 (May–June): 67–83.

Korpi, Walter. 1983. *The Democratic Class Struggle*. London: Routledge and Kegan Paul.

Korpi, Walter, and Joakim Palme. 2003. "New Politics and Class Politics in the Context of Austerity and Globalization: Welfare State Regress in 18 Countries, 1975–95." *American Political Science Review* 97: 425–446.

Krugman, Paul. 2009a. "Not Enough Audacity." *New York Times*, June 26.

Krugman, Paul. 2009b. "Obama Faces His Anzio." *New York Times*, November 5.

Leonhardt, David. 2009. "After the Great Recession." *New York Times Magazine*, May 3.

Lieberman, Robert C. 2005. *Shaping Race Policy: The US in Comparative Perspective.* Princeton: Princeton University Press.

Lindblom, Charles. 1977. *Politics and Markets: The World's Political Economic Systems.* New York: Basic Books.

McCarty, Nolan. 2007. "The Policy Effects of Political Polarization." In *The Transformation of American Politics: Activist Government and the Rise of Conservatism,* eds. P. Pierson and T. Skocpol. Princeton, NJ: Princeton University Press, pp. 223–255.

Mettler, Suzanne. 2009. "Promoting Inequality: The Politics of Higher Education Policy in an Era of Conservative Governnance." In *The Unsustainable American State,* eds. Lawrence Jacobs and Desmond King. New York: Oxford University Press.

Miliband, Ralph. 1969. *The State in Capitalist Society.* London: Weidenfeld & Nicolson.

Milner, Helen. 1997. *Interests, Institutions, and Information: Domestic Politics and International Relations.* Princeton, NJ: Princeton University Press.

Morgenthau, Hans. 1973. *Politics among Nations.* New York: Knopf.

Morgenson, Gretchen, and Louise Story. 2010. "Testy Conflict with Goldman Helped Push A.I.G. to Edge." *New York Times*, February 7.

National Archives. 2009. "The Federal Register: Executive Order of Barack Obama." (http://www.archives.gov/federal-register/executive-orders/2009-obama.html).

Nelson, William R. 2011. Statement by William R. Nelson, Deputy Director Division of Monetary Affairs, Board of Governors of the Federal Reserve System, Before the Congressional Oversight Panel, March 4. http://www.federalreserve.gov/newsevents/testimony/nelson20110304a.htm.

New York Times. 2010. "National Survey of Tea Party Supporters." April 5–12. http://documents.nytimes.com/new-york-timescbs-news-poll-national-survey-of-tea-party-supporters.

Orloff, Ann, and Theda Skocpol. 1984. "Why Not Equal Protection: Explaining the Politics of Public Social Spending in Britain, 1900–1911, and the United States, 1880s–1920." *American Sociological Review* 49: 726–750.

Page, Benjamin I., and Jeffrey A. Winters. 2009. "Oligarchy in the United States?" *Perspectives on Politics* 7(4): 731–751.

Page, Benjamin I., and Lawrence R. Jacobs. 2009. *Class War? What Americans Really Think about Economic Inequality.* Chicago: University of Chicago Press.

Pew Research Center. 2010. "Distrust, Discontent, Anger and Partisan Rancor." March 11–21. http://www.people-press.org/2010/04/18/distrust-discontent-anger-and-partisan-rancor/.

Pierson, Paul. 1993. "When Effect Becomes Cause: Policy Feedback and Political Change." *World Politics* 45: 595–628.

Pierson, Paul, and Theda Skocpol, eds. 2007. *The Transformation of American Politics: Activist Government and the Rise of Conservativism*. Princeton, NJ: Princeton University Press.

Posner, Richard. 2009. *A Failure of Capitalism: The Crisis of '08 and the Descent into Depression*. Cambridge, MA: Harvard University Press.

Schouten, Fredreka, Ken Dilanian, and Matt Kelley. 2008. "Lobbyists in Feeding Frenzy." *USA Today*, September 26.

Sheingate, Adam. 2009. "Why Can't Americans See the State?" *The Forum* 7: 1–14.

Sigelman, Lee. 1979. "A Reassessment of the Two Presidencies Thesis." *Journal of Politics* (41): 1195–2105.

SIGTARP (Special Inspector General Troubled Asset Relief Program). 2009. *Factors Affecting Efforts to Limit Payments to AIG Counterparties*. Washington, DC: Office of the Special Inspector General for the Troubled Asset Relief Program (November 17). http://www.sigtarp.gov/reports/audit/2009/Factors_Affecting_Efforts_to_Limit_Payments_to_AIG_Counterparties.pdf.

SIGTARP (Special Inspector General Troubled Asset Relief Program). 2010. Quarterly Report to Congress (January 30). http://www.sigtarp.gov/reports/congress/2010/January2010_Quarterly_Report_to_Congress.pdf.

Silverstein, Ken. 2009. "Labor's Last Stand: The Corporate Campaign to Kill the Employee Free Choice Act." *Harper's Magazine*, July.

Skocpol, Theda and Vanessa Williamson. 2011. *The Tea Party and the Remaking of Republican Conservatism*. New York: Oxford University Press.

Skowronek, Stephen. 1982. *Building a New American State: The Expansion of National Administrative Capacities, 1877–1920*. Cambridge: Cambridge University Press.

Skowronek, Stephen. 1993. *The Politics Presidents Make: Leadership from John Adams to George Bush*. Cambridge, MA: Belknap Press.

Skowronek, Stephen. 2009. "Taking Stock." In *The Unsustainable American State*, eds. Lawrence Jacobs and Desmond King. Oxford: Oxford University Press, pp. 330–339.

Smith, Rogers M., and Desmond King 2009. "Barack Obama and the Future of American Racial Politics." *Du Bois Review* 6: 1–11.

Stiglitz, Joseph. 2010. *Free Fall: America, Free Markets, and the Sinking of the World Economy*. New York: Norton.

Stolberg, Sheryl Gay. 2010. "Gentle White House Nudges Test the Power of Persuasion." *New York Times*, February 24.

Suskind, Ron. 2011. *Confidence Men: Wall Street, Washington, and the Education of a President*. New York: Harper.

Tett, Gillian. 2009. *Fool's Gold: How Unrestrained Greed Corrupted a Dream, Shattered Global Markets and Unleashed a Catastrophe*. London: Little Brown.

Thompson, Helen. 2009. "The Political Origins of the Financial Crisis." *Political Quarterly* 80 (January–March): 17–24.

Trubowitz, Peter. 1998. *Defining the National Interest: Conflict and Change in American Foreign Policy*. Chicago: University of Chicago Press.

Visser, Jelle. 2006. "Union Membership Statistics in 24 Countries." *Monthly Labor Review* (38–49).

Walker, Jack. 1991. *Mobilizing Interest Groups in America: Patrons, Professions, and Social Movements*. Ann Arbor: University of Michigan Press.

Walsh, Mary Williams. 2009. "Inquiry Asks Why A.I.G. Paid Banks." *New York Times*, March 27.

Walsh, Mary Williams. 2010a. "Fed Advice to A.I.G. Scrutinized." *New York Times*, January 8.

Walsh, Mary Williams. 2010b. "Where the Billions Went." *New York Times*, January 26.

Westin, Drew. 2011. "What Happened to Obama?" *New York Times*. August 6.

Werner, Erica. 2010. "Obama's Words Fail to Bridge Health Care Divide." Associated Press, February 3.

Wildavsky, Aaron. 1966. "The Two Presidencies." *Trans-Action* IV, December.

Wolfe, Alan. 1981. *America's Impasse: The Rise and Fall of the Politics of Growth*. Boston: South End Press.

PART II

The Legislative Crossroads

2

Institutional Empowerment and Strangulation

BUREAUCRATIC POLITICS AND FINANCIAL
REFORM IN THE OBAMA ADMINISTRATION[1]

Daniel Carpenter

ON JULY 21, 2010, President Barack Obama signed into law the Dodd-Frank Wall Street Reform and Consumer Protection Act, more commonly called the Dodd-Frank Act—named after Connecticut Senator Christopher Dodd and Massachusetts Representative Barney Frank. The Dodd-Frank Act, the most sweeping overhaul of American financial regulations since the New Deal, represents the Obama administration's main structural attack on the financial crisis of 2008 and the Great Recession that followed it. The Obama administration's financial reform proposals engendered substantial controversy and hundreds of millions of dollars in lobbying on various sides of the debate. These high stakes of financial politics reflect the massive transformations set in motion by the Act.

The Dodd-Frank Act takes large investment banks and, in some ways, fundamentally dismantles and reassembles them. One provision cleaves trading operations in derivatives and swaps from deposit-taking functions. Another provision allows only so much of a bank's capital to be deployed in proprietary trading. A critical set of provisions—largely unnoticed in the late-stage debate on the Dodd-Frank bill and the aftermath of its summer 2010 passage—establishes stringent governance of credit rating agencies (such as Moody's or Standard and Poor's) and weakens their power in the global economy and government policy making. The Act boosts the requirements for how much basic capital banks must keep on hand as they engage in lending and investing. Additionally, the Dodd-Frank Act establishes, for the first time in American history, a federal agency explicitly dedicated to the regulation of consumer financial products such as mortgages, credit cards, and commodity loans. For banks large and small, for mortgage lenders and credit card companies, and for federal and private agencies that rate and regulate risk, there will be new organizational and business models in the years to come.

To be certain, both the process and the outcome of financial reform generated broad criticism and controversy. These laments came from conservatives who saw the new regulations as far too intrusive in American and global capital markets, and from progressives who wished for a return to New Deal institutions of financial governance. Stronger versions of an independent consumer agency and of splitting derivatives operations from depository institutions were set aside, often in quieter moments of politics. Yet the momentous nature of the changes should not be understated. The politically successful proposals are notable for their breadth. As a result of the 2010 law, there will be substantial limitations upon leverage, proprietary trading, and swaps operations at major financial institutions, and relatedly, there will be stronger rules for minimum capital requirements (especially for so-called "Tier 1 capital"). A new consumer protection bureau has been added to the Federal Reserve, and the vigor with which its appointments' politics have been fought out suggests that it carries the possibility of expansive regulatory capacity and action.

At the core of the struggles over financial regulation lay contests over organizational authority, meaning, and form. In the immediacy and wake of the financial crisis, regulatory agencies that had enjoyed stable claims to policy turf and expertise quickly saw their credibility and their jurisdictions under attack. In some cases, entire classes of business firms, such as credit-rating agencies, were delegitimized and restructured. In other cases, government agencies that had been perched atop the status hierarchies of expertise, such as the Federal Reserve and the Securities and Exchange Commission (SEC), saw abiding threats to their organizational models and their power. As I have claimed elsewhere, this destabilization of organizational and professional legitimacy amounted, for a moment, to a partial democratization of finance policy networks. Older forms of expertise in financial economics and securities law were, for a time, displaced by newer forms of expertise in bankruptcy law, psychology, and behavioral economics.[2]

In the end, attempts to reshape the landscape in financial policy and regulation were only partially successful. Attempts to constrain leverage at top investment banks through stringent legislative standards were limited by a strong predilection to defer to existing regulators and international capital standards (the so-called Basel accords), and stronger versions of derivative trading restrictions were abandoned for weaker, though still constraining, alternatives. Yet in two critical areas—credit rating agency reform and consumer financial protection—substantial transformations took place, though it was change that added new powers to older organizations—a new office with oversight capabilities in the SEC and a new Consumer Financial Protection Bureau in the Federal Reserve.

I. Crisis and Reform: Some Financial Facts and Concepts

Unlike the health care debate, the essential context for financial reform was not a decades-long fight by the Democratic Party to bring American policy on a par with other advanced democracies. Instead, financial reform's place on the agenda was set and secured by a global crisis of capital, risk, and economic security, a crisis whose reach has not been equaled since the Great Depression of the 1930s. The crisis of 2008 and the "Great Recession" that followed it damaged the fortunes of the wealthy and ripped away the jobs and health insurance of the working poor, working class, and middle class. Over 8 million jobs vanished in the past three years, many of them never to return. The national housing crisis was historic in its own right—homeowners lost their shelter and their equity at record levels, with 2.3 million homes being repossessed by lenders from December 2007 to September 2010—and the housing tumult engendered a crisis in banking, with bank failures and plummeting asset values for major investments (including institutional pension accounts, retirement funds, and foundation and university endowments).

The crisis of the past two years damaged individual consumer fortunes and the accumulated wealth of the most powerful financial organizations on the planet. It hit both the consumer financial realm and the systemic financial realm[3]—and hard. Past stock market crashes were not as deeply embedded in the consumer finance market—witness the crash of 1987, the problems of Long-Term Capital Management and its international investments in 1998, and the popping of the tech and NASDAQ bubbles in 2000. In contrast to the 2008 crisis, in none of these events was the American housing market deeply implicated, and only in one was a set of overvalued household-level investments (many of them institutional, in the IT bubble of the 1990s) partially involved. At the same time, the crisis in home ownership and consumer finance is certainly lucid now, but its roots have been spreading for the better part of two decades. For a number of reasons, median income per capita has stagnated over the past decade, even as the costs of health care, education, and housing have continued to rise.[4] And even as the costs of these goods have risen, Americans are becoming more enamored with them, sacrificing long-term savings and other expenditures in order to gain access to education, health care, and owned housing.

By most accounts, the financial crisis unfolded from contexts that reveal deeply political, social and economic dimensions. The past 20 years have witnessed explicit and implicit financial deregulation, most markedly in the 1999 repeal of the Glass-Steagall Act that had formerly split commercial and depository from investment institutions in banking. This 1999 law culminated 20 years of lobbying efforts by the U.S. and global financial services industry. Income inequality has been growing in the United States and is now, by some measures, perched at levels not witnessed since the late nineteenth century. This has led to what some analysts call "surplus capital" among the wealthy, who have abundant assets with which to invest and who may compete on ever-higher returns. It has also led to the genesis of new financial and loan instruments that claim to permit financially constrained consumers to purchase homes they could not otherwise afford. So too, different analyses have revealed the degree to which the new financial instruments were aimed at ethnic and racial minorities, disadvantaged peoples whose ability to seek shelter under consumer bankruptcy laws has been deeply curtailed since the Bankruptcy Abuse Prevention and Consumer Protection Act (BAPCPA) of 2005.[5]

Changes in Financial Products

In the past two decades, lending companies began to offer new and more complicated financial products to consumers. Each of these financial products can be reduced to a contract that contains its fundamental components: a promise of the lender to provide money now in return for a series of payments by the consumer later. The explosion of credit cards over the past two decades—by 2008, the average American adult carried 10 or more of these on their person—is perhaps the most familiar evidence that financial products have revolutionized our lives. Yet it is not just credit cards but their contractual terms that have been transformed. The diversity and complexity of credit card contracts are bewildering. Most cards require no monthly fee for card use, but some still do (and many more did just a decade or more ago). Cards differ in the fees that kick in—and the transparency with which they kick in—when payments for accumulated balances come in late or not at all.

Mortgages and auto loans, too, exploded in diversity and complexity. For much of the twentieth century, the dominant form of home loan was a 30-year fixed-rate mortgage with a certain percentage of the housing value down (20 to 30 percent, usually). In recent years, however, home owners were able to purchase homes using an array of mortgages that allow purchasers with very little money down and, in addition, little or no documentation (the euphemism for these products being "no-doc" or "low-doc" home loans). And in combination with credit cards, these products were marketed with increasing sophistication to the working class, the working poor, recent immigrants, and those in particular religious and social communities where home ownership was prized both culturally and even spiritually.[6]

These new consumer products formed the building blocks for systematic products through a process called securitization.[7] Through the bundling of risk, there arose a wide range of systemic financial products—collateralized debt obligations, securitized asset bundles such as residential mortgage-backed securities (RMBS), derivatives sold institutionally as well as in individual transactions. Of these products, most of the policy attention has focused upon two sorts, first the class of financial products known as *over-the-counter derivatives*.[8] Derivatives are simply financial products derived from other financial products, and these can be traded on an exchange like that in South Korea or the Eurex institution of Europe, or "over-the-counter" between a party and a counterparty. The lack of a major exchange for derivatives trading in the United States is a peculiar feature of the American market, and one that renders the American derivatives market largely unregulated, both institutionally (through the exchanges) and governmentally.[9] The second set of products that have come in for criticism are bundles of consumer products, or bundles of those bundles—residential mortgage–backed securities and credit default swaps (CDSs). The RMBS is a bundle of mortgages, each of varying quality (where quality levels correspond to slices or *tranches*, and in which the aggregation of individual mortgages is theoretically supposed to reduce the risk). The CDS is a hedge that a party makes on another party's default on a bond or loan; it could be (and often was), for instance, a hedge that a bank makes on the probability that another bank's RMBS-backed purchase of a bond will default. Again, these hedges can be used to reduce risk, and it was not uncommon for banks (or their associates) to take out credit default swaps on some of the very loan products that they were providing to other borrowers. Again, the construction and sale of these products has been largely unregulated in the United States over the past two decades.

Political and Institutional Characteristics of the Finance Realm

The political and institutional characteristics of the finance realm also figured prominently in the production of new policy. The American financial sector has in the past decade served as one of the top contributors to congressional and presidential campaigns and has spent far more money lobbying (through payments to lobbying organizations and firms) than in direct campaign contributions. According to the Center for Responsive Politics, from 1998 to 2010 the industrial sector represented by "real estate, finance and insurance" spent over $4 billion lobbying Washington officials, placing it at the top of all aggregated sectors in lobbying, including health and energy (see Figure 2.1). In 2009 and the first quarter of 2010, when the financial reform package was making its way through Congress, this same aggregated sector spent an estimated $592.5 million.[10] Unlike the contributions of many sectors, this lobbying and contributions behavior was strategically and skillfully bipartisan, with major banks like Goldman Sachs contributing heavily to Democratic as well as Republican campaigns. Tellingly, the financial services and banking industry contributed more to the Obama campaign than to the McCain campaign in the 2008 general election cycle.

Consider next that the U.S. executive branch and the American states each possess hundreds of various agencies that regulate features of systematic and consumer finance. These range from the Federal Reserve to state insurance

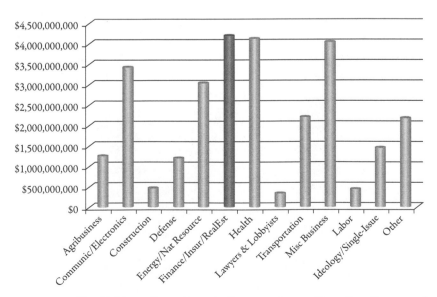

FIGURE 2.1 Total Lobbying Expenditures by Sector, 1998–2010 [from OpenSecrets.org].

regulators. At some level, these various agencies aggregate to more "administrative capacity" than in other realms of state activity, but the multiplicity of regulatory organizations in American finance also engenders the politics of boundaries. The boundaries are in part suggestive of turf wars. In other respects, the dividing lines of regulatory politics are as much about non-agency boundaries—the battles between and among professions, federalism (state versus federal authority), and even ideas and methods ("free-market economics" and "efficient markets" theories versus "behavioral finance" versus more populist approaches to regulation).

Second, the "industrial organization" of finance policy is less decentralized in Congress as compared to, say, health care. While their jurisdictions are far from watertight, the House Financial Services Committee and the Senate Finance Committee each control finance policy more than any single House or Senate committee controls health policy, environmental policy, or energy policy in their respective chambers. The two chairs of the congressional finance committees during the 111th Congress that coincided with Obama's first two years in office—Barney Frank of Massachusetts and Christopher Dodd of Connecticut—possessed experience and ties that gave each of them credibility with important financial constituencies. Yet the experience also gave each committee chair (and the committee's more experienced staff) some degree of independence from these constituencies, insofar as the expertise accumulated in each committee was substantial, and neither chair was placed in stark dependence for information upon the regulated industries. In the Obama administration, the Treasury Department occupied a critical agenda-setting role. Officials in Treasury—not only Secretary Timothy Geithner but particularly deputy and assistant secretaries, including Michael Barr and Eric Stein—spent much of the transition period and the winter and spring of 2009 writing up the administration's reform initiative.

Cross-Branch and Cross-Chamber Linkages: The Dodd-Treasury Alliance and the Filibuster

In a separated powers system, it is critical to pay attention to the linkages and the (informational and incentive) dependencies across the executive and legislative branches. Two of these are worth discussion here. First, numerous observers and participants have documented very close ties between Senator Chris Dodd and the Treasury Department. It was Dodd who, according to interviewees, helped to vocalize some of the Treasury Department's opposition to particular forms of capital requirements upon major banks, and it was the Treasury Department that later prevailed upon Dodd to give up a minor battle on those same leverage restrictions. Ties between Dodd and Treasury also figured prominently in the development of an independent consumer protection agency, the eventual placement of that agency in the Federal Reserve, and in the pitched battle over whether Elizabeth Warren would be nominated as its first director. Of course, ties between committee chairs and executive agencies have existed for well over a century—witness the long-standing portrait (sometime inaccurate but nonetheless telling) of "iron triangles" in 1950s and 1960s political science. What is interesting in this light is that no ties as strong as those between Dodd and Treasury were observed between top Treasury officials and the House Financial Services Committee or its chairman, Barney Frank. Frank and his staff maintained regular liaison with the Treasury Department and with other executive branch financial agencies, yet Frank seemed less willing to form a solid alliance with Treasury officials, both against the Republicans but also against the progressive/liberal wing of Democratic politicians.

A second linkage across the legislative players was induced by the Senate filibuster. Those interviewed repeatedly suggested that House Democrats felt it critical, in a number of policy realms, to produce unanimous or near-unanimous agreement among their caucus members so as to minimize opportunities for their Senate counterparts to defect from a Democratic coalition and thus endanger legislative prospects. This "signal-of-unity" logic was a strategy mentioned repeatedly in interviews, and it is difficult to tell whether it was pursued for all or many of the various planks in the legislation. Nonetheless, it was deemed important for the House majority (acting first) to present as unified a front as possible to the Senate majority. This cross-chamber dependency is somewhat different from that usually examined by political scientists, insofar as the supermajority institutions of the Senate induce not merely the abandonment and revision of bills in the House and even before the legislative process,[11] but also affected *the crafting of coalitions within the lower chamber and its committees.*

II. The Obama Agenda and Its Enactment: Policy Themes

The Obama Administration Response: Policy Proposals of the Spring of 2009

In the year following President Obama's inauguration, a debate raged about how to respond to the global financial crisis, both at the systemic and the consumer levels. Various reform proposals emerged from think tanks, university scholars, advocacy groups, and members of Congress. The Bush administration

Treasury Department contributed in ways that have been largely overlooked, especially by Secretary Henry Paulson, when he released a "blueprint" for financial reform in June 2007. Paulson's blueprint had little to say about derivatives regulation and consumer finance, but it called for cross-agency financial coordination, and bowed toward international capital standards by promising to complete rule-making in wake of the Basel II accords.[12]

In part because of the Treasury Department's agenda-setting role, important symbolic and structural patterns differentiated health care (where the Obama administration let Congress take the lead in drafting proposals) and financial reform (where the executive branch took the lead and Congress largely followed). The outline of reforms proposed by the Treasury Department in June 2009 was published in a heavily read and anticipated document: *Financial Regulatory Reform: A New Foundation.*[13] Much of this package of financial reforms was passed by the U.S. House of Representatives in December 2009. Like the Treasury proposal, this bill, which was reported by the House Financial Services Committee (chaired by Barney Frank), was interpreted as a bold, progressive strike against Wall Street interests on a number of fronts. The Treasury proposal and the House bill each contain a dizzying array of elements, but five common themes are of interest here.

1. Leverage restrictions and minimal capital requirements for systemic risk ("skin-in-the-game" reforms);
2. Regulation of OTC derivatives and/or requirement that they be traded on institutional exchanges;
3. Restrictions on the practices and business models of large banks (the most notable of these coming after the House bill, called the Volcker rule, which was a more recent proposal by the President in January 2010);
4. New regulations for credit rating agencies (CRAs);
5. A consumer financial protection agency.

In the months before and after this proposal, various personalities and lobbies tossed in their suggestions for reform. Harvard Law School professor Elizabeth Warren, appointed to chair the congressional oversight panel for the TARP program, became an especially forceful advocate of an independent agency to regulate consumer financial products. Her public profile, her perch at a congressional position, and her incredible skill at addressing professional and public audiences made Warren a political entrepreneur with unrivaled influence upon financial reform. Labor unions and progressive groups continued to pour resources into lobbying for the bill, though their energies were also diverted in part by the debate over health care reform.

Against these forces the various lobbies representing American and global finance entered the debate. These included the American Bankers' Association and the U.S. Chamber of Commerce. Conservative think tanks such as the American Enterprise Institute sponsored scholars and pundits—among them Charles Calomiris, Robert Hahn, Peter Wallison, and Todd Zywicki— who also expressed their doubts about financial reform and its effect upon "financial innovation." When the Obama health care reform passed Congress and was signed into law by the President, bankers' lobbies knew that financial reform was next on the national agenda, and they sprung into new and more visible forms of action.[14]

In the following sections, I take up these themes one by one, and examine the change in legislation that took place from the initial Obama proposal to the final enactment of legislation.

Capital Requirements and Leverage Restrictions

Financial reform witnessed major battles over the shape and content of capital requirements, namely the thorny question of how much "hard capital" banks should be required to keep versus how much of their capital they expose to risk-heavy trading and speculation activities. Among and within the branches of American government, these were some of the most heavily pressured and watched battles.

It was commonly understood that a critical part of the financial regulatory reform would be to require certain kinds of banks to take on less risk. A basic idea was to separate commercial banks from using their privileged position of capital access (the Fed) and institutional backstopping (FDIC guarantees for depository institutions) to take undue risks with capital. The critical question throughout this debate was how much capital to require in various categories of risk, and how those categories of risk would be defined. The most commonly referenced concept was that of "Tier 1" capital, which is essentially a bank's core investments in equity (direct company and asset investments, as differentiated from hedge funds, derivatives, or other secondary or tertiary asset markets). Well before the financial crisis, Tier 1 capital (as a percentage of assets or total capitalization) was interpreted as a measure of a bank's fiscal soundness.[15]

The Treasury Department's proposal was specific on a number of issues, but it was vague on capital requirements and on the importance of Tier 1 capital in particular. Instead, the Treasury's June 2009 blueprint suggested that stronger "prudential standards" should govern all firms and that "large, interconnected firms" should face stronger capital requirements. This more ambiguous stance was reflective of Treasury's desire that prudential standards be delegated to regulators, namely to the Fed and the Treasury itself, as represented in the umbrella oversight body established by the legislation, the Financial Services Oversight Council (FSOC). Yet the Treasury Department's ambiguity created something of a legislative vacuum, and that space was quickly filled with a proposal in the House Financial Services Committee. Working with David Moss, a business historian at Harvard, Barney Frank's committee endorsed a proposal of a maximum 15-to-1 ratio of total capital to Tier 1 capital for all regulated firms, and a lower ratio (not fully specified, but left to the FSOC) for systemically important and larger firms. This proposal, slightly modified, passed the House in December 2009.

The Senate took up the House proposal and, partly at the behest of the Treasury Department, proposed to reduce its specificity. Yet in a critical but unexpected turn of events, a juncture that happened after Dodd introduced his bill, Republican Senator Susan Collins of Maine in May 2009 offered her own proposal for leverage requirements.[16] Collins's proposal was more complicated than can be summarized fully here, but it had two critical planks: (1) a mandated 25-to-1 ratio of total capital to Tier 1 capital (lower for systemically critical firms), and (2) a tightened definition of Tier 1 capital, such that hybrid investment vehicles known as "trust-preferred securities" (TruPS) would no longer qualify as Tier 1 capital. In many respects, the Collins leverage proposal worried major banks even more than the House legislation did, and House legislators weakened it in the conference committee stage of legislation.[17] The Treasury Department again expressed its opposition to this proposal—now not only the ratios but the very concepts by which capital would be defined would be taken partially out of the Department's orbit.[18] But with Collins centrally involved in the capital requirements game, Dodd could no longer function as an effective proposal-stopper. With the victory of Scott Brown in the January 2010 Massachusetts Senate race, Collins became the kind of moderate Republican that Senate Democrats like Dodd sorely needed in order to get the bill through. Hence Collins could not be ignored. Whereas Dodd initially tried to stop the Collins proposal on behalf of the Treasury, it was later on that the Treasury Department, realizing that Collins's proposal was likely to survive and that Democrats could not afford to alienate her, asked Dodd to relent and allow the Collins proposal through the Senate. Collins's proposal also had the backing of FDIC chairwoman Sheila Bair, a Republican appointee and an experienced official widely respected among the conservative-leaning circles of American finance policy.

The final legislation embeds parts of the Collins proposal's more rigid definition of Tier 1 capital, though it delegates the question for study.[19] The exact capital requirements will, however, be delegated to "appropriate federal banking regulatory agencies"; even the recipient of delegated power is not precisely established under the statute. The final Act keeps the Collins amendment that requires bank holding companies to hold at least as much Tier 1 capital as smaller banks (a requirement calibrated by reference to the smaller bank subsidiaries of these holding companies). Banks are also forced to drop TruPS from their Tier 1 capital requirements, with a long transition phase for doing so.

The capital requirements battle was only part of the larger financial reform package, but it expressed some of the more visible patterns of financial politics during the early years of the Obama administration and the 111th Congress—the relative independence of the House Financial Services Committee from the Treasury Department (compared to the Senate Finance Committee), and the unique power of unexpected proposals from structurally and symbolically pivotal legislators. The relevant planks of the legislation will depend heavily upon regulators for their enforcement.

Proprietary Trading Restrictions

Another important battleground in the reform debate was tied to observers' understanding of the financial crisis and past battles over financial innovation. The problem of "moral hazard," as it was widely termed, was not simply one of government-backed banks abusing their protection by over-leveraging themselves. It was also the problem of government-backed banks having the status of depository institutions—the very risk-pursuant institutions were those that held the savings of the middle and working classes, and yet the very banks that would get in the most trouble by this system of incentives were the institutions that would place enormous aggregate liabilities upon the federal government in the case of hedges gone bad. In this way, institutional "moral hazard" threatened not only consumers but also the federal government's balance sheet.

Neither the Treasury proposal nor the House bill entertained serious limitations upon proprietary activities of commercial banks (the set of activities often associated with investment banks, such as foreign exchange trading, hedge fund management, or arbitrage-related operations). Yet in the midst of the financial reform debate of the fall of 2010, many commentators noticed that a critical act of the 1990s—the 1999 repeal of the Glass-Steagall Act of 1933—had not been discussed as a possible contributor to the financial crisis.

Into the vacuum stepped former Federal Reserve chairman Paul Volcker. Volcker had the bipartisan credibility of someone who once served Republican causes (he was the Fed chairman who consciously and controversially kept a lid on inflation during the early 1980s during the depth of the recession then) and who had decades-long experience in global financial policy. Volcker advanced a proposal, one favored by President Obama in January 2009 when it was announced, which required that insured depository institutions be prohibited from proprietary trading activities. Again, the Treasury Department did not endorse this proposal, and numerous commentators have suggested that its leadership (Secretary Geithner and Assistant Secretary Barr) opposed rigorous partitioning of commercial banking from proprietary trading. However, the Treasury Department's hands were somewhat tied; in February 2010, five former Treasury secretaries came out in public support of the Volcker rule, stating in a letter to the *Wall Street Journal* that "[b]anks benefiting from public support by means of access to the Federal Reserve and FDIC insurance should not engage in essentially speculative activity unrelated to essential bank services."[20]

The Volcker, rule in its strict form, was written into the Senate legislation by Oregon Democrat Jeff Merkley and Michigan Democrat Carl Levin. The clause passed the Senate, and soon after the passage of the Senate bill, the Obama Treasury Department hinted that it would support the proposal in negotiations over reconciling the House and Senate version.[21] In part due to the pivotal influence of Massachusetts Republican Scott Brown, however, the Volcker rule was diluted into what is known as "the 3-percent Volcker rule." Only a maximum of 3 percent of Tier 1 capital can be invested by large firms in proprietary activities (including hedge funds and private equity funds), and no federally insured bank's investments can compose more than 3 percent of any single hedge fund. The discretion given to regulators under the final bill is reduced compared to that of the Senate proposal and some observers see the Treasury Department as reluctant to write detailed (read: binding and specific) new rules for the enforcement of the Volcker rules.[22]

Derivatives

A third area in which large investment banks and financial institutions would be potentially constrained in financial reform appears in the regulation of derivatives markets, especially those sold "over-the-counter" between two or more counterparties and not cleared upon an exchange. It is a more complicated story than can be told adequately here, but derivatives got their start in agricultural commodities, where bundles of futures contracts, and bundles of those bundles, were the subject of massive speculation in grain, meat, and other agricultural markets from the late nineteenth century onward. It is for this reason that a regulatory agency that initially had primary authority over agricultural commodities—the Commodities Futures Trading Commission (CFTC)—began to investigate the regulation of derivatives in the 1990s. In a now legendary showdown, the chair of that commission (Brooksley Born) advanced a proposal for derivates regulation that earned the strident opposition of major financial players in the Clinton administration, mainly Fed Chairman Alan Greenspan, Treasury Secretary Robert Rubin, and (later) Treasury Secretary Lawrence Summers.

The Treasury's June 2009 proposal again gave derivatives regulation a rather ambiguous treatment, and the major proposal for regulation of derivatives (namely moving them from over-the-counter trading to institutionally regulated trading on an exchange) came in the Peterson-Frank Amendment, which was incorporated into the House legislation. There were many amendments offered to the House legislation, but two by Michigan representative Bart Stupak demonstrated the relatively moderate nature of the House bill's restrictions. Stupak proposed first that any derivative must be traded on a federally registered exchange; this proposal failed by a vote of 98–330. He then proposed that the Commodity Futures Trading Commission and/or the Securities and Exchange Commission be empowered to ban "abusive swaps." This amendment also failed. The large margins against Stupak's two amendments point to a moderate appetite for derivatives regulation in the House.

Another amendment by New York Representative Scott Murphy was intended to weaken the application of derivatives regulation to the major banks by the Murphy amendment constraining the definition of "major swap participant" in the Peterson-Frank clause to "those firms that either do a substantial amount of speculative trading or that have derivative positions that are large enough to pose a threat to the financial system." Murphy was especially interested in protecting smaller trading houses and capital firms (as opposed to major investment banks). In a surprise to House Democratic leaders and a setback for Frank and the House Financial Services Committee, this regulation-weakening amendment passed on the House floor with the votes of many Republicans as well as those of many Democrats.

The Senate bill followed the House bill in that it mandated trading on exchanges for all but a small set of derivatives. Yet, just when derivatives-trading operations felt that, with the Murphy amendment and the moderate nature of the Dodd bill, they had dodged a bullet, another unforeseen critical event happened. Senator Blanche Lincoln of Arkansas, under a serious primary challenge from Arkansas Attorney General Bill Halter, seized upon derivatives regulation as a means of demonstrating her bona fides to Arkansas Democratic primary voters. She introduced an amendment that would require all commercial banks to partition their derivatives trading units into legally and organizationally separate entities. This "spin-off" proposal surprised and alarmed major banks and their lobbyists, who were neither expecting it nor pleased with its implications. Swaps units had become important profit centers for major commercial banks in the previous decade.

The Lincoln proposal, like the Collins proposal on capital requirements and Senator Scott Brown's weakening of the bill in conference in June 2010, demonstrated the enormous shadow of the Senate filibuster. Either to weaken or to strengthen the proposal, well-positioned senators (conservative Democrats or moderate Republicans) could hold up an entire legislative package because of the necessity of having 60 votes to proceed in the Senate. Strategically, the filibuster requirement was compounded by Senator Harry Reid's refusal to call Republicans' bluff and to compel them to filibuster popular legislation.

The Lincoln spin-off provision survived the Senate intact, and various interests immediately set about trying to weaken or kill it. In some measure, as the final structure of the legislation suggests, they succeeded. In other respects, Lincoln understood that the success of the proposal would be critical to her chances for a Senate primary victory as well as the (slim) prospect of her re-election in Arkansas in a midterm season.

And perhaps most surprisingly, the fight over the derivatives provision in the conference committee (with various senators arguing for the strict Lincoln spin-off while others called for a weakening, and House conferees largely favoring a more relaxed version) deflected attention and lobbying power from other issues and planks of the legislation. As in much political bargaining, especially at such a late stage of the game, players must focus their attention upon just a few issues. It was widely expected that conferees would attempt to weaken the consumer financial protection agency or perhaps the capital requirements; yet the immense push against the stringent form of the Lincoln amendment deflected attention away from those issues. In the absence of Lincoln's primary-induced proposal, not only derivatives regulation but other planks of the Dodd-Frank Act would have looked quite different from their final, enacted form.

The final Act preserved much of Lincoln's derivatives rule, mandating a spin-off for commodity-based derivatives (agriculture and metals), energy derivatives (such as those perfected and traded by Enron before its infamous demise), and non-investment-grade credit default swap derivatives. Any commercial bank must henceforth partition these operations in a non-bank entity (one without the protections and advantages of a federal bank chapter, FDIC insurance, or the Fed's credit window). In a little-noticed but fundamental revision to Section 23A of the Federal Reserve Act, financial institutions with derivatives operations can no longer use other funds and assets to bail out their derivatives operations, and in an odd resurrection of Congressman Bart Stupak's December 2009 amendment, the Act mandates the vehicle listing of all "new derivative products" by the CFTC and the SEC (Securities and Exchange Commission).[23]

Reform and Regulation of Credit-Rating Agencies

The role of credit-rating agencies in the financial crisis of 2008 has been widely discussed. Much like the centrality of the accounting firm Arthur Andersen to the corruption and demise of Enron, it is said, credit-rating agencies (CRAs) facilitated the corruption and demise of major Wall Street firms by inflating the soundness of financial institutions and the risky mortgage-backed investments in which they were piling their capital. The Obama-Treasury proposal gave particular specificity to CRA regulation, calling for the SEC to more strictly regulate them. In a move to give the government's financial regulators more independence and expertise, the Treasury Department's proposal also called upon other government regulators to avoid using CRA ratings in their evaluations of the safety and soundness of financial institutions and asset classes. Finally, the Obama proposal banned "conflicted advising," or the marketing by CRAs of their services or evaluations to those firms whose debt or creditworthiness they were rating.

The case of CRA reform stands as one where, for all intents and purposes, the outline suggested by the Obama administration was strengthened and rendered more specific by action in the Congress. It is worth considering as something of a departure case whose trajectory of development runs counter to the general tendencies of the various reform planks, most of which were watered down or heavily amended with generalities or exceptions in the House and Senate (and often yet again in conference). Led by Massachusetts Democrat Barney Frank, the House took the Obama-Treasury proposal and specified a positive mandate for annual SEC review and reports on CRAs, including a disclosure of their potential conflicts of interest and their ratings decisions. The House also undermined a key girder of the CRAs' power, dropping the requirement that mutual funds limit their investments to top-rated investment classes—this too was Barney Frank's aspiration—and the House further added expert legal liability for CRAs, exposing them for the first time to tortiable claims at the federal level. The Obama administration's conflicted advising ban was kept.

The Senate did little to change the House bill on this front and further established an Office of Credit Rating in the SEC. Senator Al Franken introduced a controversial amendment to have a unified and systematic government rating of the various CRAs; this amendment would not survive the conference committee. The conference committee and the final bill did, however, retain the major planks promulgated by the Treasury a year earlier and severely limited the CRAs' power and legitimacy by divorcing regulatory agency judgments and mutual fund investments from the ratings.

A New Regulatory Agency for Consumer Financial Protection

The most controversial proposal of the Obama financial agenda came in the form of the resurrection of an older idea about consumer financial protection, one implemented by the Canadian government in 2002. In 2007, Harvard law scholar Elizabeth Warren published a highly influential essay in the journal *Democracy* entitled "Unsafe at Any Rate." The idea for a consumer protection agency was built upon work she had done with a new academic network named the Tobin Project, founded by Harvard Business School professor David Moss. Warren's idea was to create a separate agency for financial safety, one that echoed institutions established by the Canadian government almost a decade ago. Even during the midst of the financial crisis of the fall of 2008, little legislative or media attention was given to this idea. The idea became legislatively tangible in March 2009, when it was formally introduced to Congress as a proposal for a "Financial Products Safety Commission" by Representatives William Delahunt of Massachusetts and Brad Miller of North Carolina. Key players in the Obama administration had been attracted to the idea—some (Assistant Treasury Secretary Michael Barr and the President himself) more than others (Treasury Secretary Timothy Geithner and National Economic Council head Larry Summers)—and the Treasury included the independent agency idea in its blueprint for financial reform in June 2009.

In the year following the introduction of the Obama Treasury blueprint, it is the independent agency idea that attracted most of the attention and vitriol. Warren's brainchild was supported and attacked, surpassed only by health care and perhaps Afghanistan as front-page news and a front-burner priority for politicians. Yet other changes that are further off the radar screen have come for strong opposition from banks, lending companies, and existing federal agencies with turf and fee-based revenues to protect.

The Emergence of a Threat, and the Fed's Response

The idea for a new independent consumer agency did not become tangible or threatening to existing regulators with turf to protect until March 2009, when a bill creating a financial product safety commission (FPSC) was introduced in the House of Representatives. The announcement for this bill came on March 5, 2009.[24] The formal bill introduction to the Senate occurred on March 10th.[25] A number of web-based news sources also began to discuss the legislative proposal for a new commission around this time.[26]

In the bills introduced to Congress, and in the Obama administration's proposal as released in June 2009, the Consumer Financial Protection Agency (CFPA) posed clear threats to the turf of what may be called the "status quo regulators" of U.S. consumer finance. What was undoubtedly concerning to officials at the Fed, the Federal Deposit Insurance Corporation (FDIC), the Federal Trade Commission (FTC), and other agencies was that significant parts of their governing authority (what one might call their policy "turf") and in some cases their budgets and personnel would stand to be transferred to the new consumer agency. The FTC was one of the agencies to circle wagons most forcefully. Commissioner William E. Kovacic read the administration's bill as transferring "*all* consumer financial protection functions of the Federal Trade Commission" to the new agency. Kovacic also saw the legislation as defining "consumer financial protection functions so broadly as to include 'research, rulemaking, issuance of orders or guidance.' This expansive definition would include the Bureau of Economics' research as well as the FTC's enormously valuable public workshops and consumer education programs."[27]

Kovacic saw in the bill an affront not merely to the agency as a whole, but to its Bureau of Economics and its Bureau of Competition in particular. Indeed, Kovacic's defense of the Commission was so strong that he saw the financial crisis as a rationale for *expanding* the powers and responsibilities of the FTC: "Rather than divest the FTC of all of its consumer financial protection functions and give it hollow 'backstop authority,' a more promising approach could be to remove jurisdictional limits that currently constrain the FTC's regulatory and enforcement authority in the financial services sector."[28]

Yet given the size and expanse of the Federal Reserve—and its privileged funding structure among government agencies—it is not surprising that the Federal Reserve's mobilization against a fully independent consumer agency was larger and more forceful. Some observers saw in the CFPA proposal the largest threat to the Fed in four decades.[29] The bill passed by the House and initially considered in the Senate would have created and authorized the transfer of authorities, funds, and personnel from a number of national agencies, most notably the Federal Reserve.[30] Beyond this, the proposals had some of the CFPA's funding coming directly from the Fed. This proposed change was significant, given that the Federal Reserve's funding model differs from that of most federal agencies in that it is fee-based and less visible to the taxpayer. Of course, American consumers pay for the Federal Reserve's operations nonetheless, because banks undoubtedly pass along the direct costs of the fees (and the "indirect" administrative or compliance costs of paying them) to their customers. Banks and other lender organizations lobby against increases in these fees, and hence the size of aggregate fee revenue can only be so large before it is constrained by political resistance from banks and other fee-payers. Given such a constraint, each agency funded by fees has an incentive to capture the largest portion of the transaction and institution fee base that it can; hence the transfer of Fed funds to the CFPA would profoundly affect the Fed, even though it did not alter the balance of spending and taxation.[31]

The Fed responded in speech making and in activity, both defending its statutory and historical prerogatives in consumer protection, and pumping up its enforcement activities. Daniel Tarullo, a member of the Fed's Board of Governors, offered the first comprehensive public statement on consumer protection regulation by top Fed officials in the entire aftermath of the financial crisis on March 19, 2009.[32] Chairman Ben Bernanke did not mention regulation of consumer products in any speech following the crisis until April 2, right after (and well after) legislative energy for the proposal for consumer protection had begun. His major address on the issue came in mid-April 2009, when he addressed the issue of "consumer protection" for the first time in his response to the financial crisis. The first hint of opposition to the independent agency came in Bernanke's insistence that it would be his agency that would offer the appropriate response to government failures in financial consumer protection in testimony on July 21, 2009. This was followed by Governor Tarullo's warnings in testimony to the Senate on July 23, 2009. Then, two days after Bernanke defended his institution before Congress on July 21, and the very day that Governor Tarullo warned Congress about the costs of transferring these important responsibilities to another agency (or any agency not under the Fed's penumbra), the Fed announced the first in a set of critical proposed rules changes, to Regulation Z for mortgage disclosures. Two months later, as the House began to take up the independent agency proposal in committee, the Fed proposed that credit cards should be subject to similar regulatory reforms, and Bernanke followed on October 1 with a proposal that Congress create a council of risk regulators. This proposal, which would have the effect of retaining the status quo regulators for systemic and possibly consumer finance, echoed a plan for a council of consumer protection regulators that was then under consideration in the House, proposed by Idaho Democrat Walt Minnick. The House later defeated the Minnick plan and passed a financial regulatory reform bill that established the CFPA.[33]

In July 2009, when Fed officials proposed a second set of revisions to Regulation Z, observers of financial markets and financial regulation noted two things. First, the changes were significant, with the *Wall Street Journal* calling them "sweeping new consumer protections for mortgages and home-equity loans." The new rules compelled simplified disclosures for mortgage costs and amortization terms; they effectively banned yield spread premiums; they directed lenders to create one-page documents demonstrating the risks of loans to consumers; they forced lenders to show consumers how their rate compares with rates of borrowers with better credit.[34] Second, observers noted the clear correspondence of these rules to the turf threat posed by a CFPA. As contributors for the financial web site *fxstreet.com* stated in an interpretation of the July 2009 proposed rules,

> Bottom line: The proposed changes are in line with suggested reforms within the legislative process regarding the Consumer Financial Protection Agency (CFPA). The Federal Reserve may no longer regulate consumer financial products under certain iterations of the legislation backing the CFPA. Today's announcement is part of the feedback loop regarding this pending legislation and implications for the Federal Reserve's structure.[35]

So too, there was an odd and little noticed bump in FRB enforcement patterns, especially starting in March 2009. Using data listed on the Board's web site, announced enforcement actions against banks and lenders came at a snail's pace (just over three per month) during the very time that active foreclosures were hitting one million in statistical reports. Only when the crisis passed "from Main Street to Wall Street," in September 2008, did Fed enforcement activity (again, its own announcements) surge (to about eight and a half per month). But the Fed's announcements on its enforcement activity reached new (and unprecedented) heights when Congress took up the idea of an independent regulator in March 2009. From a post-crisis average of eight announced enforcement actions per month, the Fed nearly doubled its announcements to 16 actions per month (see Figure 2.2). Every other day, or three out of four business days per week, the Fed was publicly announcing a new enforcement action.

Regulation Comes Full Circle: The Fed Gets a Consumer Bureau

In the end, the Dodd-Frank Act placed a consumer protection agency within the boundaries of the Federal Reserve. In a proposal released on March 15, 2010, Dodd proposed placement of a "consumer bureau" inside the FRB, and in a sign that Dodd and other legislators had done their political homework, independent agency advocate Elizabeth Warren endorsed the proposal. Although it is difficult to prove, the Federal Reserve's consumer protection push from March 2009 forward probably made the agency a more hospitable location for a consumer protection bureau. I have argued elsewhere that the Fed may be a poor place for the positioning of a consumer protection bureau, given the agency's undistinguished consumer protection record, and its habit of shifting attention from consumer protection to monetary policy first, then prudential regulation second, when the chance permits. The issue has less to do with organizational capacity—there are skilled cadres of bank regulators and inspectors in the regional banks and offices of the Federal Reserve

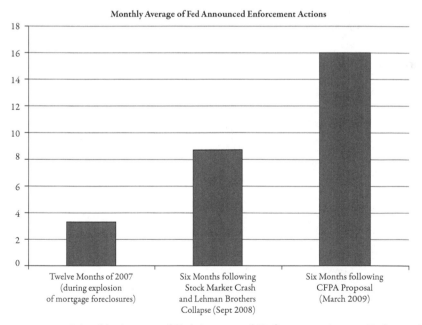

Monthly Average of Fed Announced Enforcement Actions

Twelve Months of 2007 (during explosion of mortgage foreclosures)

Six Months following Stock Market Crash and Lehman Brothers Collapse (Sept 2008)

Six Months following CFPA Proposal (March 2009)

FIGURE 2.2 Monthly Average of Fed Announced Enforcement Actions Before and After the Consumer Agency Threat.

System—than with the lack of status that consumer protection activity has at the Fed. In light of the financial crisis, the reputational threats to the Fed and the creation of the new consumer bureau, this status hierarchy may change considerably in the years to come.[36]

Nonetheless, progressive proponents of financial reform have genuine reasons to think that the new Consumer Financial Protection Bureau will have strong powers. Even though the Bureau's rules will be reviewed by an oversight council, they will not be reviewed by the Office of Information and Regulatory Affairs in the Office of Management and Budget (OMB), where cost-benefit analysis has become entrenched in the last three decades. The independent funding stream from the Federal Reserve will insulate the bureau from appropriations politics. And the legislation even included the possibility of an "interim director" appointed through the Treasury Department, temporarily bypassing the Senate confirmation process.[37]

A late-stage legislative defeat for proponents of a consumer bureau came in the "carve-out" exemption won by independent auto dealers. California Republican John Campbell introduced the amendment, which passed on the House floor and again in the Senate after being introduced by Sam Brownback. Independent auto dealers are in every congressional district and, as one congressional staffer expressed the point, "they sponsor Little Leagues and soccer games." Their ubiquitous presence was enough to overcome opposition to the amendment from the House Financial Services Committee and the Obama administration. It was an example of the power of some of the smallest "financial institutions" in the odd and complicated politics of the 111th Congress.

In the two months following the passage of the Dodd-Frank Act, perhaps the most acrimonious fight came over the appointment of Elizabeth Warren as the first director of the Consumer Financial Protection Bureau—a battle that she ultimately lost but that nonetheless is revealing. The issue did not arise until a July 15, 2010, report in the *Huffington Post* suggested that Treasury Secretary Timothy Geithner opposed Warren's appointment to the post, preferring instead his deputy Michael Barr. Progressive activists immediately and furiously set into motion, circulating a petition to the President for Warren's appointment that garnered a quarter-million signatures within a month.[38]

Liberal Democrats (including Barney Frank), skeptical economists (such as Simon Johnson and Paul Krugman), and progressive activists (SEIU and AFL-CIO on the labor side, as well as web-based progressive groups such as Progressive Change Campaign Committee) openly lobbied President Obama to nominate none other than Elizabeth Warren, brain-mother of the independent consumer regulator, to head the new agency. Republicans like Alabama

Senator Richard Shelby announced their opposition to Warren, but others (such as Senator Charles Grassley of Iowa) were viewed as possibly supportive. The Warren nomination assumed a symbolic status to the progressive wing of the Democratic Party that rivaled, if it did not surpass, the pressure that surrounded the public option concept in the national health care debate.

Senator Dodd complicated matters (perhaps intentionally, given his ties to the Treasury Department) when he repeatedly expressed concern about whether Warren would be confirmable in the Senate. On September 17, 2010, Obama stood in the Rose Garden with Warren at his side and announced his appointment of Warren as a special Assistant to the President (and to Secretary Geithner) for the purpose of managing the launch of the consumer bureau. Although some confusion set in about the precise nature of Professor Warren's authorities and powers under the post, liberal groups and union leaders hailed the appointment.

Warren immediately set about creating the structural and human foundations of the Bureau. She did so by recruiting top legal and financial talent to the agency, and by embedding an important principle in the very DNA of the agency's official structure. Warren focused regulatory attention upon two central consumer financial products—mortgages and credit cards—and placed these at the top of her organizational chart for offices where rules would be written (see Figure 2.3). That chart also reflected an important principle, namely that rule writing would be deeply affected by research organized within the Bureau. So too, Warren's first appointments—Rajeev Date (from the Cambridge Winter Center for Financial Institutions Policy) as a senior advisor; Steven Antonakes (previously Commissioner of Banks for Massachusetts) to lead depository supervision; Richard Cordry (formerly Ohio Attorney General) to head enforcement; and David Silberman (from Kessler Financial Services) to head the establishment of the credit cards unit—reflected an emphasis upon coalition-building, upon legitimacy, and upon quick and early action on mortgages and credit cards.

Political work was just as important as the structural work. In at least three deft moves, Warren began to lay the foundation for a multidimensional support coalition undergirding her agency. First, she began her appointment by striking a conciliatory stance toward the politically organized banking industry, appearing at a meeting of the Financial Services Roundtable in September 2010. Rather publicly, Warren pledged to work cooperatively with bankers' organizations and remarked that "It is now, right here at the beginning, that we have a remarkable chance to put aside misconceptions and preconceptions—whether they are yours or mine." Although some measure of distrust continued

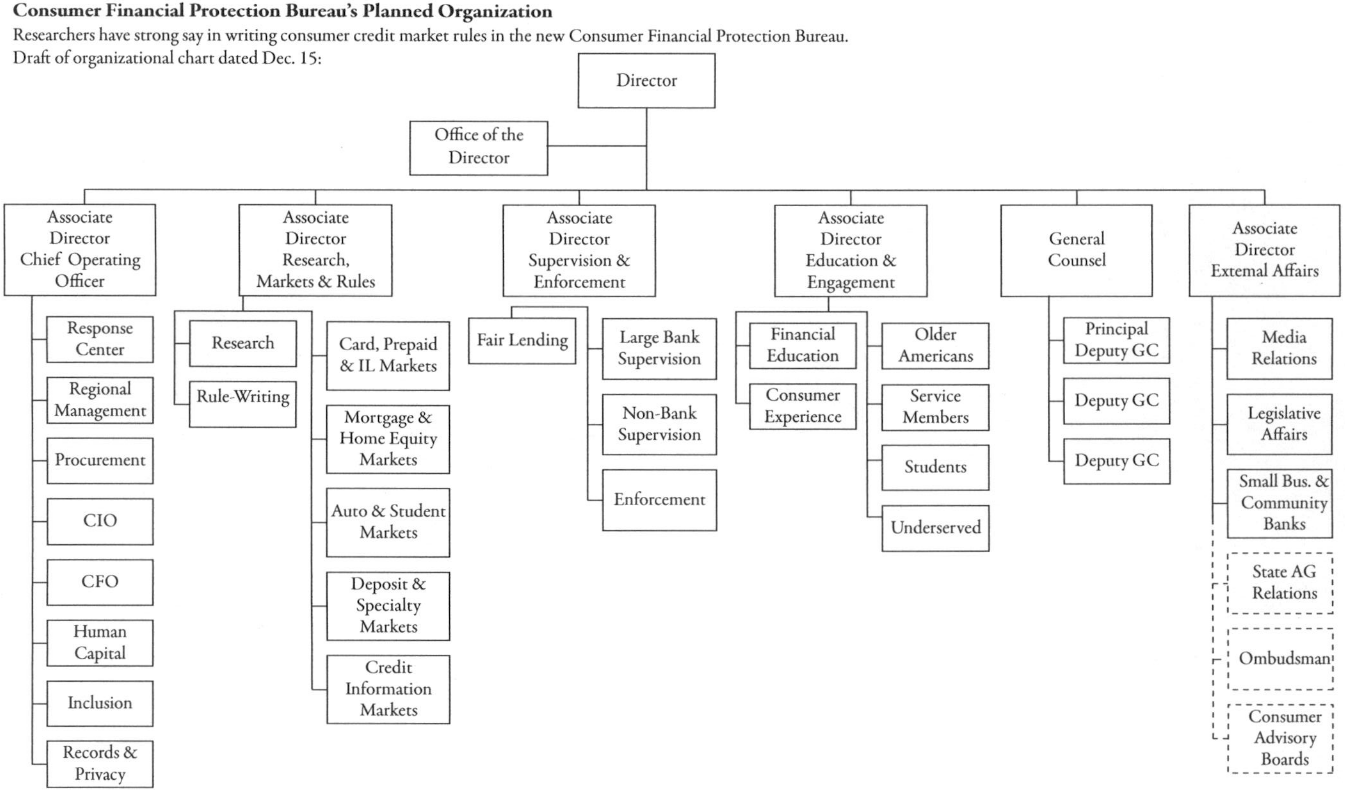

Consumer Financial Protection Bureau's Planned Organization

Researchers have strong say in writing consumer credit market rules in the new Consumer Financial Protection Bureau.

Draft of organizational chart dated Dec. 15:

FIGURE 2.3 Planned Organization Chart of the Consumer Financial Protection Bureau.

between the bankers' lobby and Warren, observers report that her public addresses had the effect of easing the tension. Second, Warren began to invite state attorneys general to participate in the establishment of the agency and even consult for the making of rules. This move had the effect of heading off federalism-based objections to the Bureau, and it also helped to cement the legitimacy judgments, and the loyalty, of the attorneys general. Finally, Warren continued to court community banks with assurances that the Bureau's policies would help them compete on a more even playing field vis-à-vis larger banks and lending companies.[39]

III. The Significance of Financial Reform and Its Legacies

On July 21, 2010, a number of critical financial reforms were struck into law in the "Dodd-Frank" Wall Street Reform and Consumer Protection Act. If there is a theme that emerges from the legislation, its politics, and the aftermath, it is that much of the real work of reform has just begun, with rule making and enforcement patterns comprising the truly significant realms of American government activity. In light of the indeterminacy of financial reform, it is incontestable that considerable institutional change is being anticipated by major American and global banks, which have already begun to consult lawyers and boards to map out strategies for separating parts of their operations from their core banking services.

Aims and Potential Moves of the New Republican House Majority

An important force shaping the evolution of financial reform will be the opposition in the House of Representatives, where Republicans won a commanding majority in the midterm elections of November 2010. Republicans voted near-uniformly against the Dodd-Frank bill in the House and all but three (Scott Brown, Olympia Snowe, and Susan Collins) voted against the bill in the Senate. While there has been considerable criticism of the Act from incoming House Financial Services Committee Chair Spencer Bachus, it remains the case that the Republicans are less likely to act forcefully to water down the Dodd-Frank bill than they are to constrain its implementation through congressional oversight. This difference stems not least from the broader popularity of the financial reform package and from the still-dubious public reputation of Wall Street and the American banking sector.

The Republican House majority aims to conduct strict oversight of the Consumer Financial Protection Bureau, but its hands are tied. While congressional Republicans can use appropriations as an oversight tool with which to control many federal agencies, the CFPB receives its funding from the Federal Reserve budget, which is financed by transaction fees, not legislative appropriations. Although some congressional Republicans have voiced their intention to return the Bureau to appropriations-based funding, this move would require a positive change in law and is unlikely to pass the Senate or the veto pen of President Obama. More likely, the early actions of congressional Republicans will focus on hearings and using publicity to shape the choices and agenda of the Bureau.

One reason that congressional Republicans may focus heavily upon administrative implementation of Dodd-Frank is that most of the critical action has been delegated to existing and new federal regulators. To some extent, this pattern confirms a long-studied array of delegation decisions in political science, whereby politicians embrace the risk of losing control over policy by taking advantage of the superior expertise and capacity of administrative organizations.[40] Yet the dynamics of financial reform in the Obama agenda gesture to a much more complicated (in some respects, more strategic but less predictable, ex ante or ex post) dynamic than political science models of delegation usually recognize. The financial realm in American politics is, as I suggested at the outset of this essay, rather well populated by agencies with considerable capacity, especially when the United States is compared to other advanced industrial democracies. Delegation, in this context, was not merely the choice of a legislature as to whether or not to hand over policy-making authority versus the trade-off in expertise forgone by entrusting policy making to congressional committees. Rather, existing financial agencies with stable funding models and thousands upon thousands of highly educated, centrally positioned, and legitimated employees lobbied aggressively for their agencies and/or their professional disciplines (quantitative finance, administrative and contracts law, behavioral finance, and others). The end result of the Dodd-Frank Act was as much due to the machinations of existing federal agencies (especially the Treasury and the Federal Reserve) as it was due to the conscious decisions of legislators about where to place delegated authority. This is all the more so in the case of the Obama financial regulation initiative because the main blueprint for the entire effort was hammered out in the Treasury Department.

As evidence that administrative and bureaucratic politics lies at the center of past and present financial reform, the most pitched battles in the wake of

President Obama's signing of the Dodd-Frank Act have come in appointments and rule making. Combined with expressions of doubt by Senators Merkley and Levin, on the one hand, and economist Simon Johnson, on the other, about the Treasury Department's seriousness in writing strong rules to enforce the Volcker provision, the fight over the Warren nomination suggests that the biggest battles of American financial reform have yet to be waged. And when they are waged, they will be fought in venues much less visible than those that hosted legislative debate over the past two years; progressive groups and consumer groups, sensing this reality, were pressing the Warren nomination for exactly this reason.

Still, the paths not taken in this saga remain informative.[41] At least four major ideas were cast aside: (1) a totally independent consumer protection agency; (2) requirements for "plain vanilla" baselines for consumer financial products; (3) the Volcker rule in its pure form; and (4) a tax on larger banks to pay for the possible costs of future bailouts. The more stringent regulation of derivatives in the original House bill is also a casualty of the process, though the Lincoln amendment to the Senate legislation helped to resurrect these restrictions.

The strangulation metaphor may be apt here because these various proposals died a relatively quiet death. There was a "pivotal politics" of the Senate filibuster and the usual expression of multiple veto points, but those veto points were as much the result of culturally and institutionally privileged elites as they were of the calculus of supermajorities. Given that moments of major institutional reform in finance come only once a generation or two, and given that general interest in reforms is often quietly weakened in the years after their enactment, obstruction by strangulation may leave a distinct policy legacy.

The coming appointments, draft rules, and early enforcement actions will tell us much about the longer arc of twenty-first century financial reform. These actions, too, are Obama administration prerogatives, and their success or failure will mark an important Obama administration legacy. The salience of appointments for rule making with new statutes is well known among administrative lawyers (yet deeply understudied in the social science literatures). This salience underscores the importance (symbolic and structural) of Obama's consumer protection bureau appointment, and will in other ways shed considerable light on the appointments of regulators—ranging from Secretary Geithner to Barr and to Warren herself—who have heretofore been principally known for their advocacy and involvement in the legislative process.

Yet the structural changes being undertaken by some of the most powerful organizations on the planet are evidence that the financial reform initiative will have broad, transformative effects.[42] Even under the most reluctant expression of rule making and enforcement, there will now be strong restrictions on leverage at the largest financial institutions, a severe weakening and dimunition of the power and discretion of credit rating agencies, a spin-off of dozens upon dozens of trading offices and derivatives and swaps operations at the nation's largest banks, and a consumer protection regulator writing and enforcing rules that do not need to pass through the OMB for review and which do not need to rely upon the congressional appropriations process for funding.

Notes

1. Text in this chapter is reproduced with permission from Daniel Carpenter, "Reconstituting the Submerged State: The Challenges of Social Policy Reform in the Obama Era," *Perspectives on Politics* 8(3) (August 2010): 825–846. For support on related and ongoing work for this project, the author thanks the Russell Sage Foundation, the National Science Foundation (SES-0351048 and SES-0076452), the Behavioral Economics and Consumer Finance Program of the Russell Sage and Alfred Sloan Foundations, and the Tobin Project. The arguments and characterizations herein are claimed by the author alone, and bear no relation to the views of these entities. For helpful comments and conversations, he also thanks Sarah Binder, Andrea Campbell, Steven Croley, Carter Dougherty, Dan Geldon, Danny Goroff, Tom Hamburger, Christopher Hood, Jeffrey Isaac, Larry Jacobs, Howell Jackson, Robert Kuttner, Des King, James Kwak, Patrick Legales, Suzanne Mettler, David Moss, Annelise Riles, Adam Sheingate, Theda Skocpol, John Skrentny, Susan Wachter, Eric Wanner, and Elizabeth Warren.

2. On the gilded network and its brief aperture in 2008 and 2009, see Carpenter 2011; for a discussion of the failures (often quite conscious) of existing regulators in the run-up to the crisis, consult Engel and McCoy (2011), Chapters 8–10.

3. Tufano 2009; Campbell 2006. For an excellent overview of the American housing finance system, consult Immergluck 2009.

4. Warren & Warren 2003; Immergluck 2009; Krugman, 2008. For a political economy interpretation of this widening trend of inequality, consult Bartels 2009.

5. On the possible linkage of Glass-Steagall's repeal to the recent explosion of bank failures, consult David Moss, "An Ounce of Prevention: The Power of Public Risk Management in Stabilizing the Financial System," Harvard Business School Working Paper. Klein 2010.

6. See the intimate connections drawn by Hannah Rosin between the "prosperity gospel" movement and the subprime mortgage crisis; Rosin 2009.

7. Engel and McCoy 2011, esp. Chapter 3 for an excellent summary of the securitization process.

8. The gross market value of these derivatives in 2009 was estimated at approximately $20 trillion; see estimates from the Bank of International Settlements "2009."

9. See, however, the well-known attempt by Commodity Futures Trading Commission head Brooksley Born to regulate these derivatives, an endeavor that was reportedly shot down by Fed Chairman Alan Greenspan, Robert Rubin, and his assistant Larry Summers during the Clinton administration. Goodman 2008; Kirk 2009.

10. Americans for Financial Reform, 2010. Skilled analyses of legislative participation make it clear that in many cases lobbyists are buying not votes but time, or, quite likely, the ability of legislators to work on setting the policy agenda; Hall & Wayman 1990. The data in Figure 2.1 come from the "Ranked Sectors" page of the "Lobbying" section of the Opensecrets.org web site: http://www.opensecrets.org/lobby/top.php?indexType=c (accessed October 1, 2010).

11. Keith Krehbiel, *Pivotal Politics: A Theory of U.S. Lawmaking* (Chicago: University of Chicago Press, 1998).

12. A summary of the Paulson proposal appears at "Treasury Releases Blueprint for Stronger Regulatory Structure"; http://www.treas.gov/press/releases/hp476.htm (accessed October 2, 2010).

13. Consult the report at http://www.financialstability.gov/docs/regs/FinalReport_web.pdf (accessed August 15, 2010).

14. Dennis & Mufson. (2010). "Bankers Lobby Against Financial Overhaul," *Washington Post*, March 19, 2010.

15. Rather misleadingly, the Treasury Department would go on to define the most systemically important and interconnected financial firms as "Tier 1 financial holding companies," or Tier 1 FHCs. "Tier 1" henceforth had the dual reference of implying the most robust kind of capital as well as the most pivotal firms in the larger financial system (firms whose possible failure would literally define "systemic risk").

16. I use the terms "capital requirements" and "leverage limitations" somewhat interchangeably here, but it is important to note that, for accounting purposes, capital requirements are usually risk-weighted valuations, whereas "simple leverage" is not risk-weighted in accounting practices used by regulators and institutional evaluators. These accounting distinctions turn out to be predictive of bank failures in Europe during the crisis; consult Tigran Poghosyan and Martin Čihák, "Distress in European Banks: An Analysis Based on a New Data Set," IMF Working Paper WP 9/09, 2009.

17. Dixon & Younglai 2010.

18. The ability of government agencies—especially regulatory agencies—to set the terms of market transactions, investments, and even scientific inquiry is a form of power that I call "conceptual power" in regulation (see Carpenter 2010 for an application to global pharmaceutical regulation).

19. This is still significant, as it privileges the Collins definition as a focal point and starting point for future discussions, and requires the Treasury Department and the Comptroller of the Currency to revisit the issue in the future.

20. Carney 2010, Johnson 2010. The former Treasury Secretaries' letter appears at "Congress Should Implement the Volcker Rule for Banks," *Wall Street Journal*, February 22, 2010.

21. Lowrey 2010.

22. Perhaps in anticipation of this reluctance, Senators Merkley and Levin have written what Simon Johnson calls a "strongly worded letter" to the Treasury Department calling for strong rules that implement the Volcker rule; http://merkley.senate. gov/newsroom/press/release/?id=CB49AE3C-B8C4-4F8F-9081- 5CD93833EFE8 (accessed August 15, 2010).

23. Dodd-Frank Wall Street Reform and Consumer Protection Act. (2010). 12 U.S.C. 5301,sections 717 and 718.

24. The timing of this bill introduction is one that I interpret as providing an important threat, although agencies such as the Fed and the FTC may have learned earlier that the bill introduction was coming. Announcement of House bill introduction on March 5th, 2009; see http://blog.affil.org/2009/03/elizabeth-warrens-financial- product-safety-commission/.

25. From the GovTrack web site (http://www.govtrack.us/congress/bill.xpd?bill=s111-566) and the Library of Congress's Thomas site (http://thomas.loc.gov/cgi-bin/bdquery/ z?d111:s.00566:). "'The Financial Product Safety Commission Bill # S.566'— status—03/10/2009: Read twice and referred to the Committee on Banking, Housing, and Urban Affairs (text of measure as introduced: CR S2975–2978); 03/10/2009: Sponsor introductory remarks on measure. (CR S2974–2975); Com- mittee/Subcommittee Activity: Banking, Housing, and Urban Affairs: Referral, In Committee."

26. See, for instance, the web report from the Left-leaning web site *The Huffington Post* on March 10, 2009: http://www.huffingtonpost.com/2009/03/10/financial- product-safety_n_173691.html; there was also discussion by the President him- self, on the "Tonight Show with Jay Leno," in the late winter of 2009; http:// www.marketwatch.com/story/new-agency-would-protect-consumers (accessed February 21, 2010).

27. Kovacic's remarks are available in a Commission-hosted publication; "The Con- sumer Financial Protection Agency and the Hazards of Regulatory Restructuring," *Lombard Street*, 23. The publication is available at the Commission's web site: http://www.ftc.gov/speeches/kovacic/090914hazzrdsrestructuring.pdf (accessed February 21, 2010).

28. Kovacic 2010.

29. *The Washington Post* 2009; On the magnitude of the threat, Vanessa Cross of Suite 101 writes that "According to financial analysts, . . . the proposed 1136 page Senate bill poses the biggest challenge to the Fed's independence since it was codified into

law in the 1970s"; Vanessa Cross, "Bipartisan Financial Reform Bill in U.S. Senate: Federal Reserve Board Chairman Bernanke Lobbies Against Reformation"; http:// business-market-analysis.suite101.com/article.cfm/bipartisan_financial_reform_ bill_in_us_senate (accessed February 21, 2010).

30. See the "Restoring American Financial Stability Act of 2009," Title X (Consumer Financial Protection Agency), Subtitle F. Section 1061. (b) "(1) Board Of Governors.—(A) Transfer of Functions.—All consumer financial protection functions of the Board of Governors are transferred to the CFPA. (B) Board of Governors Authority.—The CFPA shall have all powers and duties that were vested in the Board of Governors, relating to consumer financial protection functions, on the day before the designated transfer date." The text of the Discussion Draft is available on the web page for the Senate Banking Committee; see http://banking.senate.gov/ public/_files/AYO09D44_xml.pdf (p. 1000 of the document, accessed February 21, 2010).

31. See "Restoring American Financial Stability Act of 2009," Sec. 1018, (a)(1)(E)(i) "IN GENERAL.—Each year (or quarter of such year), beginning on the designated transfer date, and each quarter thereafter, the Board of Governors shall transfer to the CFPA from the combined earnings of the Federal Reserve System the amount estimated by the CFPA needed to carry out the authorities granted in this title, under the enumerated consumer laws, and transferred under subtitles F and H, taking into account such other sums available to the CFPA for the following year (or quarter of such year), as requested by the CFPA" Text of the Discussion Draft; see http://banking.senate.gov/public/_files/AYO09D44_xml.pdf (p. 881 of draft PDF; accessed February 21, 2010).

32. Consult Tarullo's speech at http://www.federalreserve.gov/newsevents/testimony/ tarullo20090319a.htm (accessed January 30, 2010). This statement again focuses only upon publicly archived speeches and testimony at the Federal Reserve Board's web site. The closest any Fed official came to a pronouncement about consumer protection came in remarks on March 11, 2009, by Sandra F. Braunstein, Director, Division of Consumer and Community Affairs. Braunstein spoke on "Mortgage lending reform" before the Subcommittee on Financial Institutions and Consumer Credit, Committee on Financial Services, U.S House of Representatives; see http:// www.federalreserve.gov/newsevents/testimony/braunstein20090311a.htm. These were not the remarks of a Governor, however, and even these remarks came after it was well-known that a CFPA was a real legislative threat to the Fed.

33. See http://www.federalreserve.gov/newsevents/testimony/bernanke20090721a. htm. Consult Tarullo's speech at http://www.federalreserve.gov/newsevents/testi- mony/tarullo20090723a.htm. The announcement and the rules for Regulation Z are available at http://www.federalreserve.gov/newsevents/press/bcreg/20090723a. htm (accessed January 30, 2010). On the Fed's credit card proposal, see http:// www.federalreserve.gov/newsevents/press/bcreg/20090929a.htm (accessed January 30, 2010).

34. The *Journal's* judgment appears at http://online.wsj.com/article/SB124837547483376651. html (accessed February 6, 2010).

35. The BBVN report appears at http://www.fxstreet.com/fundamental/economic-indicators/us-fed-revises-regulation-z/2009-07-24.html (accessed February 21, 2010).

36. Carpenter 2010; Chan 2010.

37. In early January 2010, President Obama announced a general review of regulations. Early interpretations of this move suggest that it was undertaken as a gesture to business executives and the business community. However, in a sign that Obama intends to shield Dodd-Frank implementation from new cost-benefit analyses, independent agencies that are critical in the administration of financial reform (such as the Fed and the CFPB, the FTC and the SEC) are exempted from this review. Lori Montgomery, "Obama Orders All Fed Agencies to Review Regulations," *Washington Post*, January 18, 2011.

38. Nasiripour, 2010; It is not known whether Geithner actually opposed Warren, and indeed Geithner denied opposing Warren for the position. Nevertheless, *The Huffington Post* story forcefully shaped on the agenda for the early establishment of the CFPB.

39. For the text of the speech to the Roundtable, consult http://pubcit.typepad.com/files/38439729-elizabeth-warren-s-speech-to-the-financial-services-roundtable.pdf (accessed January 20, 2011).

40. For the literature on delegation in political science, see Epstein and O'Halloran (1999) and Huber and Shipan (2002). Note, however, that the 848-page Dodd-Frank Act ("2,300 pages" in the jumbo congressional type referenced by bill opponents) is an example of how legislative action does not, in contrast to the assumptions of John Huber and Charles Shipan (2002), demonstrate that longer bills are those that more tightly constrain administrative discretion. Along with other enactments, the Dodd-Frank Act suggests that major legislation will often take up hundreds of thousands of pages preparing space, capacity, and funding models for agencies. Legislative length is, at least in this case, a poor measure of statutory specificity; the latter concept often requires a more nuanced reading of legislation than quantitative political scientists have been willing to give it.

41. For a summary of proposals that two prominent consumer finance specialists would recommend as additional changes to the law, consult Engel and McCoy, *The Subprime Virus*, Chapter 12, "Consumer Protection."

42. See Carpenter 2010, Chapter 10, for a similar inference strategy regarding American and global pharmaceutical companies and the power of the FDA.

References

Americans for Fairness in Lending. 2009. "Elizabeth Warren's Financial Product Safety Commission." (http://blog.affil.org/2009/03/elizabeth-warrensfinancial-product-safety-commission/) accessed May 2, 2010.

Americans for Financial Reform. (2010). "Post Passage Lobbying Statistics," citing Congress Daily report; http://ourfinancialsecurity.org/2010/08/post-passage-lobbying-statistics/ (accessed October 1, 2010).

Applebaum, Binyamin. 2009. "Deal Near on Senate Financial Reform Bill," Business Digest, *The Washington Post*, December 24.

Bank of International Settlements. 2009. *Semiannual OTC Derivatives Statistics at End-June 2009*. (http://www.bis.org/statistics/derstats.htm), accessed March 6, 2010.

BBVA Bancomer Team. 2009. "US: Fed Revises Regulation Z." (http://www.fxstreet.com/fundamental/economic-indicators/us-fed-revises-regulation-z/2009-07-24.html), accessed February 21, 2010.

Bernanke, Ben. 2008a. "Testimony Before the Joint Economic Committee" (September 24). (http://www.federalreserve.gov/newsevents/testimony/bernanke20080924a.htm), accessed January 30, 2010.

Bernanke, Ben. 2008b. "Speech at the Federal Reserve System Conference on Housing and Mortgage Markets" (December 4). (http://www.federalreserve.gov/newsevents/speech/bernanke20081204a.htm), accessed January 30, 2010.

Bernanke, Ben. 2008c. "Statement on Behalf of the Board of Governors of the Federal Reserve System" (July 14). (http://federalreserve.gov/newsevents/press/bcreg/bernankeregz20080714.htm), accessed July 3, 2010.

Bernanke, Ben. 2009a. "Speech at the Stamp Lecture" (January 13). (http://www.federalreserve.gov/newsevents/speech/bernanke20090113a.htm), accessed January 30, 2010.

Bernanke, Ben. 2009b. "Testimony Before the Committee on Financial Services." (February 10). (http://www.federalreserve.gov/newsevents/testimony/bernanke20090210a.htm), accessed January 30, 2009.

Bernanke, Ben. 2009c. "Speech at the Council on Foreign Relations" (March 10). (http://www.federalreserve.gov/newsevents/speech/bernanke20090310a.htm), accessed January 30, 2010.

Bernanke, Ben. 2009d. "Testimony Before the Committee on Financial Services" (July 21). (http://www.federalreserve.gov/newsevents/testimony/bernanke20090721a.htm), accessed July 3, 2010.

Bernanke, Ben. 2009e. "Statement on Behalf of the Board of Governors of the Federal Reserve System" (July 23). (http://www.federalreserve.gov/newsevents/press/bcreg/bernanke20090723a.htm), accessed July 3, 2010.

Board of Governors of the Federal Reserve System. 2009a. "Press Release" (March 11). (http://www.federalreserve.gov/newsevents/press/bcreg/20090311a.htm), accessed February 21, 2010.

Board of Governors of the Federal Reserve System. 2009b. "Press Release" (July 23). (http://www.federalreserve.gov/newsevents/press/bcreg/20090723a.htm), accessed January 30, 2010.

Board of Governors of the Federal Reserve System. 2009c. "Press Release" (September 29). (http://www.federalreserve.gov/newsevents/press/bcreg/20090929a.htm), accessed January 10, 2010.

Braunstein, Sandra. 2009. "Testimony Before the Subcommittee on Financial Institutions and Consumer Credit" (March 10). (http://www.federalreserve.gov/newsevents/testimony/braunstein20090311a.htm), accessed July 3, 2010.

Campbell, John. 2006. "Household Finance." *Journal of Finance* 61: 1553–1604.

Carney, John. 2010. "Treasury Department Is Already Saying That Volcker Rule Won't Change Goldman Sachs," *Business Insider*, February 2: (http://www.businessinsider.com/treasury-department-is-already-saying-volcker-rule-wont-change-goldman-sachs-2010-2), accessed August 15, 2010.

Carpenter, Daniel 2004. "Protection Without Capture: Product Approval by a Politically Responsive, Learning Regulator." *American Political Science Review* 98(4): 613–631.

Carpenter, Daniel 2010a. *Reputation and Power: Organizational Image and Pharmaceutical Regulation at the FDA*. Princeton: Princeton University Press.

Carpenter, Daniel 2010b. "Why Consumers Can't Trust the Fed." *New York Times*, March 17.

Carpenter, Daniel 2010c. "Institutional Strangulation: Bureaucratic Politics and Financial Reform in the Obama Administration," *Perspectives on Politics* 8(3) (September 2010): 825–847.

Carpenter, Daniel 2011. "The Contest of Lobbies and Disciplines: Financial Politics and Regulatory Reform in the Obama Administration," in Larry Jacobs and Theda Skocpol, eds., *Reaching for a New Deal: Obama's Agenda and the Future of American Politics*. New York: Russell Sage Foundation, 2011.

Chan, Sewell. 2010a. "A Consumer Bill Gives Exemption on Payday Loans." *New York Times*, March 9.

Chan, Sewell. 2010b. "Federal Reserve Nominees Are Clue to Its Future." *New York Times*, May 2.

Christie, Les. 2007. "Foreclosure Rates Up Big in December." *CNNMoney* (January 17). (http://money.cnn.com/2007/01/16/real_estate/December_foreclosures_up_from_2005/index.htm), accessed February 1, 2010.

Consumer Bankers' Association. 2009. "Fed Proposes Major TILA Changes for Mortgages and Home Equity Lines," *CBA Bankalert* (July 23). (http://www.cbanet.org/files/FileDownloads/Mortgage-HELOC.pdf), accessed January 23, 2010.

Cross, Vanessa. 2009. *Bipartisan Financial Reform Bill in U.S. Senate: Federal Reserve Board Chairman Bernanke Lobbies Against Reformation*. (http://business-market-analysis.suite101.com/article.cfm/bipartisan_financial_reform_bill_in_us_senate), accessed February 21, 2010.

Dennis and Mufson. 2010. "Bankers Lobby Against Financial Overhaul," *Washington Post*, March 19, 2010. Dodd-Frank Wall Street Reform and Consumer Protection Act. (2010). 12 U.S.C. 5301, sections 717 and 718.

Dixon and Younglai. 2010. "House Panel Seeks to Weaken Bank Capital Rules," June 17; Reuters. (http://www.reuters.com/article/idUSTRE65G6H820100617), accessed August 10, 2010.

Douglas, Mary. 1987. *How Institutions Think*. Syracuse: Syracuse University Press.

Engel, Kathleen C., and Patricia A. McCoy. 2011. *The Subprime Virus: Reckless Credit, Regulatory Failure and Next Steps*. New York: Oxford University Press, 2011.

Fang, Lee. 2009. "Republicans Obstruct House Proceedings to Attend Boehner's Annual Beach Party." *Think Progress*, July 24. (http://thinkprogress.org/2009/07/24/boehner-beach-party/), accessed March 8, 2010.

Federal Register. 2008. "Rules and Regulations" (October 24). (http://edocket.access.gpo.gov/2008/pdf/E8-25320.pdf), accessed January 30, 2010.

Federal Reserve Board. 2000. "Morning Session of Public Hearing on Home Equity Lending, July 27, 2000." Washington, DC (http://www.federalreserve.gov/events/PublicHearings/20000727/20000727am.htm), accessed February 21, 2010.

"Financial Product Safety Commission: Dems Want Mortgages Regulated Like Toys, Drugs." 2009. *Huffington Post* (March 10). (http://www.huffingtonpost.com/2009/03/10/financial-product-safety_n_173691.html), accessed July 3, 2010.

Fiorina, Morris, and Samuel J. Abrams. 2008. "Polarization in the American Public." *Annual Review of Political Science* 11 (June): 563–588.

Frontline (Public Broadcasting Service). 2009. "The Warning." October 20; http://video.pbs.org/video/1302794657; accessed March 6, 2010.

Goodman, Peter S. 2008. "The Reckoning—Taking Hard New Look at a Greenspan Legacy." *New York Times*, October 9.

"GOP tried to Block Warren from Heading Agency She Proposed." 2009. *Huffington Post* (October 27). (http://www.huffingtonpost.com/2009/10/27/gop-tried-toblock-elizab_n_335423.html), accessed May 2, 2010.

Hall and Wayman. 1990. "Buying Time: Moneyed Interests and the Mobilization of Bias in Congressional Committees," *American Political Science Review* 84(3): 797–820.

Heclo, Hugh, and Aaron Wildavsky. 1974. *The Private Government of Public Money*. London: Macmillan.

Holmes, Douglas. 2009. "Economy of Words," *Cultural Anthropology* 24(3): 381–341.

Holzer, Jessica. 2009. "Fed Unveils Rules to Protect Borrowers." *The Wall Street Journal* (July 24). (http://online.wsj.com/article/SB124837547483376651.html), accessed February 6, 2010.

Immergluck, Dan. 2009. *Foreclosed: High-Risk Lending, Deregulation, and the Undermining of America's Mortgage Market*. Ithaca, NY: Cornell University Press.

Johnson, Simon (2010). "The Treasury Position—On the Volcker Rule," *Baseline Scenario*, August 5; http://baselinescenario.com/2010/08/05/the-treasury-position-on-the-volcker-rule/ (accessed August 15, 2010)

Joskow, Paul. 1973. "Inflation and Environmental Concern: Structural Change in the Process of Public Utility Price Regulation." *Journal of Law & Economics* 17(2): 291–327.

Kirk, Michael. 2009. "The Warning," *Frontline*, PBS public affairs program, October 20. (http://video.pbs.org/video/1302794657; accessed March 6, 2010).

Kingdon, John. 1978. *Agendas, Alternatives and Public Policies*. Boston: Little, Brown.

Klein, Ezra. 2010. "With Financial Reform for Wall Street, Fair Is Fair." *Washington Post*, May 2.

Kovacic, William E. 2009. "The Consumer Financial Protection Agency and the Hazards of Regulatory Restructuring." *Lombard Street*, 23. Available at the FTC web site (http://www.ftc.gov/speeches/kovacic/090914hazzrdsrestructuring.pdf), accessed February 21, 2010.

Kranish, Michael. 2009. "In Fight Over Credit Rules, She Wields a Plan." *Boston Globe*, November 6.

Krause, George A., and James Douglas. 2005. "Institutional Design versus Reputational Effects on Bureaucratic Performance: Evidence from U.S. Government Macroeconomic and Fiscal Projections." *Journal of Public Administration Research and Theory* 15(2): 281–306.

Krehbiel, Keith. 1998. *Pivotal Politics: A Theory of U.S. Lawmaking*. Chicago: University of Chicago Press.

Kroszner, Randall. 2007a. "Speech at the Consumer Bankers Association" (November 5). (http://www.federalreserve.gov/newsevents/speech/kroszner20071105a.htm), accessed July 3, 2010. (http://www.federalreserve.gov/newsevents/speech/kroszner20071105a.htm), accessed July 3, 2010.

Kroszner, Randall. 2007b. "Speech at the Public Hearing under the Home Ownership and Equity Protection Act" (June 14). (http://www.federalreserve.gov/newsevents/speech/kroszner20070614a.htm), accessed July 3, 2010.

Krozner, Randall. 2008a. "Speech at the Federal Reserve System Conference on Housing and Mortgage Markets" (December 4). (http://www.federalreserve.gov/newsevents/speech/kroszner20081204a.htm), accessed January 30, 2010.

Krozner, Randall. 2008b. "Speech at the Federal Reserve Bank of Cleveland" (June 11). (http://www.federalreserve.gov/newsevents/speech/kroszner20080611a.htm), accessed July 3, 2010.

Krozner, Randall. 2008c. "Speech to Minority Depository Institutions National Conference" (July 17). (http://www.federalreserve.gov/newsevents/speech/kroszner20080717a.htm), accessed July 3, 2010.

Krugman, Paul. 2000. *The Return of Depression Economics*. New York: W.W. Norton.

Macey, Jonathan R., and Geoffrey P. Miller. 1994. "Reflections on Professional Responsibility in a Regulatory State," 63 *Geo. Wash. L. Rev.* 63 (1994–1995): 1105.

Mantell, Ruth. 2009. "Keeping Consumers Safe from Financial Products." *MarketWatch* (April 16). (http://www.marketwatch.com/story/new-agency-wouldprotect-consumers), accessed February 21, 2010.

Maor, Moshe. 2007. "A Scientific Standard and an Agency's Legal Independence: Which of These Reputation-Protection Mechanisms Is Less Susceptible to Political Moves?" *Public Administration* 85(4): 961–978.

Maor, Moshe. 2010. "Organizational Reputation and Jurisdictional Claims: The Case of the U.S. Food and Drug Administration." *Governance* 23(1): 133–159.

McCarty, Nolan, Keith Poole, and Howard Rosenthal. 2005. *Polarized America: The Dance of Ideology and Politics*. Cambridge, MA: MIT Press.

Mebane, Walter, and Jasjeet Sekhon. 2002. "Coordination and Policy Moderation at Midterm," *American Political Science Review* 96(1): 141–157.

Meyer, John, and Brian Rowan. 1997. "Institutionalized Organizations: Formal Structure as Myth and Ceremony." *American Journal of Sociology* 83: 340–363.

Nasiripour, Shahien, and Jeff Muskus. 2009. "House Passes Wall Street Reform Bill with Zero GOP Votes." *Huffington Post* (December 11). (http://www.huffingtonpost.com/2009/12/11/house-passesfinancial-re_n_389267.html), accessed March 6, 2010.

Noah, Lars. 1997. "Administrative Arm-Twisting in the Shadow of the Congressional Delegations of Authority." *Wisconsin Law Review* 5: 873.

Patashnik, Eric S. 2008. *Reforms at Risk: What Happens after Major Policy Reforms Are Enacted*. Princeton: Princeton University Press.

Pergram, Chad. 2009. "An Inconvenient Vote." *The Speaker's Lobby* (June 27). (http://congress.blogs.foxnews.com/2009/06/27/aninconvenient-vote/), accessed March 8, 2010.

Prater, Connie. 2008. "Regulators Finalize Sweeping Credit Card Rule Reforms." *Creditcard.com* (December18). (http://www.creditcards.com/credit-cardnews/fed-enacts-new-credit-card-regulations-1282.php), accessed March 16, 2010.

Reuters. 2010. "Volcker Says Must Let Big Financial Firms Fail." *CNBC* (February 14). (http://www.cnbc.com/id/35394496), accessed February 15, 2010.

Riles, Annelise. 2010. *Collateral Knowledge: Legal Reasoning in the Global Financial Markets*. Chicago: University of Chicago Press.

Rosin, Hannah. 2009. "Did Christianity Cause the Crash?" *The Atlantic* (December). (http://www.theatlantic.com/magazine/archive/2009/12/didchristianity-cause-the-crash/7764/), accessed July 3, 2010.

Schickler, Eric. 2001. *Disjointed Pluralism*. Princeton: Princeton University Press.

Skowronek, Stephen. 1982. *Building a New American State: The Expansion of National Administrative Capacities, 1877–1920*. New York: Cambridge University Press.

Sparrow, Malcolm. 2000. *The Regulatory Craft: Controlling Risks, Solving Problems, and Managing Compliance*. Washington, DC: Brookings Institution.

Steinmo, Sven, and Jon Watts. 1995. "It's the Institutions, Stupid! Why Comprehensive National Health Insurance Always Fails in America." *Journal of Health Politics, Policy and Law* 20(2): 329–372.

Sundquist, James. 1983. *The Decline and Resurgence of Congress*. Washington, DC: Brookings Institution.

Tarullo, Daniel. 2009a. "Testimony Before the Committee on Banking, Housing and Urban Affairs" (March 19). (http://www.federalreserve.gov/newsevents/testimony/tarullo20090319a.htm), January 30, 2010.

Tarullo, Daniel. 2009b. "Testimony Before the Committee on Banking, Housing, and Urban Affairs" (July 23). (http://www.federalreserve.gov/newsevents/testimony/tarullo20090723a.htm), accessed February 21, 2010.

Tedeschi, Bob. 2009. "New Lending Rules Coming Soon," *New York Times*, September 25. (http://www.nytimes.com/2009/09/27/realestate/27mort.html), accessed February 21, 2010.

Thelen, Kathleen. 2004. *How Institutions Evolve*. New York: Cambridge University Press.

Tsebelis, George. 2002. *Veto Players: How Institutions Work*. Princeton: Princeton University Press.

Tufano, Peter. 2009. "Consumer Finance." *Annual Review of Financial Economics* 1(December): 227–247.

U.S. Department of the Treasury. 2009. *Financial Regulatory Reform: A New Foundation*. Washington, DC: Treasury Department. (http://www.financialstability.gov/docs/regs/FinalReport_web.pdf) accessed June 15, 2010.

Vong, John I., and Gerald C. Lampe. 2010. "Mortgage Mash-Up: Regulatory Reform Here and Now." *Mortgage Banker* (January). (http://www.complianceease.com/opencms/opencms/CEContent/docs/articles/1-10-Mortgage-Banking-regulatory-reform-here-andnow.pdf), accessed June 15, 2010.

Warren, Elizabeth, and Amelia Warren Tyagi. 2003. *The Two-Income Trap: Why Middle-Class Mothers and Fathers Are Going Broke*. New York: Basic Books.

The Washington Post. 2009. "Deal Near on Senate Financial Reform Bill," Business Digest, December 24.

Yang, Jia Lynn. 2010. "U.S. Banks Starting to Develop Plans for Complying with Financial Overhaul Law," *Washington Post*, August 13, 2010.

3

Reconstituting the Submerged State

THE CHALLENGES OF SOCIAL POLICY REFORM IN THE OBAMA ERA

Suzanne Mettler[1]

It's time for us to change America. . . . change happens because the American people demand it—because they rise up and insist on new ideas and new leadership, a new politics for a new time. America, this is one of those moments. I believe that as hard as it will be, the change we need is coming.
—BARACK OBAMA, nomination acceptance speech, Democratic National Convention, August 28, 2008, Denver, Colorado

Eternal vigilance is the name of the game in taxation. We do not anticipate shining a light on this now-dormant proposal in coming months, but we will remain intensely focused on it.
—NATIONAL ASSOCIATION OF REALTORS, "Eye on the Hill," after opposing Obama's proposal to limit itemized deductions for individuals earning more than $250,000 as a means to raise revenues for health care reform, March 9, 2009

I voiced my opinion and voted for a Republican, and the roof did not cave in. . . . the health bill totally upsets me. First of all, do we really know what's going on with it? It's always evasive when they're talking about it.
—MARLENE CONNOLLY, North Andover, Massachusetts, after voting for Senate candidate Scott Brown, January 19, 2010

BARACK OBAMA RAN for president on the platform of change, and social welfare policies ranked among his top priorities for reform. During his campaign he denounced tax breaks and recent tax cuts that benefit the most affluent, even amidst rising economic inequality; he condemned the deteriorating condition of education, including reduced affordability of and access to higher education for young people from low- to moderate-income households; and he excoriated the skyrocketing costs of health care, the growing numbers of the uninsured, and the poor treatment that Americans often receive from insurance companies. These issues resonated with the public, because most Americans are aware of and concerned about economic inequality, and most support expanded government programs to mitigate it, particularly in the areas of education and health care (Page and Jacobs 2009).

The 2008 election offered promising indications that Obama could succeed in accomplishing his agenda. He won 53 percent of the vote, a level no Democrat had achieved since Lyndon Johnson in 1964, and his party won back control of both chambers of Congress for the first time since 1992. During his inauguration week, Obama enjoyed an approval rating of 69 percent, higher than any newly elected president of either party since Johnson.

Yet, as would soon become evident, established political arrangements present formidable obstacles to would-be reformers once they attempt the work of governance. Change requires not only new ideas and determination but also the arduous reconstitution of pre-established political relationships and modes of operation. As Stephen Skowronek explains in his analysis of such efforts in the Progressive Era, "Success hinges on recasting official power relationships within governmental institutions and altering ongoing relations between state and society" (Skowronek 1982, ix). In each area that he sought to reform, Obama confronted an existing state that is at once formidable and elusive, and thus the quest required engagement in treacherous political battles. Remarkably, his administration has now succeeded in achieving several of its major goals with respect to social welfare policy. Even so, for much of the public, the delivery on those promises fails to meet the high expectations that surrounded the president when he first took office. What can explain the shape that reform has taken and the formidable challenges that Obama has faced in accomplishing his agenda? Further, how can we make sense of why, even after scoring key victories, he has had to try to convince the public of the value of what he has achieved?

Obama confronted an established and complex policy thicket that presents tremendous challenges to reform. In contrast to presidents such as Franklin D. Roosevelt and Lyndon B. Johnson, Obama did not aim to create major new direct and visible government social programs. Neither did he seek to terminate or dramatically alter such programs, as did Ronald Reagan, who told the nation, "Government is not the solution to our problem; government is the problem," or Bill Clinton, who vowed to "end welfare as we know it."

Rather, Obama's policy objectives involved primarily attempts to reconstitute the *submerged state*—policies that lay beneath the surface of U.S. market institutions and within the federal tax system.

While its origins are not new—they date back to the middle and even early twentieth century—the "submerged state" has become a formidable presence in the United States, particularly over the past 25 years. I am referring here to a conglomeration of federal social policies that incentivize and subsidize activities engaged in by private actors and individuals. These feature a variety of tools, including: social benefits in the form of tax breaks for individuals and families; the regulation and tax-free nature of benefits provided by private employers, including health care benefits in the form of insurance; and the government-sponsored enterprises and third-party organizations that receive federal subsidies in exchange for carrying out public policy goals, such as the banks and lending associations that have administered student loans.

Over time, the policies of the submerged state have reshaped politics in two ways, both of which presented profound challenges to Obama as he sought to accomplish reform and which, paradoxically, also imperil the success of his greatest achievements thus far. First, especially during the past two decades, the submerged state has nurtured particular sectors of the market economy and they have in turn invested in strengthening their political capacity for the sake of preserving existing arrangements. As a result, the alteration of such arrangements has required either defeating entrenched interests—which has proven impossible in most cases—or, more typically, negotiating with and accommodating them, which hardly appears to be the kind of change that Obama's supporters expected when he won office. Second, such policies have shrouded the state's role, making it largely invisible to most ordinary citizens, even beneficiaries of existing policies. As a result, the public possesses little awareness of such policies, nor are most people cognizant of either what is at stake in reform efforts or the significance of their success.

I show how these dynamics combined to present challenges to Obama as he sought to achieve change in social welfare policy, and it indicates how they may likely curtail the perceived and actual political effectiveness even of his policy successes. I focus especially on tax expenditures and higher education policy, and also give some attention to health care reform. As we will see, the nature of the submerged state requires reformers to reveal its existence and how it functions to the public. To the extent that Obama has done this, it helped to facilitate the accomplishment of his goals. Yet several of the reforms that his administration has accomplished expand the submerged state further, and this means that the dynamics it promulgates are likely to continue rather than to diminish.

I. Understanding Contemporary Challenges to Reform

Despite the promising aspects of the 2008 election results for Democrats, Obama's reform agenda quickly faced formidable obstacles, two of which have been highlighted often by political observers. First, *partisan polarization* has been on the rise over the past 15 years, bringing with it an end to the bipartisan compromises on social legislation that occurred more regularly in the mid-twentieth century (McCarty, Poole, and Rosenthal 2006). As a presidential candidate, Obama often articulated a yearning to overcome such division. Yet, in the first year of the 110th Congress, polarization levels reached their highest levels yet since the end of Reconstruction (Voteview 2010 indeed, aside from three Republican senators who supported Obama's first major piece of legislation, the American Recovery and Reinvestment Act, no Republican in either chamber has voted in favor of his major social welfare priorities on final passage.

Second, although Republicans make up the minority of the U.S. Senate, the chamber's *basis of representation and rules, combined with current political geography*, gives them significantly more power than the election returns would suggest. As has been the case since the Founding, the assignment of equal numbers of senators to states with unequal representation advantages states with fewer residents. These disparities can be quite extreme: today, for each individual represented by a senator from Wyoming, a Senator from California represents 69 individuals. Overall, the partisan composition of the current Senate gives a representational bias to Republicans, since they are more likely than Democrats to represent states with small populations, and vice versa.[2] While the actual extent of this bias may appear modest, it is of critical importance because it enables the Republicans to reach the threshold level at which they can wield effective veto power. Since a rule change in the 1970s, senators in the minority have increasingly been able to use the threat of filibuster to impede the majority's legislative agenda (Sinclair 2005). The Democrats controlled 60 votes throughout much of 2009, but when Republican Scott Brown won the Massachusetts Senate seat of the late Ted Kennedy in January 2010, it ended their ability to pass legislation with a filibuster-proof supermajority.

While the importance of these political and institutional features of the contemporary polity is undeniable, focusing on them alone fails to illuminate sufficiently the politics of social policy. They offer no insight as to why Obama's supporters—so energized during his campaign—became so quiet with respect to his issue agenda. They do not indicate why policy makers have not embraced different policies, featuring mechanisms distinct from those which gained political traction. Nor do they explain why even Obama's policy achievements confront a public that appears largely unimpressed if not—like a strong vocal minority in the Tea Party movement—outwardly hostile.

A fuller explanation requires a policy-focused analytical framework, one that puts existing policy front and center and views how it has developed over time (Hacker, Mettler, and Soss 2007). Policies created or expanded in past decades have shaped the political terrain that the Obama administration confronts, and they have generated powerful dynamics that imperil reform efforts. Specifically, we need to understand the character of policies of the submerged state and the political effects they have yielded across time: the economic actors they have nurtured, whose ascent as players has reshaped the political landscape; and their obscurity to most Americans, particularly those of low or moderate incomes. Viewing the past year's developments through this lens should help us to understand why change is so difficult, the form that it has taken, and the relative degrees of success of various initiatives.

In putting forward the concept of the "submerged state," I am building on pioneering work by various scholars about the more obscure but immense aspects of American social policy. In a brief article in 1979, Paul Starr and Gosta Esping-Andersen argued that in the United States, social policy has often been created in the form of "passive intervention," through which established interests—those which would fight sweeping reform, for example, in the areas of housing and health care—have been accommodated through policy designs that channel expensive subsidies and incentives toward them (Starr and Esping-Andersen 1979). More recently, separate components of such governance have been examined in depth and detail through a few brilliant studies. Christopher Howard exposed what he termed the "hidden welfare state" of tax expenditures, showing that it competes in size, scope, and functions with the visible, traditional social programs, but that it generates distinct political dynamics (Howard 1997). Jacob Hacker revealed the politics of "private" social protections for retirement pensions and health insurance coverage, meaning those that are provided by employers but regulated and subsidized by government (Hacker 2002; also see Gottschalk 2000). Kimberly Morgan and Andrea Campbell illuminated "delegated governance," meaning the allocation of authority for many aspects of social welfare policy to non-state actors (Morgan and Campbell 2009). Here I build on and extend insights from these works, attempting to illuminate the similar political dynamics manifest across a few social welfare policy areas. In particular, insights offered by Howard and Hacker directed my attention to how the submerged state activates third-party interests that benefit from its existence, though it remains largely invisible to citizens generally (Howard 1997, 9, 93; Hacker 2002, 43).

While the foundations of the "submerged state" were established in the early and mid-twentieth century, its size and costliness have grown, especially in recent decades. Overall, as of 2006, social (non-business) tax expenditures accounted for 5.7 percent of GDP, up from 4.2 percent in 1976 (Burman, Toder, and Geissler 2008, 5). Today, the largest of these—as seen in Table 3.1—emanates from the non-taxable nature of the health insurance benefit provided by employers, followed by the home mortgage interest deduction, and then by tax-free employer-provided retirement benefits. Indicating the scope of these "submerged" dimensions relative to the clearly visible components of social welfare spending, Jacob Hacker calculated that, whereas traditional social public welfare expenditures amounted to 17.1 percent of GDP in the United States in 1995, making the nation a laggard relative to other OECD nations, the inclusion of tax expenditures and other private social welfare expenditures brought the total to 24.5 percent of GDP, placing U.S. spending slightly above average (Hacker 2002, 13–16; Garfinkel, Rainwater and Smeeding 2006, 904). Among tax expenditures, health care costs especially have ballooned over time, growing (in nominal dollars) from 77.3 billion in 1995 to 137.3 billion in 2007 (Howard 1997, 21; Burman, Toder, and Geissler 2008). Meanwhile, through another policy vehicle that also subsidizes private actors to provide social benefits, the Higher Education Act of 1965 gave incentives to banks to lend to students at low rates of interest by offering that the federal government would pay half the interest on such loans (Mettler and Rose 2009). In 1972, policy makers provided further impetus to student lending by creating the Student Loan Marketing Association (SLM, otherwise known as "Sallie Mae") to provide a "secondary market" and warehousing facility (Gladieux and Wolanin 1976, 61–62). By the 1980s and 1990s, student lending became highly lucrative for lenders but costly to the federal government; in 2009, the Congressional Budget Office estimated that $87 billion could be saved over 10 years if the system of subsidizing lenders was terminated entirely and replaced by direct lending (Congressional Budget Office 2009).

Although some individual features of the submerged state—most notably, the Earned Income Tax Credit—mitigate inequality, on net, these policies exacerbate it. First, as seen in Figure 3.1, they often bestow their benefits in an upwardly distributive fashion, as in the case of the charitable contribution and home mortgage interest deduction, and to a lesser extent, the

Table 3.1 Largest Individual Tax Expenditures: Year of Enactment
and Cost in 2011

Tax Expenditure	Year of Enactment	Estimated Cost in 2011 (billions of dollars)
Exclusion of employer contributions for medical insurance	1954	177.0
Deductibility of mortgage interest on owner-occupied homes	1913	104.5
Net exclusion of contributions and earnings for retirement plans	1974	67.1
Deduction of state and local taxes	1913	46.5
Pensions	1914–1926	44.6
Step-up basis of capital gains at death	1921	44.5
Lower tax rates on long-term capital gains	1921	44.3
Deductibility of charitable contributions (other than ed and health)	1917	43.9

Sources: U.S. Budget, Analytical Perspectives, FY 2011; Howard 1997, 176–177.

tax-free nature of employer-sponsored health insurance. Second, according to Starr and Esping-Andersen, such policies compound these inequality-generating effects. They promote consumption of higher-priced goods than individuals might choose otherwise, for instance as they buy bigger houses than they would in the absence of tax incentives. Inflated prices result, which makes non-recipients of such incentives (e.g., renters) unable to participate in the market, and this further promotes inequality. In addition, the lost revenues or excessive spending associated with operating the submerged state functions as "opportunity costs," leaving government with insufficient funds to maintain or create policies that could more effectively enhance the social welfare of low- and moderate-income citizens (Starr and Esping-Andersen 1979). This is illustrated by the growth in spending, over much of the past quarter-century, of student loans and tax credits for higher

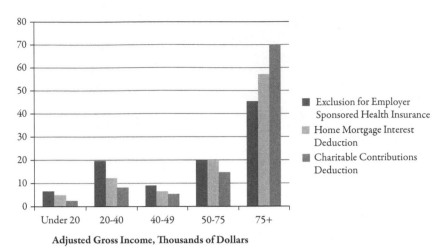

Adjusted Gross Income, Thousands of Dollars

FIGURE 3.1 Percentage of Tax Subsidy Funds Claimed by Households, by Income, 2004.

Sources: IRS Statistics of Income 2004; Leonard E. Burman, Bowen Garrett, and Surachai Khitatrakan, "The Tax Code, Employer Sponsored Insurance, and the Distribution of Tax Subsidies," in *Using Taxes to Reform Health Insurance: Pitfalls and Promises*, eds. Henry J. Aaron, Leonard Burman, (Washington, DC: Urban Institute, 2008), p. 50.

education, while the real value of Pell Grants—a more effective tool for financing college for low-income students—deteriorated in real value.

II. Interest Group Politics and the Submerged State

Ironically, when policies of the submerged state were first put in place, the affected industries were initially either indifferent or opposed, but over time, they became ardent defenders of such arrangements. For example, Christopher Howard explains that while tax breaks related to home ownership had long existed, home builders and realtors only began to mobilize to protect them after Congress began, in the late 1960s, to publish a list of them with the annual budget. Such activism paid off: "Between 1967 and 1995, the total cost of the home mortgage interest deduction increased by an average of almost 7 percent per year, adjusted for inflation" (Howard 1997, 93, 104–105). Similarly, in 1965, bankers exercised the strongest opposition to the passage of student loan policy, yet by 1993, when the Clinton administration advanced its proposal to replace the existing system with direct lending, they led the fight to preserve the system on which they had come to rely (Mettler and Rose 2009).

Developments over the past 15 years have fostered change in the degree and form of activism undertaken by these types of organizations, such that the Obama administration confronted highly sophisticated efforts to protect the status quo. Notably, the president's agenda implicated industries especially in the financial, insurance, and real estate sector—the same ones that have, collectively, procured the greatest profits in the American economy over the past quarter-century. Frank Levy and Peter Temlin show that since 1980, most private industries have experienced, at best, slow and steady growth. In the finance, insurance, and real estate sector, however, profits spiked, vastly outpacing growth in other sectors (Levy and Temlin 2007, 36–37). The fortunes of these industries emanated not from "market forces" alone but rather from their interplay with policies of the submerged state that promoted their growth and heaped extra benefits on them.

Take, for example, student lending, administered by banks and organizations within the financial sector. During the 1980s and 1990s, tuition outpaced inflation, and policy makers at the national and state level failed to maintain a constant level of funding for grants and public universities and colleges (National Center for Public Policy and Higher Education 2002, 8–9, 12, 22–30). Amid the growing partisan divide in Congress, policy makers found consensus more easily on student loans, for which they expanded borrowing limits and loosened eligibility requirements. As a result, the number and average amount of loans grew dramatically, as did lenders' profits. After lawmakers in 1996 permitted Sallie Mae to reorganize as a private company, over the next decade its stocks returned nearly 2,000 percent, compared to the S&P 500's average 228 percent gain, and its CEO became the most highly compensated in the nation, with approximately $37 million in salary, bonuses, and stock awards in 2006 (McLean 2005; Washington Post 2006). Similarly, existing political-economic arrangements bestowed extra benefits on the thriving health insurance and real estate industries.

In turn, soaring profits permitted these industries to invest in their political capacity to protect the policies that have served them well. Over the past decade, the finance, insurance, and real estate sector has poured considerable resources into both campaign contributions and lobbying, outspending all other sectors in both activities and rapidly increasing its spending over time. In the 2008 election campaign, it spent $457.4 million, through contributions to candidate committees, leadership PACs, and party committees (OpenSecrets.org 2010a). As seen in Table 3.2, between 1998 and 2009, it invested $3.892 billion dollars on lobbying.

Although the Republican leadership aggressively promoted the interests of such industries over the past decade and a half (Sinclair 2006, 308–314), their trade organizations deftly avoided committing themselves to an exclusive

Table 3.2 Spending on Lobbying by Top Five Sectors, 1998–2009

Sector	Total
Finance, Insurance, and Real Estate	$3,892,669,529
Health	$3,788,417,114
Miscellaneous Business	$3,639,000,728
Communications/Electronics	$3,210,880,162
Energy and Natural Resources	$2,741,276,475

Source: Center for Responsive Politics, OpenSecrets.org.

partisan relationship and instead maintained their traditional multipronged, bipartisan approach. First, they strived to maintain and strengthen relationships with elected officials who are inclined to support them—predominantly Republicans but also some moderate Democrats—by providing them with information, hearing their ideas, and ensuring that they will exert the energy to represent them effectively (Hall and Wayman 1990). Second, on issues characterized by a rigid partisan divide, interest groups often focused on converting a few individuals to vote for their favored position. Although political scientists have usually found little evidence of success of such efforts (Ansolabehere, de Figueiredo, and Snyder 2003), nonetheless their frequency need not be great in order to alter outcomes; currently, just destabilizing one senator's support for an issue can be enough to thwart action on a major issue. Third, interest groups have generally sought to cultivate cordial relationships with candidates and elected officials on both "sides of the aisle," as evidenced by the fact that their campaign contributions are typically distributed widely to both parties, with a slight edge to the party holding or expected to win the majority. This may help explain why on some issues, even in today's highly partisan environment, industries can count on support from both Republicans and Democrats, as we will see.

In contrast, few organizations represent the general public on social welfare issues, particularly those involving policies of the submerged state. Since the 1970s, the large broad-based membership groups that previously served as vehicles articulating the preferences of the general public have dwindled in size; in national politics, they have been replaced by advocacy organizations with no grassroots base and thus lacking comparable organizing capacity and political effectiveness (Skocpol 2003). Moreover, unlike visible policies that more readily attract group loyalty, policies of the submerged state are typically too hidden and their status too unclear to generate such affiliations (Howard 1997, 9, 114–115, 181; Mettler 2009b). Finally, some membership organizations—namely unions and the AARP—have some-times made compromises that have positioned them as either defenders of existing arrangements or as less-than-ardent advocates for reform (Gott-schalk 2000; Campbell and Skocpol 2003).

Yet the interest groups that have been nurtured by the submerged state are formidable, their power to impede reform is not absolute. Change is possible when, for example, the political credibility of such groups becomes sullied, changing circumstances lead them to alter their position, or new policy com-promises enable them to be on the side of reform. As we will see, the Obama administration has enjoyed the benefit of a few such openings.

III. Mass Politics and the Submerged State

In contrast to the 2008 presidential campaign, when fairly high rates of citizen involvement and electoral turnout helped usher Obama into office, since his inauguration supportive mass publics have been characterized by relative quies-cence. Certainly some mobilization occurred among the new grassroots compo-nent of the Democratic National Committee, "Organizing for America," and "Health Care for America Now," a coalition of several unions, MoveOn, Planned Parenthood, and other groups. Yet the most evident popular momentum took place among conservative opponents—as indicated by the Tea Party movement.

This is not surprising because, in taking on the submerged state, Obama engaged in a set of battles over policies that are obscure if not invisible to much of the public. In fact, even individuals who have themselves ever uti-lized such policies may have little awareness of them as public social benefits. Because few existing surveys permit us to examine citizens' perceptions and experiences of such policies compared to more visible ones, I designed the Social and Governmental Issues and Participation Study of 2008 (hereafter, referred to as "Governmental Issues Survey") to do so.[3] Respondents were asked, first, whether they had "ever used a government social program, or not." Later, they were asked whether they had ever benefited personally from any of 19 federal social policies, including some that belong to the "submerged state" and others which are visible and direct in their design and delivery. Table 3.3 presents the percentage of beneficiaries of each of several policies who reported that they had never used a federal social program. Notably, the six italicized policies that head the list are precisely those belonging to the submerged state: tax-deferred savings accounts, several tax expenditures, and student loans. Given the design and manner of delivery of these policies, few individuals seem to perceive them to be social benefits. Such dynamics may imperil the political effectiveness of reforms that are limited to expansions or modifications of the submerged state.

Elected officials often seem to assume, furthermore, that providing tax breaks will alter citizens' attitudes about their taxes, but the evidence suggests otherwise. I examined whether individuals' views that they paid more than their "fair share" in federal taxes might be mitigated by their receipt of tax expenditures, which effectively lightened their tax burden. Interestingly, this appears not to be the case. When Americans were asked their views about federal income taxes, 56 percent reported that they were asked to pay their "fair share," whereas 40 percent said they paid "more than their fair share."[4] The analysis of the "tax break model" in the first column of Table 3.4 shows that while the number of tax expenditures that individuals report utilizing

Table 3.3 Percentage of Program Beneficiaries Who Report That They "Have Not Used a Government Social Program"

Program	"No, Have Not Used a Government Social Program"
529 or Coverdell	64.3
Home Mortgage Interest Deduction	60.0
Hope or Lifetime Learning Tax Credit	59.6
Student Loans	53.3
Child and Dependent Care Tax Credit	51.7
Earned Income Tax Credit	47.1
Social Security—Retirement & Survivors	44.1
Pell Grants	43.1
Unemployment Insurance	43.0
Veterans Benefits (other than G.I. Bill)	41.7
G.I. Bill	40.3
Medicare	39.8
Head Start	37.2
Social Security Disability	28.7
SSI—Supplemental Security Income	28.2
Medicaid	27.8
Welfare/Public Assistance	27.4
Government Subsidized Housing	27.4
Food Stamps	25.4

Source: Social and Governmental Issues and Participation Study, 2008. Note: Submerged state policies shown in italics.

(including the home mortgage interest deduction, 529 or Coverdell accounts, HOPE or Lifetime Learning Tax Credits, or Child and Dependent Care Tax Credit) positively relates to their views of tax fairness, the relationship is not statistically significant.[5] Paradoxically, these policies, although they permit individuals to pay significantly less in taxes, do not appear related to altered views about the tax system. Instead, factors associated with public opinion on taxes include education (those who have more education are more likely to perceive the system to be fair) and income (those who have less income perceive the system to be fair), among other factors.

In contrast, experiences of benefiting from direct visible federal social programs do appear to be related to individuals' more salutary views of tax fairness. The "direct social program model," shown in the right-hand column of Table 3.4, replaces the tax breaks variable with the sum of the number of traditional, visible social programs that individuals have ever utilized. Those who had used a greater number of visible programs were significantly more

Table 3.4 Effects of Extent of Tax Expenditures and Direct Social Program Usage Experiences on Perception of Fairness of Federal Income Taxes (OLS Regression)

	Tax Break Model	Direct Social Program Model
Year of Birth	-.001 (.001)	.000 (.001)
Educational level	.029**** (.008)	.029**** (.008)
Income	-.028**** (.007)	-.020*** (.007)
African American	-.212**** (.041)	-.228**** (.042)
Hispanic	-.093* (.049)	-.082* (.049)
Female	-.130**** (.030)	-.129**** (.030)
Sum of Usage of 4 Tax Expenditures	.018 (.019)	
Sum of Direct Federal Social Programs Ever Used		.018** (.008)
R^2	.053	.053
Adjusted R^2	0.47	0.48
N	1250	1256

Source: Social and Governmental Issues and Participation Study, 2008. *p<.10, **p<.05, ***p<.01, ****p<.001; Cells show unstandardized coefficients, with standard errors in parentheses. Note: Tax fairness variable is coded as 1, "more than fair share;" 2, "asked to pay fair share;" and 3, "less than fair share."

likely to report that they paid their "fair share" in taxes; other results remained consistent with those in the first model. Thus, individuals' sense of having benefited from government through visible social programs appears to mitigate their sense of being burdened by it through taxes. Conversely, usage of policies embedded in the submerged state—the types of policies on which Obama's efforts have focused—are not associated with altered views. In short, the expansion of policies in the submerged state, even if they are aimed at low- and moderate-income Americans rather than the more typical affluent recipients, may do little to engender positive attitudes among recipients toward such policies—or, quite likely, toward the political leaders who helped bring them into being.

Neither do citizens exhibit much understanding of how policies in the submerged state function nor of the upwardly redistributive bias that many of them possess; thus they do not comprehend what is at stake in policy battles surrounding them. This is not surprising, given that political elites communicate about such policies rarely, and when they do, it is typically in muted, oblique, and contradictory ways. An experimental study to test how the provision of information about tax expenditures influenced attitudes about them found that when citizens were asked outright whether they supported particular examples of such policies, typically one out of three respondents responded that they did not know or had no opinion (Mettler and Guardino 2009).

The same study also suggested, however, that the "submerged state" need not necessarily remain hidden from ordinary Americans and visible only to entrenched powerful interests. When respondents were provided with basic facts about how such policies function and then were asked their views, the ranks of the uninformed fell to less than one in five: simple, clear, policy-relevant information facilitated opinion expression among citizens, particularly those with at least moderate levels of political knowledge. After respondents were provided with basic information about the distributive effect of the home mortgage interest deduction—the fact that it benefits mostly affluent people—*opposition grew sharply*, particularly among those with low to moderate incomes and among liberals and Democrats. By contrast, after being informed that the EITC benefited mostly those in low- to moderate-income groups, *support grew* among respondents generally, regardless of income (Mettler and Guardino 2009). This implies that if policy makers would reveal the features of the submerged state and what is at stake in reform efforts through clear communication with citizens, they could foster greater understanding of and support for reforms.

In short, in attempting to create or alter policies within the submerged state, reformers engage in a high risk endeavor in which the challenges are great and the political rewards may be very few. Their opponents will likely meet them quickly, armed and ready for battle, whereas their supporters and those of behalf of whom they engage in such struggles are unlikely to even appreciate their efforts not to mention offer assistance. Reconstituting the submerged state successfully, then, requires that reformers pay apt attention to conveying what is at stake to the public, through political communication, policy design, and the manner of program delivery.

IV. Tax Expenditures

Obama considers tax policy a centerpiece of his domestic agenda, particularly for purposes related to social welfare. He looks to it to reallocate priorities, devote resources to a wide array of purposes, mitigate rising economic inequality, and not least, raise revenues for health care reform. During the presidential campaign, Obama articulated three goals linking tax policy and social welfare: first, he planned to allow the 2001 and 2003 Bush tax cuts for the most affluent Americans to expire, restoring the higher rates on income, capital gains, and dividends that existed previously; second, he sought to scale back the regressivity of tax expenditures that favored the wealthy, restoring rules that had existed prior to the 2001 tax cuts; and third, he aimed to channel a higher proportion of tax expenditures to low- and moderate-income people, through both the creation of new policies and alterations to existing ones. For instance, he planned to make new and existing tax breaks "refundable," such that even those with no tax liability could benefit from them. Such ideas drew inspiration from the emerging field of behavioral economics, "the integration of economics and the psychology of preference formation and choice," an approach embraced by several of his advisors (Congdon, Kling, and Mullainathan 2009; Thaler and Sunstein 2008).

Early Action: The Economic Stimulus Bill

With the "American Recovery and Reinvestment Act of 2009," otherwise known as the "stimulus bill," President Obama scored several victories for his agenda within five weeks of taking office. Although this law resembled legislation enacted during Roosevelt's "First Hundred Days" inasmuch as it aimed to revive a devastated economy, it differed dramatically by making tax breaks the primary vehicle for offering relief to most Americans: in total, they amounted to $288 billion, fully 37 percent of the entire $787 billion dollar stimulus package (Recovery.gov). The largest of these was the president's signature proposal, "Making Work Pay" Tax Credits, which was based on principles like those of the Earned Income Tax Credit (EITC) but reached well up into the middle class: individuals with incomes below $75,000 and married couples with incomes below $150,000 qualified for this credit of up to $400. Second, as a means to make college more affordable, the "American Opportunity Education Tax Credit" offered up to $2,500 to reimburse low- and moderate-income families for tuition costs (U.S. Senate Finance and House Ways and Means Committees 2009). The bill also included several other tax features, including: increases in the EITC and child tax credit; one-time payments of $250 to recipients of Social Security, SSI, Railroad Retirement, Veterans' Disability Compensation, and some federal and state pensions; tax credits of up to $8,000 for first-time home buyers; and several others (Urban-Brookings Tax Policy Center 2009a).

The stimulus bill achieved the president's goals of channeling funds toward low- to moderate-income Americans, but it did so by further expanding the submerged state. In political terms, with over one out of three dollars in the stimulus bill tucked into tax breaks rather than in more obvious forms of social welfare such as relief payments or job creation, it was not clear that Americans would clearly recognize that the extra funds they received or did not owe in taxes were the result of Obama's efforts. One year later, when a CBS poll asked, "In general, do you think the Obama administration has increased taxes for most Americans, decreased taxes for most Americans, or have they kept taxes the same for most Americans?" only 12 percent responded that taxes had been decreased. In fact, 24 percent believed that the new president had increased taxes for most Americans (CBS News/*New York Times* Poll 2010). Remarkably, although 95 percent of employed Americans owed less in taxes thanks to the "Making Work Pay" tax credit in the stimulus, a policy projected to cost $536 billion over 10 years, most were unaware of it. Through an innovation prompted by behavioral economists who reasoned that small amounts of funds made available gradually would stimulate spending more reliably than a lump sum reimbursement, the new credit had been paid out automatically in the form of slightly larger earnings in workers' paychecks throughout 2009. While this approach may have prompted more spending, as intended, it seems not to have yielded enduring recognition of Obama's first major accomplishment in social welfare policy.

Obstacles to Scaling Back Regressivity

In February 2009, President Obama presented to Congress his first budget, one that contained nearly all of this campaign promises for changes in the tax code, including plans to scale back the regressivity of some tax expenditures. Obama proposed that those in the top two tax brackets—36 and 39.6 percent—should have their deductions, such as those for home mortgage interest and charitable contributions, limited to their value at the 28 percent tax bracket (Schatz 2009; Congressional Budget Office 2009, 192–193). As seen in Figure 3.1 above, those two tax deductions are especially regressive; thus altering them would facilitate progress on Obama's goal of reducing inequality. The president planned to use the saved revenues—projected to amount to $267 billion over 10 years—to help finance health care reform, for which they would provide approximately 45 percent of the needed funds.

On Capitol Hill, however, this plan met instantly with antipathy from Republicans, and it received a less-than-enthusiastic reception even from some in the President's own party. Fellow Democrat Max Baucus (MT), Chair of the Senate Finance Committee, cautioned, "Some of the reforms and offsets such as the limitations on itemized deductions, raise concerns and will require more study as we determine the best policies for getting America back on track" (Schatz 2009). In the House, Majority Leader Steny Hoyer (MD) warned, "That's going to be controversial. And, obviously, charitable contributions [present] great concern. Clearly, one of their greatest concerns will be very, very large-income donors who make very substantial contributions to very worthwhile enterprises" (Rucker 2009). Charles Rangel, Chair of the House Ways and Means Committee, also expressed reservations, noting, "I would never want to adversely affect anything that is charitable or good" (CBS/AP 2009).

What could explain such swift opposition—even from fellow Democrats—to modifying these tax breaks for the wealthy? The answer likely lies in the political power possessed by the organized groups that benefit from such provisions, starting with the real estate lobby. On the day that Obama presented his budget, Charles McMillan, president of the National Association of Realtors, wrote to him voicing opposition to proposed changes to the Home Mortgage Interest Deduction (MID). He argued that "diminishing or eliminating the MID would hurt all families, the housing market, and our national economy at a time when our housing and real estate markets are suffering, we believe it would be irresponsible for the real estate industry and federal policymakers to consider, much less support, any proposal seeking to alter the MID" (McMillan 2009). The organization circulated similar letters to all senators and representatives in Congress and published ads expressing its opposition in several newspapers (National Association of Realtors 2009a). The Financial Services Roundtable, Mortgage Bankers Association, and the National Association of Home Builders also quickly announced their opposition to any alterations to the real estate tax deductions (Mortgage Bankers Association 2009; Hoak 2009).

Such letters and ads carried weight because the real estate lobby had cultivated relationships with politicians from both parties and had done so over a long period of time and with an increasingly intense commitment of resources in recent years. In the size of its campaign contributions, it ranked among the most generous six industries in every electoral cycle at least since 1990. The $136 million it spent in the 2008 election—combining contributions from its PACs, soft money, and individual donors—was distributed widely: every member of the U.S. House received contributions that averaged $54,000, and every senator received an average of $401,000. Moreover, during 2009, the industry spent over $65 million on lobbying activities. The National Association of Realtors alone invested $19,669,268 in such activities, making it the tenth biggest spender across all types of organizations in the nation (OpenSecrets.org 2010b). While its prominence in such activities is nothing new, the amount that it invests in politics annually has soared over time, nearly quadrupling in just the past decade (OpenSecrets.org 2010c).

Though it may seem surprising, charitable organizations behaved very similarly to those in the real estate industry, spending considerable sums to protect their self-interest by protesting to the Obama administration's proposed changes in the tax code. The non-profits, foundations, and philanthropy sector spent less on such efforts than the real estate industry, but still invested considerably: it spent just one-eighth as much in campaign contributions in the 2008 election (18 million dollars), but fully half as much on lobbying in 2009—a total of about 38 million dollars (OpenSecrets.org 2010d). Philanthropists themselves appeared to be divided on whether a change in the tax law would adversely affect charitable giving, some predicting that its influence would be minor and far outweighed by the value of the achievement of health care reform (e.g., Hall 2009). Nonetheless, trade associations such as the Council on Foundations actively fought the Obama administration's proposals (Strom 2009). Throughout the ensuing debates, policy makers of both parties invoked the moral high ground associated with the philanthropic sector by expressing concerns about it far more than the real estate industry; such arguments quickly derailed the administration's primary plan for financing health care reform.

By late March, just one month after Obama introduced his proposal, the Senate had already taken action to stymie the administration's efforts to modify the two most regressive tax deductions. At Baucus's urging, Democrats endorsed a proposal offered by Republican Senator Bob Bennett (UT) requiring that health care funding not be financed through alteration of the tax benefits tied to charitable contributions (Perry 2009). A few weeks later, when the Senate Finance Committee released a report listing policy options for raising revenues to finance health care reform, it offered no discussion of Obama's preferred approach (U.S. Senate Finance Committee 2009).

From the start, the administration had sought to avoid the difficulties faced by Clinton's health care plan by leaving it to Congress to devise plans, and thus the president refrained from strongly promoting the financing plan that he favored. During a prime-time news conference in March, a reporter asked him whether he was reconsidering his approach of cutting back deductions for mortgages and charities, and whether he regretted having proposed it in the first place. Obama answered, "No, I think it's the right thing to do." Referring to the rise of economic inequality, he defended his approach as a way to "raise some revenues from people who benefited enormously over the last several years." Then, in a statement that was unusual for an elected official in its candor at revealing how an aspect of the submerged state functions, he explained:

> People are still going to be able to make charitable contributions. It just means if you give $100 and you're in this tax bracket, at a certain point, instead of being able to write off 36 (percent) or 39 percent, you're writing off 28 percent. Now, if it's really a charitable contribution, I'm assuming that that shouldn't be the determining factor as to whether you're giving that hundred dollars to the homeless shelter down the street. What it would do is it would equalize. When I give $100, I get the same amount of deduction as a bus driver who's making $50,000 a year or $40,000 a year gives that same hundred dollars. Right now, he gets 28 percent—he gets to write off 28 percent, I get to write off 39 percent. I don't think that's fair. (Obama 2009a)

Yet never did Obama offer a major speech in which he explained to the American public with similar clarity how such policies work and what difference the proposed changes would make and for whom. The issue thus remained largely invisible to the public. Without a concerted effort by the president to promote it and in the absence of public mobilization, the administration's plan continued to lose traction.

Taking Stock

Obama came into office with ambitious plans for restructuring tax expenditures and undercutting their upwardly redistributive bias. In his first year, he succeeded only in his goal of creating new tax breaks—at least temporary ones—for low- to middle-income households. But these policies further add to the size and scope of the submerged state, and they are imperceptible to most Americans.

Given that the submerged state is not nearly as visible to most Americans as it is to the interest groups that benefit from it, the task falls to reformers to

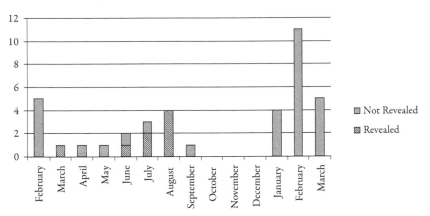

FIGURE 3.2 Obama's Public Statements on Tax Policy: Revealing the Submerged State, Feb. 2009–Mar. 2010.

Sources, Figures 3.2–3.5: White House Briefing Room web site (http://www.whitehouse. gov/briefing-room), speeches on health care, taxes, and higher education given by Barack Obama (not White House staff) as listed under "Speeches and Remarks" and Your Weekly Address" between January 2009 and March 21, 2010. Note: Health speeches include those during which Obama mentions or discusses health reform. Tax speeches include those during which Obama mentions or discusses tax cuts, tax credits, or tax expenditures (e.g., limiting the itemized deduction). Higher education speeches include those during which Obama mentions or discusses higher education, particularly education tax credits (American Opportunity Tax Credit), Pell Grants, student loans, and community colleges. Some speeches are included in multiple categories. For example, discussions of the American Opportunity Tax Credit are included in both the tax category and the higher education category. Mentions of the limit on itemized deductions are included in both the health category (as a financing option for the overhaul) and in the tax category.

reveal its key features to the public. An analysis of all speeches, press conferences, and weekly addresses given by Obama himself between his inauguration in January 2009 through March 2010 shows that he spoke about taxes 38 times. As seen in Figure 3.2, taxes were a common theme in February 2009, when Obama gave speeches focusing on the tax breaks that were part of the stimulus. After that, however, though the subject came up fairly often, it was in the context of speeches about health care reform, and took the form of brief comments about either financing or incentives and mechanisms through which the policy would operate. As indicated by the lined sections of the bars, furthermore, even direct references to taxes rarely involved statements that made explicit the actual features of the submerged state. Content analysis of the speeches revealed that on only 8 of the 38 occasions did the president actually describe how such policies functioned and who benefited. Such statements, moreover, were usually very brief: the statement in the March 2009 press conference mentioned above, for instance, occupied only 446 words in the midst of a 9,000-word news conference (Obama 2009a). The president refrained from making a full and sustained case for the financing plans that his administration put forward, and the public remained quite uninformed.

By contrast, groups benefiting from existing arrangements continued to be astutely aware of developments and poised to act when necessary to protect the status quo. As 2009 came to a close, the National Association of Realtors applauded itself for effectively "protecting the mortgage interest deduction," noting that it had "aggressively fought off changes to the MID through grassroots, advertising and similar advocacy tools" (National Association of Realtors 2009b). Subsequently, reformers had to seek other means for financing health care reform, favoring alternatives that did not face such outright opposition by established groups seeking to protect existing arrangements.

V. Higher Education Policy

A few decades ago, the United States led the world in the attainment of bachelor's degrees, but progress has stalled, particularly because of stagnating graduation rates among those from less advantaged backgrounds (OECD 2007). Obama's ambition to restore American leadership in college graduation rates required, first, a restructuring of entrenched policy arrangements, namely a subsidized lending system that has consumed funds that could have been spent instead to foster access, and which has, meanwhile, fostered increasingly divisive politics over the past decade and a half.

After enacting the legislation establishing student loans, the Higher Education Act of 1965, Democrats positioned themselves as the program's protector, while Republicans continued to object—as they had at its inception—to channeling government subsidies toward lenders. By the late 1980s, however, members of both parties became aware that student lending was expanding into a highly lucrative business, and the politics surrounding it began to shift. An official in the George H.W. Bush administration hatched the idea of direct lending by government—cutting out the banks as intermediaries—as a means to reduce overall spending for loans. A bipartisan group of congressmen led by Senator Paul Simon (D-IL) promoted the idea and won support for a pilot program in the 1992 reauthorization of the Higher Education Act. In 1993, newly elected President Bill Clinton made one of his initial goals the full replacement of existing system with direct lending. Suddenly, the lenders mobilized as never before, and a bitter fight ensued. Congress adopted only a weakened version of Clinton's plan, permitting the adoption of direct lending on a limited basis. By the time the Republicans took control of Congress in 1995, the two parties had effectively traded the positions they had each held on student lending just one decade previous, and they had adopted more stringent versions of each (Mettler 2009a, 209).

As student lenders' profits soared between 1995 and 2006, they invested in strengthening their political capacity. In campaign financing, Sallie Mae established a PAC in the late 1990s, and by 2006 it emerged as the top donor within the entire finance and credit industry; fellow student lender Nelnet ranked fifth (OpenSecrets.org 2010e). In lobbying, Sallie Mae began to rank among the top five finance and credit companies, outspending even Mastercard and American Express (OpenSecrets.org 2010e). Lenders also worked together to create several new organizations to represent their interests in Washington, D.C. Over this period, Republicans in Congress increasingly worked in tandem with lenders, attempting to seek favorable rates and terms for them.

Late in 2006, however, the lenders' stature began to decline. Heightened voter participation by young people and investigative reports into lender practices by a few journalists caught Democrats' attention. After regaining control of the House in 2007, they unveiled higher education legislation that put lenders on the defensive. Then New York State Attorney General Andrew Cuomo launched an investigation, charging that financial aid officers in many colleges and universities maintained improper relationships with "preferred lenders." An internal investigation in the U.S. Department of Education indicated that Bush administration appointees had given tacit approval to such arrangements (U.S. Department of Education

2006). In turn, in 2007 and 2008, Congress enacted and Bush signed into law two bills that put new constraints on lenders, one by placing restrictions on how colleges interacted with them, and the other by lowering subsidies and using the savings to finance increased student aid funding (Mettler 2009a, 214–225). Thus, when Obama took office, the battles he supported were already underway on the student aid front, and the opposition had been dealt several blows.

As we have seen, Obama readily achieved the American Opportunity Tax Credit as part of the stimulus bill. In 2009, Congress also boosted Pell Grant maximum grant rates to $5,550, continuing a trend of recent years. In addition, Obama—like Clinton—aimed to replace the existing student loan policy with 100% direct lending, a goal that involves reconstituting the political economy of the submerged state. He proposed to use the savings from the termination of lender subsidies to make Pell Grants an entitlement. Both objectives were articulated in the administration's first budget.

Taking on the Lenders

Just a few months into his presidency, Obama delivered a speech that revealed the inner workings of the submerged state with respect to student lending:

> Under the FFEL [Federal Family Education Loans] program, lenders get a big government subsidy with every loan they make. And these loans are then guaranteed with taxpayer money, which means that if a student defaults, a lender can get back almost all of its money from our government. Taxpayers are paying banks a premium to act as middlemen—a premium that costs the American people billions of dollars each year. Well, that's a premium we cannot afford—not when we could be investing the same money in our students, in our economy, and in our country. (Obama 2009b)

Continuing, the president directly and forcefully took on the lenders:

> The banks and the lenders who have reaped a windfall from these subsidies have mobilized an army of lobbyists to try to keep things the way they are. They are gearing up for battle. So am I. They will fight for their special interests. I will fight for American students and their families. And for those who care about America's future, this is a battle we can't afford to lose (Obama 2009b).

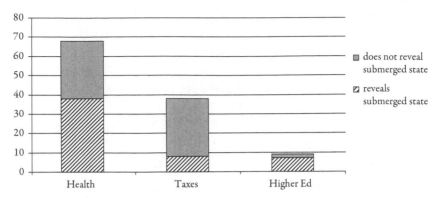

FIGURE 3.3 Frequency of Obama's Public Statements on Social Welfare Issues, Compared, Feb. 2009–Mar. 2010.

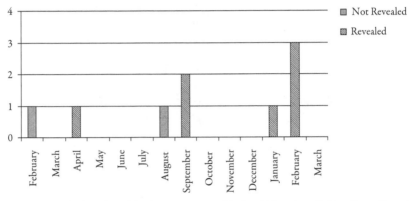

FIGURE 3.4 Obama's Public Statements on Higher Education Policy: Revealing the Submerged State, Feb. 2009–Mar. 2010.

By summer, however, health care reform efforts consumed the administration's attention, and the president rarely spoke about higher education.

As seen in Figure 3.3, Obama discussed higher education issues publicly only 9 times during his 14 months in office, compared to 68 times for health care and 38 for taxes. Figure 3.4 reveals that when speaking about higher education, Obama did usually make explicit the features of the submerged state with respect to student lending. He likely felt freer to do so on this issue because others—Cuomo, the Department of Education Inspector General, and Democratic leaders in Congress—had already begun the process. Yet because the president spoke about it so infrequently and it was vastly overshadowed by the focus on health care, the issues at stake likely remained hidden to most Americans.

The Lenders Fight Back

The lenders, on the other hand, continued to focus on the issue. Realizing that existing arrangements were unlikely to endure, in July 2009 they put forward a proposal that ceded ground to the administration by assuming the end of subsidies to lenders. Nonetheless, the plan featured a continuing role for themselves: they would originate, service, and collect payments on student loans, in exchange for fees paid to them by government.

The U.S. House of Representatives quickly repudiated the lenders' plan. Education and Labor Committee Chairman George Miller spoke out against it and introduced his own bill, one that followed Obama's lead on core principles and effectively ended the FFEL program. The Committee approved a version that met the President partway: on Pell Grants, it recommended regular annual increases but retention of discretionary authority for Congress to set the base award (Field 2009b), and on student loans, it permitted lenders to compete to service loans but not to originate them. In September, the full House approved the measure (Lewin 2009; U.S. Congress 2009b).

In the Senate, however, it appeared that changes to student lending would prove more contentious. Already in the spring of 2009, Nebraska Senator Ben Nelson, in whose state lender Nelnet employs one thousand individuals, voiced his opposition to direct lending (Howard 2009). Senate leaders decided to put the issue on hold while grappling with health care legislation. Senate rules permit per session just one budget reconciliation vote, in which a simple majority—unstoppable by filibuster—may approve legislation that is strictly related to the budget. Leaders realized that they might ultimately need to combine elements of the higher education policy with health care reform in such a bill, so they delayed action throughout the autumn.

Lenders used the delay to organize the opposition, both at the grassroots and elite levels. Sallie Mae mobilized workers and residents in towns where it employs the greatest numbers. In Fishers, Indiana, for example, over 81,000 individuals signed a petition urging Congress to preserve a role for lenders. At a rally of company employees, hundreds of whom donned matching T-shirts that read "Protect Indiana Jobs," Sallie Mae CEO Albert Lord attempted to stir populist anger, declaring, "There's Washington, and then there's the rest of the country. This is the rest of the country" (Nelson 2009; Lichtblau 2010). Meanwhile, in Washington, D.C., lenders set the goal of gaining support from at least five moderate Democratic senators to retain the FFEL program, and they spent millions on lobbying (Alarkon 2009; Knight 2009; Dreas

2009). Sallie Mae alone devoted over $4 million to such activities in 2009, the second-largest amount it had ever spent in one year.

By November, the lenders appeared to be gaining ground: analysts predicted that Obama's proposal lacked the support of enough senators to pass (Dreas 2009). The next month, Democratic Bob Casey from Pennsylvania led 11 moderate Democrats in support of an alternative to the House bill that would allow lenders to continue to originate government-backed loans and to be awarded fees by the federal government for doing so (Boles 2010 The prospects for the achievement of Obama's goals looked increasingly uncertain. Just as in the tax policy realm, vested interests of the submerged state seemed far more aware of what was at stake in reform efforts than ordinary citizens, and they proved ready and able to mobilize, whereas the general public remained quiescent.

Remarkably, however, in an eleventh-hour stroke of good fortune for the Obama administration, Democratic leaders ultimately found that including the higher education legislation with health care reform in the March 2010 budget reconciliation bill helped it to meet the criteria for cost-savings that would help ensure passage. Despite the dim prospects in December for the administration's higher education proposals to acquire support from even 50 Democratic senators, 56 came on board when the direct lending plan that some disliked was combined with the party's top agenda item, health care reform. In what represented the most significant shift from submerged to visible governance achieved by Obama to date, the existing system of student lending was terminated and replaced entirely by direct lending.

VI. Health Care Reform

By 2008, the idea was widely accepted that the U.S. health care system was in crisis. Health care costs had climbed to 16 percent of the U.S. GDP—more than the percentage spent in any other OECD nation and twice that of the average (Robert Wood Johnson Foundation 2009). The nation has long been the only one in the Western industrialized world that lacks national health insurance, yet the U.S. government itself spends substantially more than other countries on health care—on Medicare and Medicaid and the subsidization of employer-provided health care. The percentage of Americans with employer-provided private insurance benefits fell from 69 percent to 60 percent between 2000 and 2005 alone (Quadagno and McKelvey 2008, 12); one in six Americans were uninsured (Swartz 2008, 33).

As a result, health care reform hit the political agenda again in 2009 as it has approximately every 15 years since 1920. Each time, the issue has consumed the attention of policy makers and the media for months of intense drama, protracted battles, and deal-making between the political parties and with interest groups (Hacker 2008, 107; Blumenthal and Morone 2009). That health care reform would require Herculean efforts by the President and congressional leaders was a given; that such efforts would guarantee success was anything but. And yet, this time, the reformers won.

A full recounting of the tumultuous saga of 2009–2010 and a comprehensive analysis of the issues involved lies well beyond our scope here. Rather, the analytical framework featured throughout this article will be utilized to consider the briefly the challenges the Obama administration faced on the issue and the level of success it has achieved. As much or even more than other aspects of the submerged state, existing arrangements for the health care system have long fostered powerful vested interests, complicating the quest for reform. Over the past decade, the amount that strictly health-related groups have spent on lobbying—$3.788 billion dollars—ranked second only to spending by the finance, insurance, and real estate sector, and much of the lobbying by the latter industries—as well as by other miscellaneous business groups—also focused on health care (OpenSecrets.org 2010f). And, just as in the other areas of the submerged state, government's role in subsidizing private actors in the provision of health care is largely hidden from ordinary citizens.

Interest Group Politics

Throughout the long history of struggles over health care reform in the United States, interest groups have played leading roles—primarily as antagonists. Some of this activism preceded the development of existing policies. The American Medical Association (AMA), for instance, opposed national health insurance as early as 1920 and impeded its inclusion in New Deal legislation (Hacker 2002, 188, 207). Health insurance companies sought and achieved special tax-exempt status in the early twentieth century, and then worked to strengthen and expand their government-subsidized role (Hacker 2002, 203, 239–242).

The policies, in turn, reshaped politics, particularly among labor unions. These organizations found greater leverage in negotiating with employers for private health insurance benefits than in seeking government-sponsored coverage, so they became lukewarm supporters at best and often opposed reform (Gottschalk 2000). By the 1993–1994 reform cycle, when labor's power and circumstances had changed dramatically from its zenith in the postwar era, it refrained from a strong endorsement of Clinton's plan—in part, holding out for a stronger alternative, and in part, disillusioned by the president's support for the North American Free Trade Agreement (Gottschalk 2000; Skocpol 1997, 78–80). In fact, few groups—with the exception of the American Nurses Association and a coalition of black and Hispanic doctors—expressed firm support for the Clinton proposal (Skocpol 1997, 95–96).

Viewed against this daunting history, during 2009 the Obama administration and congressional Democrats achieved significant success in working together with key interests—namely doctors, labor, drug companies, and the AARP—to create a stronger coalition of support for health care reform than in the past. First, although the AMA signaled early on that it would oppose a government-sponsored insurance plan, in a dramatic reversal it lent its support. It even endorsed the House plan, complete with the "public option," of which it disapproved, because it had won several modifications it favored within the Medicare payment reform plan (Pear 2009; Glendinning 2009; Rohack 2009; Geiger and Hamburger 2009). Second, organized labor played a more active and constructive role in pushing for the adoption of health care reform than in the past. The Service Employees International Union (SEIU), AFL-CIO, and American Federation of State, County, and Municipal Employees all strongly supported the adoption of the "public option," and thus favored the House plan (Klein 2009; MacGillis 2008). But rather than only disparaging alternatives, unions actively promoted the legislation: they ran ads, they showed up at town meetings to counter the arguments of opponents, and they mobilized in states and districts of swing voters. Said organizer Dennis Rivera, "We're running this like a presidential campaign, and our candidate is health care reform" (Greenhouse 2009). Third, the pharmaceutical industry cooperated in supporting reform. Although Obama had lambasted it throughout the 2008 campaign, once elected he and Senator Baucus worked closely with its leaders—as well as the AARP—to broker an agreement about how to reduce the cost of drugs purchased through the Medicare prescription drug benefit, and about its "doughnut hole" provision that required seniors to pay the full price of some prescriptions. The result, while granting some leverage to the drug companies, generated $80 billion in savings to help finance health care reform, and also brought the AARP on board (Tumulty and Scherer 2009; Hamburger 2009; Attkisson 2009,Young 2009b; Young 2009c).

While this degree of cooperation among stakeholders brought reform closer to being realized than ever before, some powerful interests remained opposed. Insurance companies and business groups, which continued to benefit most from the existing arrangements of the submerged state, allied themselves and mobilized vigorously against proposed changes. Unlike the drug companies, insurance companies refused to cooperate in cost cutting. America's Health Insurance Plans, a trade group of several large insurance companies, collected funds from its members—Aetna, Cigna, Humana, and others—to finance television ads disparaging the main proposals being developed in Congress. The U.S. Chamber of Commerce facilitated the ad buys (Stone 2010). For its part, the Chamber of Commerce also poured $144 million into lobbying, outspending all other organizations and businesses during 2009 (OpenSecrets.org 2010gAs we saw in examining tax policy, furthermore, the demise of the Obama administration's proposed limitations on tax deductions for wealthy Americans involved organizations that might seem to have little to do with health care reform—the real estate industry and charitable organizations. Their action thwarted the bill's progress at a critical juncture and prompted leaders to advance instead a tax on high-priced employer-provided health insurance. That plan, because it would have affected a significant number of low- and moderate-income Americans, involved greater political risks. But that story lies beyond our scope here.

Revealing Reform to the Public

In using the bully pulpit during his 14 months in office, Obama prioritized health care reform. As seen in Figure 3.3, he spoke out on that issue far more than higher education and taxes combined. Possibly the timing of these speeches, which did not begin until summer, was a bit delayed: at that point,

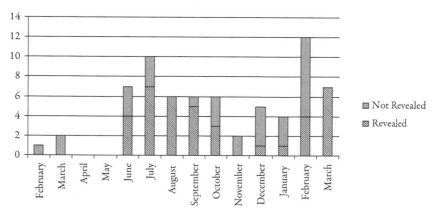

FIGURE 3.5 Obama's Public Statements on Health Care Reform: Revealing the Submerged State, Feb. 2009–Mar. 2010.

opponents had already mobilized to depict the "public option" as a "government takeover" and to stoke concerns about new taxes on existing health benefits, and support had begun to diminish.

The complexity of health care reform, furthermore, involving efforts to alter practices carried out between government, employers, and insurance companies, makes it difficult to explain to the public. As seen in Figure 3.5, Obama made public statements on the subject 68 times, and on 38 of those occasions he attempted to reveal what was at stake in reconstituting the submerged state. In some cases, he described how existing arrangements benefited private interests. For example, at an on-line town hall meeting in July, he said:

> About two-thirds of the costs of the reforms will come from reallocating money that is already being spent in the health care system but isn't being spent wisely. So it doesn't involve more spending; it just involves smarter spending. And I'll just give you one example. Over the next 10 years, we will spend $177 billion in unwarranted subsidies to insurance companies under something called. Medicare Advantage. Now, this does not make seniors healthier. People who are signed up for this private insurance subsidized program don't get any better care than those who aren't. The subsidies don't go to the patients; they go to the insurance companies. Now, think if we took that $177 billion and helped families so that they could have insurance, and that we could have preventive care. (Obama 2009c)

The next month, in Montana, he once again talked about the need to "eliminate subsidies to insurance companies."

> I just think I would rather be giving that money to the young lady here who doesn't have health insurance and giving her some help, than giving it to insurance companies that are making record profits. (Obama 2009d)

The president also tried to explain how differently situated citizens—those with insurance already and those without it—would experience the benefits that came with reform.

Obama did less, however, to illuminate the cost of health care reform and how it would affect ordinary Americans. The public thus likely found little clarity and assurance on questions that likely most concerned many: how it would be paid for, and whether and to what extent they personally would be burdened by new costs. Without making these dimensions of the submerged state visible to the public, Obama may have left uncertain Americans more easily swayed by the arguments of opponents, who repeatedly equated health care reform with higher taxes.

While citizens may have received insufficient information about how reform would affect them, what they could observe clearly in media coverage were the numerous special deals that lawmakers made in the process of arriving at a bill. Repeatedly, congressional leaders and the President negotiated with stakeholder interest groups and with a handful of individual lawmakers whose votes were deemed crucial. Each of these interactions resulted in the negotiation of privileged treatment for particular parties, whether Nebraskans, union members, or drug companies. While such agreements helped move this major legislation aimed for the general public closer to passage, it likely appeared to many citizens as excessive catering to special interests. Such politics likely strike many—particularly independents, who have less knowledge of the political process generally—as undemocratic, and at odds with the open and accessible forms of governance that Obama had promised during his campaign. Massachusetts voter Marlene Connally, quoted in one of the opening quotations of this paper, articulated this view when she called the reform plans "elusive."

At Last

Time and again, the hopes of reformers have been dashed in the pursuit of health care reform, and yet this time, despite the obstacles, they prevailed. After 90 years of effort, the achievement is momentous. It promises to expand health care coverage to 32 million Americans and, by imposing new regulations on insurance companies, to grant people greater security that they will not be denied coverage, for example if they have a pre-existing condition. In some significant ways, the policy expands the visible state, particularly by making many more Americans eligible for Medicaid. In other ways, however, it enlarges the submerged state, by channeling many more toward private insurance and offering them tax breaks to help pay for it. Other aspects of reform use state action to modify the action of private actors. This raises the question: How will Americans view the reformed health care system once it is underway—as accountable to citizens, through government, or as a system that is not subject to public control? Time will tell, but the Obama administration may influence the outcome, first through how it communicates about the meaning of reform and next through the process of policy delivery.

VII. Visible and Submerged Success

In the realm of social welfare issues, Barack Obama set out to transform exist-ing policies within the submerged state. He sought to harness this vast set of arrangements and to make it more inclusive and responsive to the needs of ordinary citizens, and to curtail the extent to which it channels public funds toward powerful sectors of the economy and affluent citizens. This has been an ambitious reform agenda. Such change requires the reconstitution of long-established relationships between government and economic actors. Organi-zations and industries that have long benefited from the established system of public subsidies and incentives have been willing and able to invest tremen-dous resources in preserving those arrangements. Paradoxically, in defending them, they and their allies in elective office have routinely depicted reform proposals as attempts at "government takeovers," as if to imply that govern-ment were not already central to the existing arrangements.

Reconstituting the submerged state has been doubly difficult; though the stakes have been highly apparent to the groups that have benefited from them, they were not very visible to most Americans. Most people perceived only the market at work: they have little awareness that many of the social benefits they receive emanate from a submerged state that is structured by public policy and subsidized by government. Neither do they realize that many such policies disproportionately benefit wealthy citizens. They are unlikely to know the extent to which government policy promotes the profitability of some industries by offsetting their costs in serving citizens, whether as con-sumers or borrowers. The functioning and effects of the submerged state remain murky, if not largely hidden, to most citizens.

Yet, despite the shrouded nature of the submerged state, citizens have been able to observe—illuminated in the media's spotlight—the activities of re-formers who attempt to engage in its reconstitution. The problem is that, without perceiving what is at stake, citizens likely viewed reformers as simply playing "politics as usual," making deals with powerful interests. The process of reforming the submerged state is inherently messy and conflictual, far from idealized notions of change. It may have reinforced some citizens' views that government should not be trusted with complicated matters—that the pri-vate sector can handle them better and without such controversy.

In his first 14 months in office, Barack Obama accomplished numerous of his major goals with respect to social welfare policy, as we have seen. Yet, as shown in Table 3.5, the scorecard indicates that the new policies do as much or more to expand the submerged state as they do to reduce its scope. The end of

Table 3.5 Effects of the Obama Presidency on the Submerged State

Termination of Existing Programs	Reductions in Scope and New Regulations of Private Actors	Expansions in Scope
Subsidies for banks/ lenders of student loans	Subsidies for Employer Provided Health Benefits (via tax on "Cadillac plans," to begin in 2018) New regulations of health insurance companies, re: preexisting conditions, children through age 26, etc.	Making Work Pay Tax Credit American Opportunity Education Tax Credit Expansions of several other existing tax credits One-time tax credits: Cash for Clunkers, first-time homebuyers, installation of energy-efficient windows, etc. More individuals to receive subsidized health insurance benefits

the existing bank-based system of student lending and its replacement with direct lending represents the most significant curtailment of the submerged state—even though lenders will continue to have a role in servicing loans. In the area of tax expenditures, the Obama administration achieved the creation of new and expanded policies for low- to moderate-income people. Several aspects of health care reform, as discussed above, also expand on the submerged state. Thus, the submerged state endures, albeit in altered form, promising that the political dynamics it engenders will continue to challenge reformers.

VIII. Postlude

Usually presidents are rewarded on Election Day for the enactment of landmark legislation. After the remarkable passage of the Civil Rights Act of 1964, Lyndon Johnson won a huge victory and gained even larger Democratic majorities in Congress; the same was true of Roosevelt after he signed into law the Social Security Act of 1935, and that was at a time with an unemployment rate double that of 2010: 20 percent, compared to 10 percent. The Affordable Care Act of 2010 compares to both of those in terms of its scope and significance, and yet, Obama did not reap such rewards. Instead, opponents gained steam. By September, 61 percent of Americans told pollsters that they favored repeal of the health care reform law (Rasmussen Report 2010). In the November election, Republicans took control of the House, gaining 63 seats, the largest gain in a midterm year since 1938. It was, to use Obama's words, a "shellacking" of the administration and the Democrats.

While the different outcomes in 2010 owe in part to other factors, one cannot explain our contemporary politics without understanding the submerged state. Certainly the devastated economy, sharp partisan polarization, and the contemporary media each played a part in political developments. But the president's ability to receive credit for what his administration had achieved was undermined greatly by the fact that so many Americans were unaware of the policies that had been restructured or newly created. Neither did they grasp how such reforms channeled resources and rights to the vast majority of ordinary Americans.

The submerged nature of much of the Affordable Care Act, compounded by the results of the election, will make it difficult to sustain. Once the new Republican-controlled House convened in January, it took little time before voting to repeal the law. Without support in the Senate, the blanket repeal will not go further, but the party will likely try to chip away at specific provisions and to undermine implementation, while meanwhile it works its way through the courts.

Interestingly, the House Republicans have not signaled that they will attempt to restore bank-based student lending. Consistent with their stance in 2009 and 2010, as much as they are publicly critical of direct lending, they seem resigned to the fact that the credit crisis has ruled out alternatives that emanate from the private sector. Yet, at the same time, officials in the U.S. Department of Education have let the opportunity pass them by to make the new loans more visible to students, so that they would better grasp government's role in enabling them to attend college. As one told me, "From the customer perspective, it will not be very different—students will barely know the difference. It is a government program, like before, and run by private actors, like before" (Interviews 2010).

As 2010 came to an end, two events during the lame-duck Congress exacerbated the trends in tax policy that occurred during the early months of the Obama administration, expanding the submerged state further. First, when a bipartisan commission named by Obama to address the deficit floated a proposal to scale back the Home Mortgage Interest Deduction, the plan was immediately shot down. Just as it had throughout 2009, the real estate lobby quickly lambasted the idea, and Democrats on Capitol Hill piled on—despite the fact that the plans would have made the policy far less regressive than it is currently (Luhby 2010). The commission report subsequently lost any remaining steam when it failed to gain the necessary approval of 14 out of 18 members required for it to go to Congress for a vote. Next, Obama made an agreement with congressional Republicans to extend the Bush tax cuts for two more years—including those which aid the most affluent the most. The package that Congress proceeded to pass included, among other things, a payroll tax break that would benefit all Americans but, just like the tax cuts in the stimulus bill, would do so in a way that few would notice. Taken together and on balance, these policies would fail to mitigate inequality, and the benefits they would channel to ordinary Americans would be delivered a way that would elude many. Despite the administration's efforts to do much to improve citizens' lives, little of it had occurred in a manner that would enable them to see the outcome.

Revealing Governance

Successful reconstitution of the submerged state requires reformers to accomplish several tasks. First, they must either *regroup or defeat* the interest groups that have been empowered by existing arrangements. If circumstances allow and meaningful agreements can be reached, some groups might be brought on board to cooperate in reform, as the Obama administration succeeded in doing with respect to health care reform. Outright defeat of groups that benefit from current policies is unlikely, given the extent to which they were empowered. It worked in 2010 with respect to student lenders only because those groups had already been weakened substantially over time: the creation of pilot programs for direct lending in the early 1990s created an entering wedge, a base on which reformers could build until their ideas became more widely acceptable. As this indicates, a new policy alternative can be established alongside existing arrangements as an interim approach that can facilitate more extensive reform later on.

Second, reformers must *reveal* to the public how existing policies of the submerged state function and who benefits, what is at stake in reform, who will gain, and what the costs will be. In each of the three policy areas considered here, Obama has done more than other political leaders to expose the deeply obscured arrangements, but more focused and sustained attention is warranted. The tasks of reform may have proceeded more easily throughout 2009–2010 if political leaders had attempted to communicate to the public earlier, more often, and more deliberately about these matters. Even now that reform has been achieved, political leaders need to continue to inform the public about what has changed and how new policies will function.

Third, reformers must *revamp policies*, either through redesigning them or at least by guiding their delivery to make them more visible to citizens. The primary way to engage in this meaningfully is for policies to be restructured so that they no longer subsidize the interests and groups they have promoted in the past, or at least so that such support is curtailed. The change to direct lending represents quite a complete reconstitution of one policy area. The health care reform bill offers a more modified approach by retaining the existing system of private health insurance, but making it subject to mechanisms that regulate private actors and slightly curtail the extent of subsidization. But administrators should seek means to make the benefits of the submerged state more evident to citizens, for example by providing a summary sheet to individuals with their tax return that notes the amount accrued through each type of tax expenditure, or by indicating what private health insurance would cost individuals in the absence of public subsidies.

When Obama first declared his candidacy, and later, as he assumed the highest office in the land, he promised that his presidency would help Americans to "reclaim the meaning of citizenship," "restore our sense of common purpose," and "restore the vital trust between people and their government." While efforts to reconstitute the submerged state may have appeared distant from or antithetical to such goals, it is crucial to their achievement because, to the extent that it has succeeded, it diffuses the power of special interests relative to that of the public. Now, if the Obama administration can successfully reveal the remaining aspects of submerged state to citizens through new features of policy delivery, it may enable them to participate in a more meaningful way.

Notes

1. An earlier version of this chapter appeared in *Perspectives on Politics* 8(3) in September 2010, pp. 803–824. I am grateful to Julianna Koch for excellent and extensive research assistance on this paper. Grants from the Russell Sage Foundation and the Spencer Foundation supported the Social and Governmental Issues and Participation Survey of 2008, some results of which are discussed herein. For helpful comments on an earlier version of this paper, I am thankful to E.J. Dionne, Larry Jacobs, Kimberly Johnson, Desmond King, Adam Sheingate, Helen Thompson, and participants at a March 2010 conference held at Nuffield College, Oxford University, "Reconstituting the American State: The Promise and Dilemmas of Obama's First Year." The conference was sponsored by the Mellon Trust Fund.

2. If we conceptualize each Senator as hypothetically representing half of the population of the state from which they were elected and then calculate the total number represented by each party in that manner, I calculate that Democrats currently represent 63 percent of all Americans (192 million) while controlling only 59 seats, whereas Republican Senators represent only 37 percent (112 million) of Americans yet hold 41 seats.

3. The Social and Governmental Issues and Participation Study of 2008 consisted of a telephone survey of 1,400 Americans, including a national random sample of 1,000 plus over-samples of 200 low-income individuals and 200 25–34 year olds. It was conducted by the Cornell Survey Research Institute, from August–September 2008. The response rate was 34 percent, calculated according to AAPOR guidelines.

4. Of the remainder, 3 percent said they paid less than their "fair share," and 1 percent explained that they do not pay taxes.

5. EITC is not included in this analysis both because it is designed in a way that appears to make its existence as a social benefit more apparent, given that those without tax liability may claim it, and because organizations have publicized its availability in low-income communities in recent years and helped eligible individuals to claim it.

References

Alarkon, Walter. 2009. "Beneficiaries of Sallie Mae, Nelnet Fight Obama's Student-Aid Proposal." March 9. *The Hill*.

America's Health Insurance Plans. 2009a. "AHIP Statement on House Passage of H.R. 3962" November 7. (http://www.ahip.org/content/pressrelease.aspx?docid=28730).

America's Health Insurance Plans. 2009b. AHIP Statement on Senate Health Care Reform Legislation" December 19. (http://www.ahip.org/content/pressrelease.aspx?docid=28997).

Ansolabehere, Stephen, John M. de Figueiredo, and James M. Snyder, Jr. 2003. "Why Is There So Little Money in U.S. Politics?" *Journal of Economic Perspectives* 17(1): 105–130.

Attkisson, Sharyl. 2009. "White House & Big Pharma: What's the Deal?" CBS News. August 10. (http://www.cbsnews.com/stories/2009/08/10/eveningnews/main5231143.shtml)

Blumenthal, David, and James A. Morone. 2009. *The Heart of Power: Health and Politics in the Oval Office*. Berkeley: University of California Press.

Boles, Corey. 2010. "Alternate Senate Student Loan Plan Would Retain Role for Banks." *Dow Jones News Wire*. (http://www.advfn.com/news_Alternate-Senate-Student-Loan-Plan-Would-Retain-Role-For-Banks_40615283.html), accessed March 1, 2010.

Burman, Leonard, Eric Toder, and Christopher Geissler. 2008. "How Big Are Total Individual Income Tax Expenditures, and Who Benefits from Them?" Discussion

Paper No. 31. The Urban-Brookings Tax Policy Center. (http://www.taxpolicycenter.org/UploadedPDF/1001234_tax_expenditures.pdf), accessed March 1, 2010.

Campbell, Andrea Louise, and Theda Skocpol. 2003. "AARP at Risk of Medicare Blowback." *Albany Times Union*, November 30. Originally written for Newsday. (http://www.nysaaaa.org/News%20Headlines/Editorial_Medicare_TU_12-03-03.pdf), accessed March 1, 2010.

CBS/AP. 2009. "Top Dems Question Tax Deduction Proposal." *CBS News/Politics*. (http://www.cbsnews.com/stories/2009/03/05/politics/100days/economy/main4844012.shtml), accessed January 29, 2010.

CBS News/*New York Times* Poll. 2009. "The Tea Party Movement," February 5–10. (http://www.cbsnews.com/htdocs/pdf/poll_Tea_Party_021110.pdf), accessed March 1, 2010.

Congdon, William, Jeffrey R. Kling, and Sendhil Mullainathan. 2009. "Behavioral Economics and Tax Policy." National Bureau of Economic Research, Working Paper 15328 (http://www.nber.org/papers/w15328).

Congressional Budget Office. 2009. "An Analysis of the President's Budgetary Proposals for FY 2010." http://www.cbo.gov/ftpdocs/102xx/doc10296/TablesforWeb.pdf, accessed June 15, 2010.

Delisle, Jason. 2010. "Senator Conrad's Choice on Student Loan Bill." Higher Ed Watch. New America Foundation, January 19. (http://higheredwatch.newamerica.net/blogposts/2010/senator_conrads_choice_on_student_loan_bill-26445), accessed March 1, 2010.

Dreas, Maryann. 2009. "Private Lenders Focus on Jobs in Student Loan Fight." *The Hill*. (http://thehill.com/business-a-lobbying/69873-private-lenders-focus-on-jobs-in-student-loan-fight), accessed March 1, 2010.

Field, Kelly. 2009. "On Higher-Education Spending, the White House and Congress Agree, to a Point." *Chronicle of Higher Education*. August 17. (http://chronicle.com/article/On-Education-Spending-the/48007/?sid=wb&utm_source=wb&utm_medium=en)

Garfinkel, Irwin, Lee Rainwater, and Timothy M. Smeeding. 2006. "A Re-examination of Welfare States and Inequality in Rich Nations: How In-Kind Transfers and Indirect Taxes Change the Story." *Journal of Policy Analysis and Management* 25(4): 897–919.

Geiger, Kim, and Tom Hamburger. 2009. "Healthcare Reform Wins over Doctors Lobby." *Los Angeles Times*, September 15. (http://articles.latimes.com/2009/sep/15/nation/na-lobbying-ama15).

Gladieux, Lawrence E., and Thomas R. Wolanin. 1976. *Congress and the Colleges: The National Politics of Higher Education*. Lexington, MA: Lexington Books.

Glendinning, David. 2009. "AMA Backs House health System Reform Bill That Includes Medicare Pay Overhaul," July 27. (http://www.ama-assn.org/amednews/2009/07/27/gvl10727.htm).

Gottschalk, Marie. 2000. *The Shadow Welfare State: Labor, Business, and the Politics of Health Care in the United States*. Ithaca, NY: Cornell University Press.

Greenhouse, Steven. 2009. "Dennis Rivera Leads Labor Charge for Health Reform" *New York Times*, August 26. (http://www.nytimes.com/2009/08/27/business/27union.html).

Hacker, Jacob S. 2002. *The Divided Welfare State: The Battle over Public and Private Social Benefits in the United States*. New York: Cambridge University Press.

Hacker, Jacob S. 2008. "The New Push for American Health Security." In *Health at Risk: America's Ailing Health System—and How to Heal It*, ed. Jacob S. Hacker. New York: Columbia/SSRC, pp. 106–137.

Hacker, Jacob S., Suzanne Mettler, and Joe Soss. 2007. "The New Politics of Inequality: A Policy-Centered Perspective." In *Remaking America: Democracy and Public Policy in an Age of Inequality*. New York: Russell Sage Foundation, pp. 3–23.

Hamburger, Tom. 2009. "Obama Gives Powerful Drug Lobby a Seat at the Health Care Table." *Los Angeles Times*, August 4. (http://articles.latimes.com/2009/aug/04/nation/na-healthcare-pharma4).

Hall, Holly. 2009. "Charitable-Giving Plan Divides Nonprofit Groups and Worries Donors." *Chronicle of Philanthropy*, March 2. (http://philanthropy.com/article/Charitable-Giving-Plan-Divides/63030/), accessed January 29, 1010.

Hall, Richard L. and Frank W. Wayman. 1990. "Buying Time: Moneyed Interests and the Mobilization of Bias in Congressional Committees." *American Political Science Review* 84(3): 797–820.

Hoak, Amy. 2009. "This Week's Real Estate Stories." In *Marketwatch: Real Estate Weekly*, February 27. (http://www.marketwatch.com/story/plan-limit-mortgage-deduction-draws-realty).

Howard, Christopher. 1997. *The Hidden Welfare State: Tax Expenditures and Social Policy in the United States*. Princeton, NJ: Princeton University Press.

Howard, Ed. 2009. "Nelson Cited as Emblematic of Administration's Problems," Nebraska State Paper. April 1, 2009, (http://nebraska.statepaper.com/vnews/display.v/ART/2009/04/01/49d355604df9c), accessed October 30, 2011.

Interviews. 2010. Conducted by the author with congressional and agency staff, lobbyists, and representatives of organizations in Washington, D.C., April through June.

Kaiser Family Foundation. 2010. "Focus on Health Care: Side-by-Side Comparison of Major Health Care Reform Proposals." (http://www.kff.org/healthreform/sideby-side.cfm), accessed March 1, 2010.

Klein, Rick. 2009. "Labor on Line in Health Care Debate," ABC News, September 7. (http://abcnews.go.com/Politics/labor-line-health-care-debate/story?id=8492718).

Knight, Danielle. 2009. "Lobbying Showdown over the Future of Student Loans." Huffington Post Investigative Fund, July 29. (http://huffpostfund.org/stories/2009/07/lobbying-showdown-over-future-student-loans), accessed March 1, 2010.

Levy, Frank, and Peter Temlin. 2007. "Inequality and Institutions in 20th Century America." Industrial Performance Center, MIT, Working Paper Series. MIT-IPC-07-002.(http://web.mit.edu/ipc/publications/pdf/07-002.pdf).

Lewin, Tamar. 2009. "House Passes Bill to Expand College Aid." *New York Times*, Sept. 18.

Lichtblau, Eric. 2010. "Lobbying Imperils Overhaul of Student Loans." *New York Times*. February 5.

Luhby, Tami. 2010. "Mortgage Tax Break in the Cross-hairs." *CNNMoney.com*. December 2. (http://money.cnn.com/2010/12/02/news/economy/mortgage_interest_deduction/index.htm), accessed January 30, 2011.

MacGillis, Alec. 2008. "Obama Rallies Labor in Fight for Health-Care Reform," *Washington Post*, September 16.

McCarty, Nolan, Keith T. Poole, and Howard Rosenthal. 2006. *Polarized America: The Dance of Ideology and Unequal Riches*. Cambridge, MA: MIT Press.

McLean, Bethany. 2005. "Sallie Mae: A Hot Stock, A Tough Lender." *CNN Money*. December 14. (http://money.cnn.com/2005/12/14/news/fortune500/sallie_fortune_122605/index.htm).

McMillan, Charles. 2009. Letter to Honorable Barack Obama, from National Association of Realtors. February 26. (http://www.realtor.org/government_affairs/mortgage_interest_deduction/mid_obama_budget_proposal), accessed January 28, 2010.

Mettler, Suzanne. 2009a. "Promoting Inequality: The Politics of Higher Education Policy in and Era of Conservative Governance." In *The Unsustainable American State*, eds. Lawrence Jacobs and Desmond King. New York: Oxford University Press, pp. 197–222.

Mettler, Suzanne. 2009b. "Visible Lessons: How Experiences of Higher Education Policies Influence Participation in Politics." Unpublished paper. Available from author at sbm24@cornell.edu.

Mettler, Suzanne, and Matt Guardino. 2009. "Revealing the 'Hidden Welfare State': How Policy Information Influences Public Attitudes about Tax Expenditures." Unpublished, available upon request from sbm24@cornell.edu.

Mettler, Suzanne, and Deondra Rose. 2009. "Unsustainability of Equal Opportunity: The Development of the Higher Education Act, 1965–2008." Prepared for delivery at the Annual Meeting of the American Political Science Association. Toronto, Ontario, Canada. September 3–6.

Morgan, Kimberley J., and Andrea Louise Campbell. 2009. "Exploring the Rube Goldberg State." Paper prepared for delivery at the Annual Meeting of the American Political Science Association, Toronto, Ontario, Canada. September 3–6.

Mortgage Bankers Association. 2009. Press Release, "MBA Raises Concern over Limit on Mortgage Interest Deduction in Federal Budget," February 27. (http://www.mbaa.org/NewsandMedia/PressCenter/67934.htm), accessed January 28, 2010.

National Association of Realtors. 2009a. "In This Issue: March 2009 Update." *In Eye on the Hill*. (http://www.realtor.org/fedistrk.nsf/4fca10aeb5e60f4f86257414007015d5/582f268be308a76285257570063330e?OpenDocument), accessed January 28, 2010.

National Association of Realtors. 2009b. "In This Issue: 2009 NAR Public Policy Accomplishments." *In Eye on the Hill*. http://www.realtor.org/fedistrk.nsf/4fca10aeb5e60f4f86257414007015d5/5ac57ca353ec4a3885257685007b4540?OpenDocument. Accessed January 28, 2010.

National Center for Public Policy and Higher Education. 2002. *Losing Ground: A National Status Report on the Affordability of American Higher Education*. San Jose, CA: National Center for Public Policy and Higher Education.

Nelson, Libby. 2009. "Sallie Mae Fights for Student-Loan Role in a Campaign that's All About Jobs," November 22. *Chronicle of Higher Education*. (http://chronicle.com/article/Sallie-Mae-Fights-for-Stude/49224/), accessed March 1, 2010.

Obama, Barack. 2007a. "Announcement for President." February 10. (http://www.barackobama.com/2007/02/10/remarks_of_senator_barack_obam_11.php), accessed March 1, 2010.

Obama, Barack. 2008a. "Remarks of Senator Barack Obama: Super Tuesday." February 5, 2008. (http://www.barackobama.com/2008/02/05/remarks_of_senator_barack_obam_46.php).

Obama, Barack. 2009a. "Transcript: President Obama's News Conference." *New York Times*, March 23. (http://www.nytimes.com/2009/03/24/us/politics/24text-obama.html?pagewanted=all), accessed January 29, 2010.

Obama, Barack. 2009b. "Remarks by the President on Higher Education," April 24, 2009. (http://www.whitehouse.gov/the_press_office/Remarks-by-the-President-on-Higher-Education), accessed February 26, 2010.

Obama, Barack. 2009c. "Remarks by the President in Town Hall on Health Care," August 14, 2009. (http://www.whitehouse.gov/the_press_office/Remarks-by-the-President-in-town-hall-on-health-care-Belgrade-Montana), accessed February 26, 2010.

Obama, Barack. 2009d. "Remarks by the President in an Online Town Hall on Health Care," July 1, 2009. (http://www.whitehouse.gov/the_press_office/Remarks-of-the-President-in-an-Online-Town-Hall-on-Health-Care-Reform), accessed February 26, 2010.

OECD. 2007. "Education at a Glance: OECD Briefing Note for the United States." (www.oecd.org/edu/eag2007).

OpenSecrets.org. 2010a "Finance, Insurance, & Real Estate, Sector Profile 2008" (http://www.opensecrets.org/lobby/indus.php?id=F&year=2008) accessed January 28, 2010.

OpenSecrets.org. 2010b. "Lobbying: National Association of Realtors, Client Profile, Summary 2009." Center for Responsive Politics web site. (http://www.opensecrets.org/lobby/clientsum.php?lname=National+Assn+of+Realtors&year=2009), accessed January 28, 2010.

OpenSecrets.org. 2010c. "Real Estate: Long-term Contribution Trends." Center for Responsive Politics. (http://www.opensecrets.org/industries/indus.php?ind=F10), accessed January 28, 2010.

OpenSecrets.org. 2010d. "Non-profits, Foundations, and Philanthropists." Center for Responsive Politics. (http://www.opensecrets.org/industries/indus.php?ind=W02), accessed January 29, 2010.

OpenSecrets.org. 2010e. "Finance/Credit Companies." Center for Responsive Politics. (http://www.opensecrets.org/pacs/industry.php?txt=F06&cycle=2008), accessed January 29, 2010.

OpenSecrets.org. 2010f. "Ranked Sectors." (http://www.opensecrets.org/lobby/top. php?indexType=c), accessed January 29, 2010.

OpenSecrets.org. 2010g, "Top Spenders, 2009." (http://www.opensecrets.org/lobby/ top.php?showYear=2009&indexType=s), accessed January 29, 2010.

Page, Benjamin I., and Lawrence R. Jacobs. 2009. "No Class War: Economic Inequality and the American Public." In *The Unsustainable American State*, eds. Lawrence Jacobs and Desmond King. New York: Oxford University Press, pp. 135–166.

Pear, Robert. 2009. "In Divide over Health Care Overhaul, 2 Major Unions Withdraw from a Coalition." *New York Times*, March 6. (http://www.nytimes.com/2009/03/07/ us/politics/07health.html).

Perry, Suzanne. 2009. "Meaning of Senate Language on Charitable Deductions in Eye of Beholder." *Chronicle of Philanthropy*. April 3. (http://philanthropy.com/blog-Post/Meaning-of-Senate-Language-on/10961/), accessed January 29, 2010.

Quadagno, Jill, and J. Brandon McKelvey. 2008. "The Transformation of American Health Insurance." In *Health at Risk: America's Ailing Health System—and How to Heal It*, ed. Jacob S. Hacker. New York: Columbia/SSRC, pp. 10–31.

Rasmussen Reports. 2010. "61% Favor Repeal of Health Care Law." September 20, 2010. (http://www.rasmussenreports.com/public_content/politics/current_events/health-care/september_2010/61_favor_repeal_of_health_care_law), accessed December 2, 2010.

Recovery.gov web site. 2010. "Track the Money." (http://www.recovery.gov/Pages/ home.aspx), accessed January 23, 2010.

Robert Wood Johnson Foundation. 2009. "Talking about Quality, Party I: Health Care Today." (http://www.rwjf.org/pr/product.jsp?id=45110), accessed March 1, 2010.

Rohack, J. James. 2009. "AMA Reaction to President Obama's Address on Health System Reform," September 9. (http://www.ama-assn.org/ama/pub/health-system-reform/news/september-2009/obama-health-reform-address.shtml).

Rucker, Philip. 2009. "Obama Defends Push to Cut Tax Deductions for Charitable Gifts." *Washington Post*, March 26, p. A02.

Runningen, Roger, and Ryan J. Donmoyer. 2009. "Obama Asks Volcker to Lead Panel on Tax-Code Overhaul." Bloomberg.com. (http://www.bloomberg.com/apps/ news?sid=a8yCQsJfpb24&pid=20601087), accessed January 26, 2010.

SEIU. 2009. Press release. "SEIU Tells Lincoln, Nelson, Landrieu and Lieberman: We're Adopting Your States," November 17. (http://www.seiu.org/2009/11/seiu-tells-lincoln-nelson-landrieu-and-lieberman-were-adopting-your-states.php).

Schatz, Joseph J. 2009. "Obama's Budget Proposal Alters the Typical Tax and Spend Equation." *CQ Weekly*, March 2, pp. 480–481.

Sinclair, Barbara. 2006. *Party Wars: Polarization and the Politics of National Policy Making*. Norman: University of Oklahoma Press.

Skocpol, Theda. 1997. *Boomerang: Health Care Reform and the Turn Against Government*. New York: W.W. Norton.

Skocpol, Theda. 2003. *Diminished Democracy: From Membership to Management in American Civic Life.* Norman: University of Oklahoma Press.

Skowronek, Stephen. 1982. *Building a New American State: The Expansion of National Administrative Capacities, 1877–1920.* New York: Cambridge University Press.

Social and Government Issues and Participation Study. 2008. Survey conducted by Survey Research Institute, Cornell University. Principal Investigator, Suzanne Mettler. Contact sbm24@cornell.edu for more information.

Starr, Paul, and Gosta Esping-Andersen. 1979. "Passive Intervention." *Working Papers for a New Society,* July/August. (http://www.princeton.edu/~starr/articles/articles68–79/Starr_Esping-Andersen_Passive_Intervention.pdf), accessed March 1, 2010.

Stone, Peter H. 2010. "Health Insurers Funded Chamber Attack Ads." *National Journal,* January 12. (http://undertheinfluence.nationaljournal.com/2010/01/health-insurers-funded-chamber.php).

Strom, Stephanie. 2009. "Limiting Deductions on Charity Draws Ire." *New York Times,* February 27. (http://www.nytimes.com/2009/02/27/us/27charity.html), accessed January 29, 2010.

Swartz, Katherine. 2008. "Uninsured in America: New Realities, New Risks." In *Health at Risk: America's Ailing Health System—and How to Heal It,* ed. Jacob S. Hacker. New York: Columbia/SSRC, pp. 32–65.

Thaler, Richard H., and Cass Sunstein. 2008. *Nudge: Improving Decisions about Health, Wealth, and Happiness.* New Haven, CT: Yale University Press.

Tumulty, Karen, and Michael Scherer. 2009. "How Drug-Industry Lobbyists Won on Health Care," *Time,* October 22. (http://www.time.com/time/politics/article/0,8599,1931595,00.html).

Urban-Brookings Tax Policy Center. 2009a. "Tax Stimulus Report Card, Conference Bill, as of February 13, 2009." (http://www.urban.org/publications/411839.html), accessed January 26, 2010.

Urban-Brookings Tax Policy Center. 2009b. "Tax Proposals in the 2010 Budget." (http://www.taxpolicycenter.org/taxtopics/2010_budget.cfm), accessed January 26, 2010.

U.S. Congress. 2009b. House of Representatives. Clerk. "Final Vote Results for Roll Call 719." (http://clerk.house.gov/evs/2009/roll719.xml), accessed September 21, 2009.

U.S. Congress. Joint Committee on Taxation. 2006. "Estimates of Federal Tax Expenditures for Fiscal Years 2006–2010." (http://www.jct.gov/s-2-06.pdf), accessed March 1, 2010.

U.S. Department of Education, Office of Inspector General. 2006. "Review of Financial Partners' Monitoring and Oversight of Guaranty Agencies, Lenders, and Servicers." Final Audit Report. September. (http://www2.ed.gov/about/offices/list/oig/auditreports/a04e0009.pdf).

U.S. Senate Finance Committee. 2009. "Description of Policy Options: Financing Comprehensive Health Care Reform: Proposed Health System Savings and

Revenue Options," May 20. (http://finance.senate.gov/newsroom/chairman/download/?id=8a3deecc-59d2-4530-ba0e-8862a05ed714), accessed March 1, 2010.

U.S. Senate Finance and House Ways and Means Committee. 2009. "The American Recovery and Reinvestment Act of 2009—February 12, 2009. Full Summary of Provisions." (http://finance.senate.gov/press/Bpress/2009press/prb021209.pdf), accessed January 23, 2010.

Voteview web site. 2010. "Party Polarization: 1879–2009. Updated January 4, 2010." (http://www.voteview.com/).

Wall Street Journal. 2009. "Senate Finance Bill: Drug Industry Likes It, Unions Don't." Health Blog, October 14, 2009. (http://blogs.wsj.com/health/2009/10/14/senate-finance-bill-drug-industry-likes-it-unions-dont/tab/article/).

Washington Post. 2006. "Top 100 Executives by Total Compensation." (http://projects.washingtonpost.com/post200/2006/executives-by-compensation/).

Young, Jeffrey. 2009a. "AMA Endorses Senate Healthcare Reform Bill." *The Hill*, December 21. (http://thehill.com/homenews/senate/73249-ama-endorses-senate-health-bill).

Young, Jeffrey. 2009b. "AARP Endorses House Healthcare Reform Bill." *The Hill*, November 5. (http://thehill.com/homenews/house/66533-aarp-endorses-house-healthcare-bill).

Young, Jeffrey. 2009c. "Reid Vows Help For Medicare Drug Costs." *The Hill's Blog Briefing Room*, December 14. (http://thehill.com/blogs/blog-briefing-room/news/72221-reid-vows-help-for-medicare-drug-costs).

Zeleny, Jeff. 2010. "Blogging the Massachusetts Senate Race." *New York Times*, January 19, 2010. (http://thecaucus.blogs.nytimes.com/2010/01/19/blogging-the-mass-senate-race/?hp).

PART III

Structural Crossroads: Political Economy and Racial Orders

4

Situating Obama's Response to the Crisis

FINANCE, REGULATION, AND THE AMERICAN STATE

Leo Panitch[1]

> ... Don't hamper us from getting the banking system back on track.
> —PRESIDENT BARACK OBAMA, *March 23, 2009 (cited in Ward 2009)*

AS RALPH MILIBAND put it in *The State in Capitalist Society* (1969), "[R]eform always and necessarily falls short of the promise it was proclaimed to hold: the crusades which were to reach 'new frontiers,' to create 'the great society,' to eliminate poverty, to assure justice for all" (Miliband 2009, 198). Miliband pointed out that, although governments promising such reforms are usually elected at moments of "adverse conditions" economically, the actual reforms they introduce usually fall short of the promise because they aggravate a crisis of capital accumulation. Although he wrote this 40 years ago, it almost seems as if he were speaking directly to those who were initially enthusiastic about Obama and now lament his lack of ambition and commitment to principle. Miliband counsels that elected leaders who take office under adverse conditions should "treat these conditions as a challenge to greater boldness, as an opportunity to greater radicalism, and as a means, rather than an obstacle, to swift and decisive measures of reform. There is, after all, much that a genuinely radical government, firm in purpose and enjoying a substantial measure of popular support, may hope to do on the morrow of its electoral legitimation, not despite crisis conditions but because of them" (Miliband 2009, 73).

This chapter argues that Obama's response to the crisis that he inherited had less to do with his reluctance to alienate the coalition of corporate and financial elites that helped finance his election campaign, and certainly much less to do with any sudden embrace of neoliberal ideas, than with the systemic structural linkages between capital and the state. What determined Obama's actions was the assumption of responsibility for sustaining capital accumulation and managing capitalism's contradictions that comes with occupying the highest offices in the American state.

"They say they won't intervene. But they will." With these words, Robert Rubin, Bill Clinton's Treasury Secretary, responded to Paul O'Neill, who when he became the first Treasury Secretary under George W. Bush, had openly criticized his predecessor's interventions in the face of what Rubin called "the messy reality of global financial crises" (Rubin and Weisberg 2003, 297, emphasis added). The dramatic combination of financial crisis and state intervention since the summer of 2007 proved Rubin more correct than he could have imagined. The Obama presidency continued and expanded the most wide-ranging state interventions in the economy since the New Deal—from the financial rescue that Bush initiated to the finance reform legislation of 2010 and very extensive administrative actions by the Treasury and Federal Reserve.

Whatever the scale of the intervention, however, it does not really constitute a break with state practices over the past three decades, as has been mistakenly assumed by those—whether from the Right or the Left—who have understood the era of neoliberalism in terms of an ideological determination to free markets from states. Indeed, rather than trying to understand the relationship between states and markets in the neoliberal era in the context of financial deregulation, it may be more useful to see it in terms of financialization, developing through the agency of both old and new regulatory bodies.

To be sure, this is not meant to deny that changes in the mode of regulation played an important role in producing the financial developments that led to the crisis. Instead, it is to propose that we situate such measures within a wider context of financialized relations of class power. What has been called deregulation was less determined by an ideological commitment to neoliberalism than by a series of pragmatic decisions, usually driven by the exigencies of the moment, to remove barriers to financial dynamics that had already gathered decisive momentum within the old form of regulation. Indeed, oftentimes such restrictions were removed only after they had ceased to have any practical effect, as was largely the case with the repeal of the Glass-Steagall Act at the end of the 1990s. Moreover, even with the removal of some restrictions, Donald Mackenzie was certainly still correct to write in 2005 that "to conceive of the changes in the global financial markets since the early 1970s as 'deregulation,' the withdrawal of the state cannot survive serious study of the regulation of financial markets. The modern American financial markets are almost certainly the most highly regulated markets in history, if regulation is measured by volume (number of pages) of rules, probably also if measured by extent of surveillance, and possibly even by vigour of enforcement" (Mackenzie 2005, 569).

Yet the era of neoliberalism has at the same time been one long history of financial volatility—with the American state leading the world's states in intervening in a series of financial crises. Almost as soon as he was appointed as head of the Federal Reserve, Alan Greenspan immediately dropped buckets of liquidity on Wall Street in response to the 1987 stock market crash. In the wake of the Savings and Loan crisis, the public Resolution Trust Corporation was established in 1989 to buy up bad real estate debt. In Clinton's first term, Wall Street was saved from the consequences of bond defaults during the 1995 Mexican financial crisis by Rubin's use of the Stabilization Exchange Fund. (This Treasury kitty, established during the 1930s, has once again been called into service in the recent crisis.) During the Asian crisis two years later, Rubin and his undersecretary Larry Summers dictated the terms of the IMF loan to the South Korean government. And in 1998 (not long after the Japanese government nationalized one of the world's biggest banks), the head of the New York Federal Reserve summoned the CEOs of Wall Street's leading financial firms and told them that they would not be allowed to leave the room until they agreed to take over the insolvent hedge fund, Long-Term Capital Management (LTCM). These quick interventions by the Fed and Treasury, most of them without waiting upon congressional pressures or approval, showed that they were aware of the disastrous consequences that the failure to act quickly to contain each crisis could have on both the domestic and global financial system.

The financial crisis that began in 2007 was met with a continuation of this practice. What stood out is the depth and breadth of the interventions by the U.S. Treasury and Federal Reserve after 2007 as the scale and scope of the crisis became increasingly clear. Finally, amidst a dramatic series of bankruptcies and takeovers during the course of a week in September 2008, the U.S. government undertook to buy virtually all the illiquid assets on the balance sheets of financial institutions in the US, including those of foreign-owned firms. The Fed and Treasury needed to act not only as lender of last resort, but also, by taking responsibility for buying and trying to sell all those securities that couldn't find a value or market in the current crisis, as *market maker of last resort* (Buiter 2008). We now know that Federal Reserve Chairman Ben Bernanke had warned Treasury Secretary Hank Paulson the year before that this might be necessary, and Paulson had agreed. "I knew he was right theoretically," he said. "But I also had, and we both did, some hope that, with all the liquidity out there from investors, that after a certain decline that we would reach a bottom" (New York Times 2008). Yet the private market has no secure bottom without the use of state power.

The fundamental relationship between capitalist states and financial markets cannot be understood in terms of how much or little regulation is promulgated. It needs to be understood in terms of the guarantees that the state provides to property, as measured above all in the promise not to default on its bonds—which are themselves the foundation of financial markets' role in capital accumulation. But not all states are equally able, or trusted as willing, to honor these guarantees. The American state came to act in the second half of the twentieth century as an entirely new kind of imperial state precisely because it took utmost responsibility for honoring these guarantees itself— while promoting a world order of independent nation-states which the new empire would expect to behave as capitalist states, and would discipline accordingly (Panitch and Gindin 2003).

Only at a purely *ideological* level was neoliberalism about the retreat of public institutions from social and economic life or a return to a pre-Keynesian era of non-intervention. Neoliberal *practices* have not entailed institutional retreat from finance; just the opposite—they have involved the expansion and consolidation of the networks of institutional linkages that sustain the imperial power of American finance. Of course it is by now commonplace to assert that states and markets should not be seen as really opposed to one another. But such claims have tended to remain rather perfunctory, and most research has remained guided by the mistaken notion that financial expansion has been accompanied by the attenuation of the state. The practical effects of neoliberal ideologies are not well represented in those discourses themselves. To assume that neoliberalism reshaped the world in the image of its own discourse—that is, that it replaced political relations with economic logics and public decision making with market rationalities— is to attribute too much positive force and coherence to neoliberal ideas. It was only on the most stylized and superficial reading of the neoliberal era that the state could be seen to have withdrawn in the first place.

It might be thought that the exposure of the state's role in the recent financial crisis would once and for all rid people of the illusion that capitalists don't want their states involved in their markets, or that capitalist states could ever be neutral and benign regulators in the public interest of markets. Unfortunately, the widespread call today for the American state to "go back" to playing the role of such a regulator reveals that this illusion remains deeply engrained. One of the ironies of neoliberalism is that its ideology of pulling back the state actually coincided with an era in which the state's linkages to finance became ever more blatant. Understanding the relationship between the state and finance in the United States requires an appreciation of its roots, a history that is much older and goes much deeper than neoliberalism.

I. The State and Finance Before World War II

In October 1907, near the beginning of the "American century," and exactly a hundred years before the onset of the recent financial crisis, the United States experienced a financial crisis that, for anyone living through it, would have seemed as great. Indeed, there were far more suicides in that crisis, as "Wall Street spent a cliff-hanging year" that spanned a stock market crash, an 11 percent decline in GDP, and accelerating runs on the banks (Chernow 1990, 121). At the core of the crisis was the practice of trust companies drawing money from banks at exorbitant interest rates and, without the protection of sufficient cash reserves, lending out so much of it against stock and bond speculation. The result was that almost half of the bank loans in New York had questionable securities as collateral. When the trust companies were forced to call in some of their loans to stock market speculators, interest rates zoomed to well over 100 percent on margin loans and still could not attract funds. The U.S. financial crisis spread across the Atlantic, as European investors started withdrawing funds from the United States.

Whereas European central banking had its roots in "haute finance" far removed from the popular classes, U.S. finance was enmeshed in the lives of many Americans. The dependence of small farmers on credit had made them hostile to a central bank that they recognized would serve bankers' interests. In the absence of a central bank, both the U.S. Treasury and Wall Street relied on J. P. Morgan to organize the bailout of 1907. As Henry Paulson did with Lehman's a century later, Morgan let the giant Knickerbocker Trust go under in spite of its holding $50 million of deposits for 17,000 depositors ("I've got to stop somewhere," Morgan said). This only fueled the panic and triggered runs on other financial firms including the Trust Company of America (leading Morgan to pronounce that "this is the place to stop the trouble"). Using $25 million put at his disposal by the Treasury, and calling together Wall Street's bank presidents to demand that they put up another $25 million "within ten or twelve minutes" (which they did), Morgan dispensed the liquidity that began to calm the markets (Chernow 1990, 123–125).

When the Federal Reserve was finally established in 1913, this was seen as Woodrow Wilson's great victory over the unaccountable big financiers. As Ron Chernow's monumental biography of Morgan put it, "From the ashes of 1907 arose the Federal Reserve System: everyone saw that thrilling rescues by corpulent old tycoons were a tenuous prop for the banking system" (Chernow 1990, 128). Yet the main elements of the Federal Reserve Bill had already been drafted by the Morgan and Rockefeller interests during the previous Taft administration; and although the Fed's corporatist and decentralized structure of regional federal reserve boards reflected the compromise that the final Act made with populist pressures, its immediate effect was actually to cement the "fusion of financial and government power" (Rothbard 1999; Livingston 1986). The state assumed responsibility for capital both by establishing the Fed as the "banker's bank"—that is, a largely passive regulator of bank credit and a lender of last resort—and by cementing the close ties between the Federal Reserve Bank of New York and the House of Morgan. William McAdoo, Wilson's Treasury Secretary, described the advantages of the Federal Reserve Act's provisions that allowed U.S. banks to establish foreign branches as helping to lay the basis for the United States "to become the dominant financial power of the world and to extend our trade to every part of the world" (cited in Broesamle 1973, 129).

In its early decades, the Fed began as "a loose and inexperienced body with minimal effectiveness even in its domestic functions" (Arrighi 1994, 272). This was an important factor in the crash of 1929 and in the Fed's perverse role in contributing to the Great Depression. Class pressures from below produced FDR's union and welfare reforms, but the New Deal is misunderstood if it is simply seen in terms of a dichotomy of purpose and function between state and capitalist actors. While the Morgan empire was brought low by an alliance of new financial competitors and the state, the New Deal's financial reforms, which were introduced before the union and welfare legislation, protected the banks as a whole from hostile popular sentiments. The New Deal regulatory structure restrained competition and excesses of speculation, not so much by curbing the power of finance, but rather through the fortification of key financial institutions via a corporatist "network of public and semi-public bodies, individual firms and professional groups" that existed in a symbiotic relationship with one another, distanced from democratic pressures (Moran 1991, 29). The Fed stepped in to oversee fixed interest rate ceilings and brokerage fees and the new boundaries established between commercial and investment banks, on which basis the New York investment banks were to grow ever more powerful. Despite the hostility of capitalists to FDR's union and welfare reforms, the New Dealers struck what they themselves called their "grand truce" with business by the time World War II began (Brinkley 1995, 89-90). Even though the Treasury's Keynesian economists (who took the lead in rewriting the rules of international finance during World War II) were regarded suspiciously by New York bankers, Wall Street helped constitute the new international regulatory order established at the conference in Bretton Woods, New Hampshire, in 1944.

Since World War II, the American state has been not just the dominant state in the capitalist world, but the state responsible for overseeing the expansion of capitalism to its current global dimensions and for organizing the management of its economic contradictions. The American state has done this not by displacing other states, but rather by penetrating and integrating them into its orbit. This included the internationalization of these states in the sense of their taking responsibility for global accumulation within their borders and cooperating in setting the international rules for trade and investment. As New York became the world's financial centre and the American state the world's creditor, it also moved to become the guarantor of capitalist banking as well. This helps explain why the American state took responsibility for making international capitalism viable again after 1945. With the fixed exchange rate of the dollar to gold established at Bretton Woods, the US currency effectively became the global currency, and fundamental store and measure of value in the international arena. When it proved by the 1960s that those who held US dollars would have to suffer a devaluation of their funds through inflation, the fiction of a continuing gold standard was abandoned. The world's financial system was now explicitly based on the dollar as American-made "fiat money," backed by an iron clad guarantee against default of US Treasury bonds, which were now treated as "good as gold" (Panitch and Gindin 2004).

II. The State and Finance in the Postwar Era

In the postwar period, the New Deal regulatory structure acted as an incubator for financial capital's growth and development. The strong position of Wall Street was institutionally crystallized via the 1951 Accord reached between the Federal Reserve and the Treasury, which was designed to ensure that "forces seen as more radical" within any administration would find it difficult, at least without creating a crisis, to implement inflationary monetary policies (Epstein and Shor 1995, 27; Dickens 1995, 1998). The Fed now stopped making Treasury bonds available only at a fixed price but joined with investment banks in creating a market in these bonds whereby dealers could take speculative positions and thus allow "market forces" to determine Treasury bond prices (Herzel and Leach 2001, 57-63). Bond traders could thus increase the cost of running government deficits, and this allayed Wall Street's lingering concerns that Keynesian commitments to the priority of full employment and fiscal deficits might prevail in the Treasury. In the 1950s, profits in the financial sector were already growing faster than in industry. By the early 1960s, the securitization of commercial banking (selling savings certificates rather than relying on deposits) and the enormous expansion of investment banking (including Morgan Stanley's creation of the first viable computer model for analyzing financial risk) were already in train. With the development of the unregulated Euromarket in dollars and the international expansion of U.S. multinational corporations, the playing field for American finance was far larger than New Deal regulations could contain.

Both domestically and internationally, the baby had outgrown the incubator, which was in any case being buffeted by inflationary pressures stemming from union militancy and public expenditures on the Great Society programs and the Vietnam War. The bank crisis of 1966, the rise of pension funds that complained about non-competitive brokerage fees protected by New Deal regulations, the series of scandals that beset Wall Street by the end of the decade—all this foretold the end of the corporatist structure of brokers, investment banks, and corporate managers that had dominated domestic capital markets since the New Deal, culminating in Wall Street's "Big Bang" of 1975. Meanwhile, once the Bretton Woods fixed exchange rate system collapsed by the early 1970s, due to inflationary pressures on the dollar as well as the massive growth in international trade and investment, all those who held U.S. assets had to live with the fluctuating value of the U.S. dollar. This laid the foundation for the derivatives revolution by leading to a massive demand for hedging risk to offset the dollar's oscillations by trading futures and options in exchange and interest rates. The Commodity Futures Trading Commission (CFTC) was created in 1974, less to regulate this new market than to facilitate its development (Melamed 1992, 43, 77-78; Bryan and Rafferty 2006).

It was not so much neoliberal ideology that broke the New Deal system of financial regulations as it was the contradictions that had emerged within that system. If there was going to be any serious alternative by the 1970s, this would have required going well beyond the old regulations and capital controls, and introducing qualitatively new policies to undermine rather than protect the social power of finance. Ironically, one of the origins of the new financial system was the 1977 Community Reinvestment Act (CRA), which was promoted by the left wing of the Democratic Party during the Carter administration. CRA required commercial banks to allocate 5 percent of their working capital for home and small business loans in poor communities, against fierce opposition from the banks. Yet, in fact, it did little for local economic development and ultimately contributed to the great housing collapse and financial breakdown of 2007. CRA's concessions to the banks from the government-sponsored mortgage companies, Freddie Mac and Fannie Mae, would encourage the secondary mortgage securities market to relieve the burden of banks being required to make loans to poor people.

In countries where socialist politics were stronger, the nationalization of the financial system was forcefully advanced by the mid-1970s. The Left in the British Labour Party was able to secure the passage of a conference resolution to nationalize the big banks and insurance companies in the City of London, albeit with no effect on a Labour Government that embraced one of the IMF's first structural adjustment programs. In France, the *Programme Commun* of the 1970s led to the Mitterand government's bank nationalizations at the beginning of the 1980s, but this was carried through in a way that ensured that the structure and function of the banks were not changed in the process. In Canada, directly elected local planning boards, which would draw on the surplus from a nationalized financial system to create jobs, were proposed by the Left as the first step in a new strategy to get labor movements to think in ways that were not so cramped and defensive (e.g. Panitch 1986). Such alternatives—strongly opposed even by social democratic politicians, who soon accommodated themselves to the dynamics of finance-led neoliberalism and the ideology of efficient free markets—were soon forgotten amidst the general defeat of labor movements and socialist politics that had dawned by the end of the 1970s and the onset of the Thatcher and Reagan era. Financial capitalists took the lead in demanding the defeat of those domestic social forces they blamed for creating the inflationary pressures that undermined the value of their assets. The further growth of financial markets, increasingly characterized by competition, innovation, and flexibility, was central to the resolution of the crisis of the 1970s.

III. The State and Finance in the Neoliberal Era

Perhaps the most important economic aspect of the neoliberal era was the central role that the state played in disciplining and integrating labor into new capitalist markets as workers, consumers, savers and home owners. The industrial and political pressures from below that characterized the crisis of the 1970s could not have been countered and defeated without the discipline that the new financial order of mobile capital placed upon unions and the workers they represented. Shareholder value was in many respects a euphemism for how the discipline imposed by the competition for global investment funds was transferred to the high-wage proletariat of the advanced capitalist countries. New York's and London's access to global savings simultaneously came to depend on the surplus extracted through the high rates of exploitation of the new working classes in "emerging markets." At the same time, the very constraints that the mobility of capital had on working-class incomes in the rich countries had the effect of further integrating these workers into the realm of finance. This was most obvious in terms of their increasing debt loads amidst the universalization of the credit card. But it also pertained to how workers grew more attuned to financial markets, as they followed the stock exchanges and mutual funds in which their pension funds were invested, often cheered by rising stocks as firms were restructured without much thought to the layoffs involved.

Both the explosion of finance and the disciplining of labor were a necessary condition for the dramatic productive transformations in this era. The leading role that finance came to play over the past three decades, including the financialization of industrial corporations and the financial sector's distinction for taking the largest share of profits, has often been viewed as undermining production and representing little else than speculation and a source of unsustainable bubbles. But this fails to account for why this era—a period that was longer in duration than the "golden age"—lasted so long. In fact, the era between the crisis of the 1970s and the outbreak of the current crisis has been one of capitalist dynamism, including significant technological revolutions, involving not just the deepening and expansion of capital, but also the radical restructuring of corporations and firms and indeed of capitalist social relations and culture in general. This was especially the case for the United States itself, where financial competition, innovation, flexibility, *and* volatility accompanied the reconstitution of the American material base at home and its expansion abroad. Overall, the era of finance-led neoliberalism experienced a rate of growth of global GDP that compares favorably with earlier periods of capitalist development over the last two centuries (Maddison 2001, 265).

It is, in any case, impossible to imagine the globalization of capitalist production without the type of financial intermediation in the circuits of capital imparted by derivatives and other financial instruments that help offset the risks associated with flexible exchange rates, interest rate variations across national borders, uncertain transportation and commodity costs, and so on.

Moreover, as competition to access more mobile finance intensified, this imposed discipline on firms (and states) that forced restructuring within firms and reallocated capital across sectors. Operating by the rules of new finance, venture capital flowed to the new information and bio-medical sectors, which have become leading arenas of accumulation. At the same time, the U.S. investment banks spread their tentacles abroad for three decades through their global role in corporate mergers and acquisitions and initial public offerings of corporate stock. Relationships between finance and production, including their legal and accounting frameworks, were radically changed around the world in ways that increasingly resembled American patterns. This was reinforced by the bilateral and multilateral international trade and investment treaties (pioneered by the Canada-US Free Trade Agreement and its successor, NAFTA), which were increasingly concerned with opening up other economies to New York's and London's financial, legal, and accounting services.

The commitment by the Federal Reserve—via the high interest rates of the "Volcker shock" of 1979 to 1982—to anti-inflation policies at the expense of stable employment was designed to guarantee the value of Treasury bills as the global store of value. This was a defining moment of U.S. state intervention precisely because of its implications in terms of the class and power relations that have characterized the neoliberal era. Like the current moment, it started in the run-up to a presidential election—that is, *before* Reagan's election—with bipartisan congressional support and industrial capital backing the new leading role this marked for financial capital in the United States and abroad. As the American state took the initiative, by its example and its pressure on other states around the world, to give priority to low inflation as a much stronger and ongoing commitment than before, this bolstered finance capital's confidence in the substantive value of lending; and after the initial astronomical interest rates produced by the Volcker shock, this soon made an era of low interest rates possible.

Throughout the neoliberal era, the enormous demand for U.S. bonds and the low interest paid on them has rested on the confidence the Volcker shock gave to financial markets everywhere that the Fed and Treasury were committed above all to an anti-inflation policy priority as part and parcel of guaranteeing the value of U.S. bonds. This was reinforced by the defeat of American trade unionism in the late 1970s and early 1980s, highlighted first by the concessions forced on the UAW as part of the conditions the Carter administration imposed on Chrysler in saving it from bankruptcy, and then by Reagan's deliberate breaking of the Air Traffic Controllers' union. But this defeat was itself related to the earlier defeat labor suffered with the passage of the Airline Deregulation Act in October 1978, which it correctly foresaw as having the effect of driving down wages and benefits via the removal of price controls as well as leading to the concentration of industry once price competition drove out small carriers. The fact that its leading sponsor in the Senate was Edward Kennedy, and that President Carter himself had put deregulation of the transportation industries near the top of his legislative agenda, was a key indicator of the "convergence of attitudes between the liberal left and the conservative right" that Allan Greenspan had already noted by the mid-1970s (Greenspan 2007, 72).

Coming in advance of the anti-statist rhetoric represented politically by Reaganism and Thatcherism, this harbinger of changing state-market relations did not foretell the end of regulation, of course—any more than Keynesianism had, conversely, meant the suppression of markets. Insofar as the state's restructuring of its regulatory rules to facilitate competition over prices was about the creation of "freer markets," this involved "the reformulation of old rules and the creation of new ones"—and this would indeed soon prove even more the case in finance and telecommunications than it did in transportation (Vogel 1996, 3). The defeat of American trade unionism was especially related to the intense competition in financial markets domestically and internationally. This played itself out in terms of financial capital putting pressure on firms to lower costs through restructuring in order to access financial markets, as well as reallocating capital across sectors, especially through venture funds to support new technologies.

Of course, deregulation was as much a consequence as the cause of the intense competition in financial markets and its attendant effects. The "Americanization of finance" in other states, involving U.S. banks increasingly operating directly abroad and domestic banks competing with them by emulating their practices, also played an important corollary role in both spreading deregulation *and* bringing it back home—along with the flow of global savings from abroad to the U.S. economy. By 1990, this competition had already led to banks scheming to escape the reserve requirements of the Basel bank regulations by creating "structured investment vehicles" to hold these and other risky derivative assets. It also led to the increased blurring of the lines between commercial and investment banking, insurance, and the real estate sector of the U.S. economy. Competition in the financial sector fostered all kinds of new instruments that allowed for high "leveraging" (i.e., increasing the ratio of loans to bank reserves) of the funds that could be accessed via low interest rates. This meant that there was an explosion in credit and the effective money supply, and this lay behind the asset inflation that characterized the whole era. (This was highly ironic: the talisman of monetarist theories, which are usually thought to have founded neoliberalism, was limiting—not expanding—the growth in money supply as the foundation for economic stability.).

The world beat a path to US financial markets not only because of the demand for Treasury bills, and not only because of Wall Street's linkages to US capital more generally, but also because of the depth and breadth of those financial markets. All this was reinforced by the American state's readiness to throw further liquidity into the financial system whenever a specific asset bubble burst—while imposing austerity on economies in the Global South as the condition for the liquidity that the IMF and World Bank provided to their financial markets at moments of crisis. This was a central component of the uneven and often chaotic making of global capitalism over the past quarter century.

Financing the American Dream

What has been called the "American dream" has always materially entailed promoting the integration of the popular classes into the circuits of financial capital, whether as independent commodity farmers, as workers whose paychecks were deposited with banks and whose pension savings were invested in the stock market, as consumers reliant on credit, and not least as heavily mortgaged home owners. This incorporation of the mass of the American population was as or more important to the dynamism and longevity of the finance-led neoliberal era than the degree of supposed "deregulation" of financial markets. But it also helped to trigger the current crisis—and the massive state intervention in response to it.

The scale of the current crisis, which significantly has its roots in housing finance, cannot be understood apart from the defeat of American trade unionism since the early 1980s and how this played out in the first years of the twenty-first century. In spite of stagnating wages and growing class inequality, this defeat did not bring about an absolute deterioration of living standards for most American working families. This is because high levels of consumption, including increasingly expensive health care, were sustained by the lower prices of consumer goods produced by cheap labor abroad, by the accumulation of household debt rather than saving, and by the intensification of family labor—more family members working longer hours under more severe working conditions. Constrained in what they could get from their labor for two decades, and dependent on debt for consumption, working-class families were drawn, however, into the logic of asset inflation not only through the institutional investment of their pensions, but also through the one major asset they held in their own hands (or could aspire to hold)—their family home. It was the inegalitarian effects of neoliberal policies that pushed Americans to base many of their financial decisions on the belief, amply encouraged by both the private and public institutions enmeshed in the U.S. financial system, that home ownership was risk-free and guaranteed annual increases in equity.

The attempted integration via bank and credit markets of poor African American communities, so long the Achilles' heel of working-class integration into the mythology of the American dream, was an especially notable aspect of the neoliberal era. As the Great Society public expenditure programs of the 1960s ran up against the need to redeem the imperial state's anti-inflationary commitments, financial markets came to be seen as the mechanism for doing this. One of the great ironies of the legacy of the civil rights and feminist movements was that as banks and credit card companies were pressed to develop color- and gender-blind risk models—creating greater opportunity for more and more people to become debtors (with higher interest rates, of course, for those with lower incomes)—they also subjected more and more people to the patterns of discipline, subordination, and crisis within contemporary financial markets. Beginning in the 1980s, amidst the Reagan administration's assault on labor rights and public services, home owners tried to take advantage of the "wealth effect" of rising home values by using that as collateral to take on more debt. The reorganization of the mortgage sector in the wake of the Savings and Loans crisis of the 1980s, including through the increased bundling and selling of mortgages as securities, fostered the link between consumption and real estate values. This combined with the allure of home ownership to create a self-reinforcing spiral of growing market demand and rising home prices. As the 1990s dawned, the Clinton administration especially sought to integrate working-class black and Hispanic communities into mainstream housing markets through its promotion of wider access to financial services and market-based alternatives to public housing and income supports in order to "end welfare as we know it."

By the end of the decade, such unsettling events as the Asian financial crisis and the collapse of the dot-com boom increased the risk of investments in the stock market, whether directly or through pension funds. In this context, the housing market emerged as a key source of wealth for many American wage earners, embodying the one significant asset they could actually hope to possess. All these developments served both to extend the reach of financial relations and to establish the growth of household debt as a key anchor of American financial growth. Of course, the desire to realize the American dream of home ownership on the part of so many of those who had previously been excluded was one thing; actual access to residential markets was another. They could only do so in such unprecedented numbers by the end of the twentieth century because financial intermediaries were frantically creating domestic mortgage debt in order to package and resell it in the market for structured credit. Already well under way during the 1990s, the trend was given a great fillip by the Bush administration's determination to open up competition to sell and trade mortgage-related securities, as well as by the Fed's lowering of real interest rates in the aftermath of the dot-com meltdown in spring 2000 and following 9/11.

With most middle-class income earners already in the market, mortgage companies structured loans in such a way as to capture consumers who could not otherwise have afforded homes. The majority of these loans were adjustable rate mortgages (ARMs) with initial two-year fixed-rate periods at lower interest rates. In addition, a growing number of mortgage providers offered debtors the option of limiting their monthly payments to the interest or even less, so that the principal would increase over time. By 2006, subprime loans represented 28 percent of total U.S. mortgages, and subprime mortgage-backed securities had become the largest component of the American market for asset-backed securities, accounting for nearly half of all issues (Weaver 2008). Commercial banks competed to extend residential mortgages to nearly anyone and then combined these mortgages into new "derivative" securities, which they sold on to other financial intermediaries (including the special investment vehicles they used to create the "shadow banking system"), as well as to the government-sponsored mortgage corporations Fannie Mae and Freddie Mac. The possibility of earning fees on debts that could be moved off their balance sheet made banks more willing to increase their exposure to low-income households, knowing very well the risks that they would not be able to pay their debts as interest rates rose.

The bubble in mortgage finance that emerged inside the U.S. housing sector was supported and reinforced by the tendency among developing economies, above all China, to peg their currencies to the dollar and to recycle their growing export earnings into the American market, including mortgages. But even beyond this, private capital flowed from around the world to the nodes of the global circuit of capital located in the United States. This raised asset prices, lowered interest rates, and intensified competitive pressures on investors to procure higher yields through greater leveraging and innovative securitization to stretch the boundaries of risk. Between 2000 and 2006, house prices rose faster than during any other period in recent U.S. history, with medium real home prices growing from $169,428 to $276,324 (National Association of Realtors n.d.). Encouraged by rising home prices and by mortgage tax deductions, growing segments of the home-owning working class sustained their consumption as wages stagnated by taking out second mortgages on the bubble-inflated values of their homes. The acceleration of mortgage-backed securitization, taking place amidst rising house prices that seemed to increase the wealth and creditworthiness of those borrowing, gave rise to the acceptance of lower standards by regulatory agencies, acting with the connivance of both parties in Congress. The Republicans opened up competition to sell and trade mortgages and mortgage-backed securities to all comers. But this was a policy that was only sustainable via the flow of global savings to the United States, not least to the apparent Treasury-plated safety of Fannie Mae and Freddie Mac securities as government-sponsored enterprises.

Much of this edifice of financial obligations was built through the "shadow banking system," which did not fall under the Federal Reserve's regulatory purview and therefore was not subject to constraining rules such as reserve requirements. The shadow banking system opened up to a wider world of structured finance, where mathematical wizards used complex models to build "nested structures of Russian dolls" (Feruson and Johnson 2009) - a complex and opaque world of asset-backed securities where already speculative derivative instruments were based on other derivatives and seemingly protected by a variety of insurance instruments (mostly credit default swaps). It was thus a long chain of neoliberal connections that led to the massive funding of mortgages, the hedging and default derivatives based on often high-risk mortgages, their treatment as safe low-risk investments by bond rating agencies such as Moody's, and their spread onto the books of many foreign institutions. The great New York investment banks, whose traditional business was corporate and government finance, were themselves fully involved in buying and selling the derivatives based on mortgages sold in poor communities in the United States and then repackaged and resold many times over. It also included the world's biggest insurance company, AIG, which had made a massive business of selling under-funded insurance on these derivatives, even while subject to the highly regulated insurance regime in the United States. The worlds of high and low finance had never been so closely interconnected than in this volatile mix of global capital movements, insecurity, and poverty that had developed by 2007.

The Federal Reserve emphatically made the case that "information processing technologies had enabled creditors to achieve significant efficiencies in collecting and assimilating the data necessary to evaluate risk"; and it increasingly defined its role as that of promoting financial education for the masses. "Like all learning," as Greenspan put it, "financial education is a process that should begin at an early age and last throughout life" (Greenspan 2005). It certainly got people to think of themselves as investors by thinking of family homes as an asset. But neoliberalism never delivered on its promise of a hidden hand equilibrating financial markets alongside a mass public of informed, financially literate borrowers and investors. This was borne out by the sale of derivatives around the world based on mortgages whose risk was scarcely evaluated at all. And it was borne out by the success that mortgage brokers had in manipulating people into taking out expensive loans by using a variety of techniques—balloon mortgages, teaser rate, adjustable rates, hiding the real terms in the small print, among others—designed to confuse borrowers as to the real cost of their loan, as well as the fact that many subprime loans with frightening interest rates went to households that would have easily qualified for a regular mortgage loan with less exploitative terms. Securitization techniques, as they had evolved over the past decade, produced tremendous pressure on, or temptation for, brokers to pursue ever more aggressive sales strategies. Predatory lending was not eradicated; rather, it went mainstream.

Had the Federal Reserve and the Treasury been so inclined, they certainly could have made considerably more efforts to impose some regulations (or to get other regulators to do so) to limit the banks' practices. Certainly Rubin's experience at Goldman Sachs had taught him that there were "situations where derivatives put additional pressure on volatile markets" and that "many people who used derivatives didn't fully understand the risks they were taking" (although Larry Summers, his deputy at the Treasury, thought Rubin "'was overly concerned with the risk of derivatives") (Rubin and Weisberg 2003). But their own structural ties to the markets meant that there was not much they were inclined to do. Their authority over the financial system had largely been based on their capacity to steer markets already strongly biased in favor of expansion, hence their support for the legislation in 1993 that exempted new hybrid derivative instruments from regulation by the Commodity Futures Trading Commission, which had, as we have seen, been established to sustain the emergence of modern financial derivatives exchanges two decades earlier. Brooksley Born (appointed by Clinton to head the CFTC in 1996) had expressed concerns that contagion from the Asian financial crisis might be brought home by speculative "over the counter" derivative trading that was being funded by New York's biggest banks. Her fears were realized by the collapse of Long-Term Capital Management hedge fund in the fall of 1998: "This episode should serve as a wake-up call about the unknown risks that the over-the-counter derivatives market may pose to the U.S. economy and to financial stability around the world" (Born 2001). But this yielded not only strong opposition from senators in the pockets of Enron, like Phil Gramm, but also from both the Treasury and the Fed. "Regulation of derivative transactions that are privately negotiated by professionals is unnecessary." Greenspan said. "Regulation that serves no useful purpose hinders the efficiency of markets to enlarge the standard of living" (Faiola et al 2008). But, apart from such neoliberal nostrums, what especially determined the Fed's and Treasury's position on this was the fear that to start regulating over-the-counter derivate swaps now would actually spark a crisis that they might not be able to contain due to the "legal uncertainty" this would create regarding the trillions of dollars in contracts involved, according to the 1999 *Report of the President's Working Group on Financial Markets* that Summers and Greenspan coauthored (Summers et al. 1999).

Of course, the exercise of pragmatism in public policy making is itself not unrelated to its exercise in terms of personal well-being. Once the Commodity Futures Modernization Act was passed on Summer's watch in the dying months of the Clinton administration to reinforce the relationship between derivatives markets and the CRTC, Summers relocated to the presidency of Harvard, which seemed to suggest a greater independence from financial capital that did Rubin's shuffle back to Wall Street (moving from Goldman Sachs to Citibank). But if Summers's appointment as Senior Economic Advisor to the Obama administration apparently stood in contrast to the pipeline that seemed to link Wall Street to Washington, this assumption was soon negated when it was disclosed that in 2008 Summers had "collected roughly $5.2 million in compensation from hedge fund D. E. Shaw" as well as over "$2.7 million in speaking fees from several troubled Wall Street firms and other organizations" (Rucker and Stephens 2009). What could clearly be seen at work here was the complex intertwining of public and private careers and interests that informed the relationship between state and market institutions, especially those that linked Wall Street with Washington, D.C. In the absence of a traditional bureaucracy in the American state, leading corporate lawyers and financiers have moved between Wall Street and Washington ever since the age of the "robber barons" in the late nineteenth century. Taking time off from the private firm to engage in public service has been called the "institutional schizophrenia" that links these Wall Street figures as "double agents" to the state. While acting in one sphere to squeeze through every regulatory loophole, they act in the other to introduce new regulations as "a tool for the efficient management of the social order in the public interest" (Gordon 1984, 53, 58, 65-66). Not to mention the thousands of lower-level links, this connection defined the role played by individuals like McChesney Martin and Douglas Dillon in the Eisenhower and Kennedy administrations no less than that of Robert Rubin, Henry Paulson, Larry Summers, and Timothy Geithner in the Clinton, Bush, and Obama administrations.

It is partly for this reason that the popular protest and discontent triggered by a long history of financial scandals and crises in the United States, far from undermining the institutional and regulatory basis of financial expansion, have repeatedly been pacified through the processes of further "codification, institutionalization and juridification," as rules became more elaborate, as the regulatory institutions applying them acquired more resources, and as the courts were increasingly involved in interpreting them (Moran 1991, 13). And far from buckling under the pressure of popular disapproval, financial elites have proved very adept at not only responding to these pressures but also using them to create new regulatory frameworks that have laid the foundations for the further growth of financial capital and the reproduction of class and institutional power. The capital adequacy rules that states adopted for banks from the 1980s onward had precisely that effect. Nor is this a matter of simple manipulation of the masses. Most people have an interest, however contradictory, in the daily functioning and reproduction of financial capitalism because of their dependence on it: from access to their wages and salaries via their bank accounts, to buying goods and services on credit, to paying their bills, to investing their savings. They depend on it, moreover, for the very roofs over their heads, let alone the investment in their homes as assets for retirement. So much was this the case that by the first decade of the twenty-first century, American capitalism was enveloped in a financial system premised on a massive funding of mortgages and consumer credit. And this was facilitated by the jumble of derivative and securitized instruments which, once wrapped in the triple-A status bequeathed by the somnambulant rating agencies, could be spread onto the books of a wide variety of financial institutions both at home and abroad.

What Triggered the Great Recession

The way in which finance had been used in the neoliberal era to sustain the American dream eventually triggered the first great economic crisis of the twenty-first century. When a housing bubble bursts, it affects not just the financial system, but the whole economic system in a way that stock market meltdowns do not. This is so because of the way in which housing bridges finance and the rest of the economy—most directly, the construction industry, as well as furniture and appliances. Because the real estate value of the home accounts for most family's wealth by far, any significant decline in that value can undermine consumer confidence. The housing boom had reached its peak by the end of 2004 and began to really weaken in the second half of 2005, when inventories of unsold homes jumped up and house prices began to decline. The problems in the residential mortgage market can be traced directly to households' growing mortgage payment burdens. In the short term, Americans were able to manage this burden by (re)financing at attractive interest rates and cashing in the equity in their homes. But this, of course, only added to the structural burden. Meanwhile, as families pressed against the limits of continually increasing their total working hours, the real income of the median U.S. household fell between 1999 and 2005 (US Census Bureau n.d.). In 2005, when the teaser period of ultra-low interest rates began to end (in some cases, rates on subprime mortgages doubled or even trebled), the average national variable mortgage rate jumped from 5.3 percent to 6.2 percent (Kirchhoff and Keen 2007). During the same period, the Fed (once again feeling the need to offer inflation-proof guarantees as the world's central banker) decided to step on the brakes and raised the federal funds rate by a full four percentage points between mid-2004 and mid-2006. This translated into even higher interest premiums on subprime issues. By 2006, the delinquency rate on subprime mortgages rose by 4.4 percent; in 2007, by 16.7 percent (US Census Bureau 2005, 2006, 2007).

On the eve of the crisis, subprime residential mortgage–backed securities and mortgage-linked collateralized debt obligations still comprised 60 percent of the American market for asset-backed securities. The dramatic growth of securitized subprime mortgages meant that the whole financial system had become extremely vulnerable to the volatility in this segment of the market. Select investors began to view the market as inflated and to back away from mortgage-backed securities. As it became clear that the growth of this market was largely dependent on the continued entry of low-income borrowers and that the default rate of non-prime borrowers vastly exceeded actuarial projections, the value of structured instruments came under pressure and their supply slowed down. From 2006 to 2007, the issuance of asset-backed securities slumped by 29.4 percent, led by a 69.1 percent collapse in the new supply of collateralized debt obligations and subprime mortgage–backed securities (Weaver 2008). Since the expansion of securitized mortgage debt had taken place through the construction of complex chains of interconnected financial networks, the malaise in the mortgage market spread quickly to other sectors. The globalized nature of American finance meant that foreign investors who were major players in the U.S. markets took immediate losses. The collapse of the U.S. housing bubble was also spread internationally because of the complex ways that collateralized mortgages are constructed, with the result that broad segments of the financial sectors in Europe as well as North America were quickly drawn into the collapse of non-prime risk. Moreover, since the risk in subprime mortgages had been spread through their packaging in derivatives with more secure forms of debt, the subprime crisis undermined the econometric equations that valued these assets in global markets. Mortgage-backed securities, which were held broadly by financial institutions around the world, now became difficult to value and to sell, and this produced a contagion throughout securitized financial and inter-bank markets.

Crisis Management from Bush to Obama

As the financial crisis broke out in the summer of 2007, the newly appointed chairman of the Fed, Ben Bernanke, could draw on his academic work as an economist at Princeton University on how the Depression could have been avoided (Bernanke 2000), and Treasury Secretary Henry Paulson could draw on his own illustrious career (like Rubin's) as a senior executive at Goldman Sachs (Paulson 2010). Both the Treasury and Federal Reserve staff worked closely with the Securities Exchange Commission and Commodity Futures Trading Commission under the rubric of the President's Working Group on Financial Markets that had been set up in 1988, known on Wall Street as the "Plunge Protection Team." The central problem they faced was that large amounts of debt were owed by U.S. households that were simply incapable of generating the income streams needed for their repayment. In an era when few data are not recorded and analyzed, banks had ended up holding assets that they were unable to value. Once a debt had been "securitized"—that is, sliced up, mixed with a variety of other debts, and then sold as a new composite asset–backed security—there was little hope of tracing the value of the resulting new "asset." Former Treasury Secretary Paul O'Neill summarized the nature of the problem facing debt markets in this way: "If you had ten bottles of water and one bottle had poison in it, and you didn't know which one, you probably wouldn't drink any one" (Solomon 2008).

During 2007, the U.S. Treasury organized, first, a consortium of international banks and investment funds and then an overlapping consortium of mortgage companies, financial securitizers, and investment funds to take concrete measures to calm the markets. As it had done a decade earlier during the Long-Term Capital Management crisis, Treasury officials convened the CEOs of the nation's ten largest commercial banks in September 2007 (Mollenkamp et al. 2007). This time, however, the attempt to use the Treasury's authority to get the major banks to act to stabilize the system did not succeed: no one would invest in debt backed by subprime mortgages, which were at the heart of the problem. For its part, the Federal Reserve acted as the world's central bank by repeatedly supplying other central banks with dollars to provide liquidity to their banking systems, while doing the same for Wall Street. The global attraction and strength of American finance was seen to be rooted in its depth and breadth at home; when the crisis hit in the subprime security market at the heart of the empire, it shook the banking systems of many other countries. The scale of the American government's intervention has certainly been a function of the consequent unraveling of the crisis throughout its integrated domestic financial system, yet it is also important to understand this in terms of the American state's imperial responsibilities—namely, to manage the contradictions of global capitalism and to coordinate the responses to the crisis—and the eventual "exit strategies" out of the crisis—by finance ministries and central banks.

The American state's responsibilities for managing global capitalism led the Fed to repeatedly pump billions of dollars via foreign central banks into inter-bank markets abroad, where banks balance their books through the overnight borrowing of dollars from other banks. An important factor in the nationalizations of Fannie Mae and Freddie Mac was the need of the U.S. government to confirm its commitment to never default on its debt obligations to foreign investors, including the Japanese and Chinese central banks, who had invested in the securities of these "government-sponsored enterprises". It is for this reason that even those foreign leaders who have opportunistically pronounced the end of American "financial superpower status" have credited the US Treasury for "acting not just in the U.S. interests but also in the interests of other nations" (German Finance Minister Peer Sienbrück cited in Benoit 2008).

The United States was not being altruistic in playing this role internationally, since not to do it would have risked a run on the dollar. But this is precisely the point. *The American state cannot act in the interests of American capitalism without also reflecting the logic of American capitalism's integration with global capitalism both economically and politically.* This is why it is always misleading to portray the American state as merely representing its "national interest" while ignoring the structural role it plays in the making and reproduction of global capitalism.

Both the Treasury and Federal Reserve staff continued to work through the President's Working Group on Financial Markets to facilitate regulatory cooperation and quick policy responses to coordinate their activities with the Securities Exchange Commission and Commodity Futures Trading Commission. As 2008 began with stock markets in Asia and Europe shaken at the prospect of a serious American recession, the Fed undertook a large emergency cut in interest rates. By March it had undertaken another coordinated move with the other central banks, supplying them with dollars to provide liquidity to their banks, while simultaneously making no less than $200 billion available to Wall Street's investment banks. Yet even this could not save all the banks. The headlines that greeted St. Patrick's Day 2008—"Wall Street Quakes as the Parade Passes By"—revealed that the Fed had directed, overseen, and guaranteed JP Morgan's takeover of Bear Stearns to the tune of $30 billion. Essentially, the Fed had agreed to take full responsibility for the risk associated with low-grade investments. Ironically, Bear Stearns had been the lone major investment bank that had refused to cooperate with the Fed-engineered bailout of Long-Term Capital Management a decade before.

The Bear Stearns crisis was somewhat of a watershed, as it made clear to regulators just how deep the cracks in the system ran and how forceful and effective the regulatory response would have to be. By the end of the month, the Treasury issued its long-awaited "Blueprint for a Modernized Financial Regulatory Structure" (in preparation since March 2007, before the onset of the crisis). Apart from announcing plans for the further formalization of coordination of the interventions undertaken by the U.S. and British Treasuries, the "Blueprint" was primarily designed to enhance the Fed's regulatory authority over the whole financial system, not least over the investment banks for whom it now was so openly the lender of last resort. The Fed now placed a staff of analysts inside each of Wall Street's investment banks in order to collect important information. Yet the Fed was at the same time stymied by the fact that what had been such a key monetary policy instrument during the Greenspan era—the announcements of marginal charges of the federal funds rate—did not have much leverage in a situation where the inter-bank loans had become almost fully paralyzed by anxiety-driven, liquidity-hoarding behavior. With the Fed rapidly approaching a situation in which interest rates could not be lowered any further, it dramatically expanded its programs for helping the banks by "repurchasing agreements" ("repos"), thereby hugely enhancing its capacity to provide liquidity and sector-specific support. Through a related program (the Term Securities Lending Facility), the Fed transferred what was then a stunning $219 billion in risky assets from financial institutions to its own books in the months following the Bear Stearns collapse.

But all of this state intervention, however much it was founded on a legacy of relatively successful efforts to contain crises in the past, could not prevent this crisis from assuming still greater proportions. Although most serious analysts thought the worst was over in spring of 2008, by the summer Fannie Mae and Freddie Mac were also being undone by the crisis. By September, so were the great New York investment banks. The problem they all faced was that there was no market for a great proportion of the mortgage-backed assets on their books. As financial capital's risk-evaluation equations unraveled, so did the ability of financial markets to judge the worth of financial institutions' balance sheets. Banks became very reluctant to give each other even the shortest-term credits. Without such inter-bank credit, any financial system will collapse.

The unprecedented scale of interventions in September 2008 can only be understood in this context. The interventions involved pumping additional hundreds of billions of dollars into the world's inter-bank markets; the nationalizations of Fannie Mae, Freddie Mac, and AIG; the seizure and fire sale of Washington Mutual to prevent the largest bank failure in U.S. history; a blanket guarantee on the $3.4 trillion in mutual funds deposits; a ban on short-selling of financial stocks; *and* Paulson's $700 billion "Troubled Asset Relief Program" (TARP) to take on toxic mortgage assets. The takeover of Fannie Mae and Freddie Mac created little additional liquidity in markets for mortgage-backed securities, let alone in those subprime market segments where Freddie and Fannie had no presence. During the following week, two major investment banks found themselves heading for disaster. One catastrophe was averted when, through regulatory orchestration, Merrill Lynch was sold to Bank of America, but another was not—the American government's reluctance to extend financial guarantees complicated last-minute efforts to have the old firm of Lehman Brothers bank taken over, with the result that it was forced to file for bankruptcy. The Fed and Treasury once again convened Wall Street CEOs and urged them to arrange a private-sector bailout. But the reluctance to make substantial funds available from the public purse turned out to be a serious miscalculation. Lehman had massive exposure in the markets for securitized products and complex derivatives, and its failure sent shockwaves through the markets. As significant as the losses was the message to global investors about the central operating assumption of global capitalism in our time—namely, the U.S. government's capacity to understand the dynamic interconnections in the financial system and to meet its commitment to support its key institutional pillars.

If the government derived one benefit from letting Lehman sink, it was that it lent some credence to the idea that market discipline was not only for ordinary people, but also for Wall Street firms. But it was not permitted to enjoy such newfound ideological coherence as the financial system shook in the fall of 2008. AIG, the world's largest insurance company, had been forced to write off massive amounts of funds, and when the rating agencies downgraded the company's debt, they effectively brought it to the brink of insolvency. Its failure would have sent markets around the world in a tailspin, but behind-the-scenes rescue efforts had already been set in motion, and the Federal Reserve quickly made available a sizable lifeline in September 2008. The Federal Reserve had already gone well beyond the normal boundaries of its regulatory remit by extending help to investment banks, and it now ventured into even newer territory as it took responsibility for the survival of an insurance company whose commitments constituted a key pillar of the markets for securitized products and complex derivatives. On the same day that AIG's problems became fully apparent, the price of stock in Reserve Primary, the largest and oldest fund operator in the short-term money market (the safest investments after cash and bank deposits) fell below one dollar. It took the Treasury's insurance of all money market deposits to stabilize the situation.

September 2008 raised the prospect that the Treasury was slipping into an endless series of interventions that would have entangled them in patchworks of ad hoc financial arrangements. In this situation, it proposed a sweeping plan that, it hoped, would serve to flush sufficient toxic debt out of the system to restore its liquidity. In early October 2008, Congress was finally induced to pass the $700 billion TARP fund under the Economic Stabilization Act. The Treasury had justified getting these astronomical amounts from Congress in order to save the banks by being able to buy up their toxic assets. In the wake of the markets showing anything but vitality in the following weeks, it exploited the latitude the Act gave it by purchasing equity stakes in financial institutions to provide them with more capital, the mammoth financial conglomerate of Citigroup, above all. Investors began betting against it, sending the share price down more than 60 percent. After having been approached by senior Citigroup officials, regulators at the Federal Reserve, Treasury, and the FDIC announced a plan to prop it up. All this meant, as the US state began accumulating equity stakes, is that for a period it actually owned a very significant part of the nation's financial system. But this had nothing to do with the imposition of effective democratic public control. The Bush administration was committed to socializing risk, but it was most certainly not interested in socializing control of the financial system. The fact that both the Treasury and Fed did not ask for much in return for this highlighted the political contradictions the crisis posed for a Republican administration, as the socialization of bankers' losses was increasingly seen to be both ineffective and unfair.

This was a factor that had already played its part in the outcome of the November 2008 election. But in fact, as Paulson's memoir makes very clear, Obama had far better appreciation for the Treasury's management of the crisis than had Senator McCain. Through his private discussions with Obama at the height of the crisis, Paulson recognized that Obama "genuinely seemed to want to do the right thing. He wanted to avoid doing anything publicly— or privately—that would damage our efforts to stabilize the markets and the economy" (Paulson 2010, 13-14). Obama's appointment of Timothy Geithner as his own Secretary of the Treasury was predicated on this. As head of the New York Federal Reserve Bank, Geithner was especially seen as "onside" with Wall Street, and had been at the epicenter of the Bush government's response to the crisis. He now went out of his way to emphasize that their objective was to keep banks in private hands, and that any government control over banks' operations would be strictly temporary. This left the Obama administration with the same dilemmas and contradictions as its predecessor faced in its last months in office—namely, the provision of massive public assistance to a financial sector that was now, in its own self-interest, extremely reluctant to lend. The Financial Stability Plan that Geithner unveiled in February and March 2009 to deal with the persistent illiquidity of financial markets followed what had gone before: it extended Treasury purchases of bank stock, and it built on the TARF program (the Term Asset-Backed Securities Loan Facility) announced just before the end of the previous administration in December 2008. For its part, the Fed devoted as much as a trillion dollars to purchasing from the banks the now unmarketable derivatives on their books, and announced a framework for financial sector regulatory reform, which closely followed Paulson's 2007 plan to expand its supervisory authority.

One new element, resembling the private-public partnerships that had become so common under neoliberalism, was a plan for five "asset management funds" to be set up along the lines of the government's Resolution Trust Corporation during the Savings and Loan crisis. The Financial Times' Martin Wolf accurately summed up the essence of the plan: "Under the scheme, the government provides virtually all the finance and bears almost all the risk, but it uses the private sector to price the assets. In return, private investors obtain rewards—perhaps generous rewards—based on their performance via equity participation, alongside the Treasury. I think of this as the 'vulture fund relief scheme'" (Wolf 2009). In the end, this scheme did not have to be used because the scale of the rest of the bailout of the big banks was sufficient to restore their profitability for the most part. When the Federal Reserve released the results of the "stress test" that it had conducted of the 19 largest U.S. bank holding companies in May 2009, it found that, with the help of government purchase of bank stocks and bad assets, 9 of them already had adequate capital. The requirement it put on the others to immediately develop and implement a detailed plan for the regulators to raise additional capital put most of Wall Street's banks in the position to start paying back their loans from the government and buy back their stock. In addition to the direct government bailouts, banks regained their footing with the help of their profits on the fees from marketing government bonds and on the spread between the government's inexpensive charges for funds and the interest they then charged to lenders.

The one real innovation of the new administration, not heralded as part of its Financial Stability Plan, was the announcement in March 2009 that the Fed would begin to purchase hundred of billions of dollars of long-term Treasury bonds to help improve conditions in private credit markets. By keeping down the interest costs on its deficit that the government would have to pay, this made more viable its undertaking of the most extensive fiscal stimulus (outside of wartime) in American history. This purchasing of government debt by its central bank ("quantitative easing," as it was now called)—and the relative lack of public attention or critical comment—was a measure of how the crisis had shaken the ruling class circles, as well as the mainstream economists who advise them. At almost any time since World War II, anyone suggesting such direct and massive pump-priming would have been judged economically illiterate. A sell-off of Treasuries by other purchasers would have been predicted, amidst a massive run on the dollar. That nothing like this occurred may be a measure of what the crisis has finally proved about global capital's recognition—as well as that of the other capitalist states—of the central role of the U.S. state in keeping the system going.

The greatest political danger that both the banks and the state faced was the scandal over bonuses paid to managers in bailed-out firms, even as unemployment continued to climb and as banks refused loans to those they now deemed not credit-worthy. The real "moral hazard" was the fear of widening for permanent bank nationalization. But just as the Labour Government in the United Kingdom set up its provision of massive public capital to the banks in the fall of 2008 so that they would still "operate on a commercial basis at arm's length" from any government direction or control (Hampton and Kingman 2008), so did the U.S. Treasury, no less under Geithner than under Paulson, draw back from taking direct control over companies in which it became the major stockholder. The congressional furor that enveloped Geithner over the millions in bonuses paid to AIG executives within months of his taking office was directly related to the untenable position in which this action put members of Congress, who had insisted that autoworkers agree to renegotiate their contracts as a condition for rescuing the car companies. The obvious class bias that this entailed went all the way back to the beginning of the neoliberal era when Volcker was put on the Chrysler board at the insistence of Congress to oversee UAW concessions during the Chrysler bailout. The difference now was that the grotesque salaries and bonuses that bankers paid themselves—which somehow had seemed acceptable when Wall Street was facilitating a new wave of capitalist globalization—could no longer be as easily defended by politicians, or be quite so admired in the media. Joining in the vilification of financiers has always been a central trope of the populism commonly practiced by American politicians. A particularly memorable instance of how U.S. elites must accommodate to—and at the same time overcome—a populist political culture was Henry Paulson's declaration before the House Financial Services Committee, as he tried to get his TARP plan through Congress, that "the American people are angry about executive compensation and rightfully so" (Stout 2008). This was rather rich, given that he had been Wall Street's highest-paid CEO, receiving $38.3 million in salary, stock, and options in the year before joining the Treasury, plus a midyear $18.7 million bonus on his departure, as well as an estimated $200 million tax break against the sale of his almost $500 million share holding in Goldman Sachs—as was required to avoid conflict of interest in his new job (Bowers 2008). When Paulson appeared before the congressional hearings to defend his TARP plan to save the financial system, he acknowledged that Wall Street's exorbitant compensation schemes are "a serious problem." But Paulson immediately added, "We must find a way to address this in legislation *without undermining the effectiveness of the program*" (cited in Stout 2008, emphasis added).

The accommodation to the culture of populism was also seen at work in both McCain's and Obama's campaign rhetoric against greed and speculation (even though Wall Street investment banks were among their largest campaign contributors and supplied some of their key advisers). President Obama made the identical appeal that Paulson had six months earlier, when his Treasury Secretary's new plan for leveraging private investments with massive public subsidies to save the financial system was rolled out amidst the mass outrage over the millions paid out to the very executives who had created the mess. "You've got a pretty egregious situation here that people are understandably upset about," Obama said, referring to these bonuses. "So let's see if there are ways of doing this that are both legal, that are constitutional,,that uphold our basic principles of fairness, *but don't hamper us from getting the banking system back on track*" (cited in Ward 2009). Like Paulson before him, Obama was signaling that really attacking the class inequality that is embedded in American capitalism would endanger working people's immediate interests in not losing what little they have as subordinate class participants in the financial system. Given that market efficiency could no longer credibly be claimed to explain why the basic principles of fairness should not be taken too far, Obama's "but" spoke volumes about how social justice is trumped by class hegemony in a capitalist society.

Nowhere is the class bias embedded in this system—for which Obama assumed responsibility with his election to the presidency—more clearly seen than in the role the Fed and Treasury both played under his administration in preventing the "pay czar" that Obama himself had appointed from drastically cutting the grotesque amounts that the executives of the bailed-out companies (even those effectively taken over by the U.S. government) paid to themselves (Brill 2010). This included not only the executives of financial firms like AIG, Bank of America, and Citigroup, but also Chrysler and General Motors, exactly at the same time that the condition imposed on the bailouts of those industrial giants required the UAW to agree to massive concessions on wages, pensions, and working conditions, with the explicit goal of setting an example for all other workers. The differential treatment of company executives and workers was also explicitly justified in terms of the need to compensate the former in order to preserve capitalist incentives and restore profits and competitiveness, to get them to cooperate in "saving the economy." Thus was the system of class power and inequality that generated the crisis reinforced as the American state intervened to "save the economy."

How ironic, but how typically so, that Obama should have made a show of calling the chief executives of 12 major financial institutions to the White House just before the end of 2009. The day before he had gone on television to proclaim "I did not run for office to be helping out a bunch of fat cat bankers." His main message to the bankers was that "America's banks received enormous assistance from American taxpayers to rebuild their industry—and now that they're back on their feet we expect an extraordinary commitment from them to help rebuild our economy." As for financial sector reform, Obama expressed his frustration over the "big gap between what I am hearing here in the White House and in the activities of lobbyists on behalf of those institutions" (Financial Times 2009). As Goldman Sachs showed a surge in its net income for 2009 to a record $13.4 billion while unemployment remained stuck at 10 percent, Obama's frustration at the palpable political costs (which were not mollified by Goldman's promise to reduce its annual bonus pool from $22 billion to $16 billion and to donate $500 million to charities) led him to propose two new measures in January 2010. One was a "financial crisis responsibility fee" on the largest banks, projected to raise $90 billion over 10 years. The other, prominently associated with Paul Volcker's reform proposals in 2009 (Working Group on Financial Stability 2009), was to prohibit deposit-taking banks from proprietary activities (i.e., using their own capital to speculate as well as to operate their own hedge funds).

The Fed and Treasury's lack of enthusiasm for even such modest proposals had less to do with the activities of lobbyists than the problematic implications for a highly integrated financial system. The responsibility fee could have untoward implications for the "repo market" in U.S. Treasury securities, further limiting lending by banks and complicating the practice of monetary policy. And isolating banks' own proprietary trading would be very difficult, given how much of their capital was necessarily involved in helping clients carry out trades in stocks, bonds, and derivatives. Indeed, the integration of commercial and investment banking combined with the integration of the American states and financial markets in global capitalism makes any return to the watertight compartments of the "Glass-Steagall" New Deal reforms virtually impossible. Even Volcker spoke not in terms of reviving Glass-Steagall but only of returning to its "spirit," and this was reflected in the vagueness in Obama's proposals. As with the 1930s reforms—which the banks were closely involved in devising and implementing, and which became the foundation for the recovery and enormous expansion of U.S. banking—the final form taken by today's much more limited measures are as likely to strengthen Wall Street as weaken it.

The Failure of the Left

The financial crisis of the first decade of the twenty-first century afforded an opportunity that could have been used by a genuinely radical government to nationalize the banks and turn them into a democratic public utility. This opportunity has so far been wasted. Its displacement in 2010 with minor reforms, presented in a way that led to headlines like "Obama Declares War on Wall Street" and "Banks Face Revolutionary Reform," captures the essence of populism, and bespeaks its limits. Meanwhile, in the wake of the American Left's failure to develop lasting and effective political vehicles in the course of opposing neoliberalism over the last three decades, political resistance to the financial crisis was largely spontaneous and sporadic, and almost entirely defensive. This was evident in the few-and-far-between outbursts of direct action in reclaiming and occupying houses by anti-poverty and shelter activists in various cities, the isolated factory occupations by workers demanding proper severances and pensions, the rejection of further concession demands by employers (such as by Ford workers), the student and teacher revolt across California against university cutbacks. As crucial an element as local and sectoral resistance must be for any progressive change, the degree of political organization necessary for it to be sustained and effective has been missing. Most of the inherited problems of the Left that constrained effective political opposition to neoliberalism have been reinforced through this crisis. Nor least among these are purely defensive trade unionism, narrow public interest lobbying, and the misconceived call for "more" regulation of the financial sector.

The remarkable "flexibility" that the U.S. state has had in terms of the resolution of the crisis is directly related to the basic weaknesses of the Left. This has given it additional room for maneuver in the world market in coordinating and negotiating the international response to the crisis. And this also helps explain why the capitalist class in the United States has shown so few divisions around what type of regulation to impose on financial markets. It has been able to take advantage of labor market insecurities, rewriting collective bargaining agreements while the American state finds new ways to reconstitute neoliberalism globally. Elements of finance may still be in disarray, but the capitalist class in general has retained the resources, power, and the organizational support of the state to restructure and recast and pursue their political interests. Certain economic crises in the past—the Great Depression of the 1930s above all—have created openings and opportunities for *both* capitalists and workers. But the lack of any comparable strategic resources on the part of labor and the Left more broadly in North America—crucial for sustaining struggles through time, transmitting them across communities, and developing new political capacities—were made even more evident by this crisis.

But much else may yet be clarified by this crisis. Even if the discourse of neoliberalism successfully obscured the extent to which states have played a crucial role in making capitalist globalization happen, it should no longer be able to obscure the extent to which states are encumbered with the responsibility for keeping it going in face of the financial volatility to which their economies have been increasingly exposed. This is especially the case with the

United States, "as the country responsible for managing the international financial system, a role that other countries have accepted and, indeed, consented to through decades of past practice," according to two leading U.S. political scientists who had close ties to the foreign policy establishment in the 1990s. "This authority, in turn, rests on a perception of the reliable American stewardship of international financial markets" (Kahler and Lake 2009, 267). If this perception in the 1980s had rested on the pivotal role of the American state in the fight against inflation, so was it reinforced in the 1990s by the pivotal role it played in containing the financial crises that attended the growing international mobility of finance.

Despite widespread expectations that these international perceptions would be undermined by the current crisis, there is as of yet little concrete evidence that this is the case. Indeed, since the crisis began, it is the ruling classes, not the labor movements, that have seized the crisis as an opportunity. Even while the public stands disgusted with the speculative orgy that neoliberalism unleashed, even while the mythology of market fundamentalism has been discredited, and even while public sentiment is hostile to the bank bailouts—the response of capitalist states has been to shore up, however they can, the very model that brought the economy to ruins. In June 2010 the leaders of the G-20, meeting in Toronto, declared that they were holding fast to free markets, which, since the onset of the crisis, had been "the right choice." And they pledged to "renew for a further three years [their] commitment to refrain from raising barriers or imposing new barriers to investment or trade ... [and] to rectify such measures as they arise." They also promised to "minimize any negative impact on trade and investment of [their] domestic policy actions, including fiscal policy." What has been so significant about this crisis is that the further assault on trade unions and the social entitlements of working classes that this portended has been evident in many countries in Europe, and it has been especially evident in the United States itself.

How will the political effects of this come to be registered? The rhetoric of U.S. Republicans and conservatives for state withdrawal from finance appears to reveal an utter disconnect from the interests they claim to serve, although it is explicable in terms of playing to a populist recognition of how closely finance and state have been aligned in the neoliberal era and how far the measures taken since the crisis are mainly about reproducing, as they are, the "too-big-to-fail" relationship on a more secure footing. It is, of course, most unlikely that any new Republican administration would act much differently. When Newt Gingrich opposed President Clinton's U.S. bailout of Mexico in the financial crisis of 1994 (echoing Michel Camdessus, the sophisticated managing director of the IMF, in calling it "the first crisis of the twenty-first century"), Robert Rubin believed that "many members of Congress probably meant to oppose us without actually stopping us". Even Newt Gingrich was quoted as saying there would be a "huge sigh of relief from Congress once the administration took responsibility for the rescue plan because the legislators "understood what needed to be done but didn't want to vote for it" (Rubin and Weisberg 2003). This would become a familiar congressional maneuver in subsequent crises, but it effectively gave the Treasury license to do "what needed to be done" so as to "restore market confidence." This has also proven to be the case in the current crisis. The political Right in the United States has been more determined to take advantage of the crisis, not to break the link between the state and finance, but to once and for all break the power of state employees.

Note

1. This paper, originally prepared for the "Dilemmas of the Obama Presidency" Conference, Nuffield College, March 11–12, 2010, partially draws on the final chapter (with Martijn Konings, Sam Gindin, and Scott Aquanno) of *American Empire and the Political Economy of Global Finance* (Palgrave, 2009), and Chapters 3, and 4 (with Greg Albo and Sam Gindin) of *In and Out of Crisis* (PM Press, 2010).

References

Arrighi, Giovanni. 1994. *The Long Twentieth Century*. London: Verso.

Benoit, Bertrand. 2008. "US 'Will Lose Financial Superpower Status.'" *Financial Times*, September 25.

Bernanke, Ben. 2000. *Essays on the Great Depression*. Princeton, NJ: Princeton University Press.

Born, Brooksley. 2001. "International Regulatory Responses to Derivatives Cases: The Role of the U.S. Commodity Futures Trading Commission." *Northwestern Journal of International Law & Business* 21(3).

Bowers, Simon. 2008. "Wall Street Man." *The Guardian*, September 26.

Brill, Stephen. 2010. "What's a Bailed-Out Banker Worth?" *New York Times Magazine*, January 3.

Brinkley, Alan. 1995. *The End of Reform: New Deal Liberalism in Recession and War*. New York: Alfred A. Knopf.

Broesamle, John J. 1973. *William Gibbs McAdoo: A Passion for Change, 1863–1917*. Port Washington, NY: Kennikat Press.

Bryan, Dick, and Michael Rafferty. 2006. *Capitalism with Derivatives: A Political Economy of Financial Derivatives, Capital and Class*. London: Palgrave.

Buiter, Willem. 2008. "The Fed as the Market Maker of Last Resort: Better Late Than Never." *Financial Times*, March 12, 2008.

Chernow, Ron. 1990. *The House of Morgan*. New York: Simon & Schuster.

Dickens, Edwin. 1995. "US Monetary Policy in the 1950s: A Radical Political Economy Approach." *Review of Radical Political Economics* 27(4).

Dickens, Edwin. 1998. "Bank Influence and the Failure of US Monetary Policy during the 1953–54 Recession." *International Review of Applied Economics* 12(2).

Epstein, Gerald A., and Juliet B. Shor. 1995. "The Federal Reserve-Treasury Accord and the Construction of the Postwar Monetary Regime in the United States." *Social Concept*.

Faiola, Anthony, et al. 2008. "What Went Wrong?" *Washington Post*, October 15.

Ferguson, Thomas, and Robert Johnson. 2009. "Too Big to Bail: The 'Paulson Put,' Presidential Politics, and the Global Financial Meltdown, Part I: From Shadow Financial System to Shadow Bailout." *International Journal of Political Economy* 38(1).

Financial Times. 2009. "Obama in Tough Talk to 'Fat Cat' Bankers." *Financial Times*, December 15.

Greenspan, Alan. 2005. "Consumer Finance." *Federal Reserve Fourth Annual Communities Affairs Research Conference*, Washington, DC, April 8.

Greenspan, Alan. 2007. *The Age of Turbulence*. New York: Penguin.

Gordon, Robert G. 1984. "'The Ideal and the Actual in the Law': Fantasies and Practices of New York City Lawyers, 1870–1910." In Gerald W. Gewalt, *The New High Priests: Lawyers in Post-Civil War America*. Westport, CT: Greenwood Press.

Hampton, Philip and John Kingman. 2008. "Mandate to Protect Taxpayers' Investment." *Financial Times*, November 13.

Herzel, Robert, and Ralph F. Leach. 2001. "After the Accord: Reminiscences on the Birth of the Modern Fed." In Federal Reserve Bank of Richmond, *Economic Quarterly* 87(1), Winter.

Kahler, Miles, and David Lake. 2009. "Economic Integration, Global Governance: Why So Little Supranationalism?" In Walter Mattli and Ngaire Woods, eds., *The Politics of Global Regulation*. Princeton, NJ: Princeton University Press.

Kirchhoff, S., and J. Keen. 2007. "Minorities Hit Hard by Rising Costs of Subprime Loans." *USA Today*, April 25.

Livingston, J. 1986. *Origins of the Federal Reserve System: Money, Class and Corporate Capitalism, 1890–1913*. Ithaca, NY: Cornell University Press.

Mackenzie, Donald. 2005. "Opening the Black Boxes of Global Finance." *Review of International Political Economy*, 12(4).

Maddison, Angus. 2001. *The World Economy: A Millennial Perspective*. Paris: OECD.

Melamed, Leo. 1992. *Leo Melamed on the Markets: Twenty Years of Financial History as Seen by the Man Who Revolutionized the Markets*. New York: Wiley.

Miliband, Ralph. 2009. *The State in Capitalist Society* (1969). London: Merlin Press.

Mollenkamp, C., et al. 2007. "Rescue Readied by Banks Is Bet to Spur Markets." *Wall Street Journal*, October 15.

Moran, Michael. 1991. *The Politics of the Financial Services Revolution*. London: Macmillan.

National Association of Realtors. n.d. "S&P/Case-Shiller Home Price Index." Washington, DC: *National Association of Realtors*.

New York Times. 2008. "A Professor and a Banker Bury Old Dogma on Markets." *New York Times*, September 20.

Panitch, Leo. 1986. "A Socialist Alternative to Unemployment." *Canadian Dimension* 20(1), March.

Panitch, Leo, and Sam Gindin. 2003. "American Empire and Global Finance." *Socialist Register 2004*. London: Merlin.

Panitch, Leo and Sam Gindin. 2004. "Finance and American Empire." *Socialist Register 2005*, London: Merlin.

Paulson, Henry M. 2010. *On the Brink: Inside the Race to Stop the Collapse of the Global Financial System*. New York: Business Plus.

Rothbard, Murray N. 1999. "The Origins of the Federal Reserve." *The Quarterly Journal of Austrian Economics* 2(3), Fall.

Rubin, Robert, and Jacob Weisberg. 2003. *In an Uncertain World: Tough Choices from Washington to Wall Street*. New York: Random House.

Rucker, Philip, and Joe Stephens. 2009. "Top Economics Aide Discloses Income: Summers Earned Salary From Hedge Fund, Speaking Fees From Wall St. Firms." *Washington Post*, April 4.

Solomon, D. 2008. "Questions for Paul O'Neill: Market Leader." *New York Times*, March 30.

Stout, David. 2008. "Paulson Gives Way on CEO Pay." *New York Times*, September 24.

Summers, Lawrence H., et al. 1999. "Over-the-Counter Derivatives Markets and the Commodity Exchange Act." *Report of the President's Working Group on Financial Markets*, November.

U.S. Census Bureau. 2005. "Statistical Abstracts of the United States, 2004." Washington DC: *The National Data Book: Banking, Finance and Insurance*.

U.S. Census Bureau. 2006. "Statistical Abstracts of the United States, 2005." Washington DC: *The National Data Book: Banking, Finance and Insurance*.

U.S. Census Bureau. 2007. "Statistical Abstracts of the United States, 2006." Washington DC: *The National Data Book: Banking, Finance and Insurance*.

U.S. Census Bureau. n.d. "Historical Income Tables." (http://www.census.gov/hhes/www/income/histinc/incpertoc.html).

Vogel, Steven K. 1996. *Freer Markets, More Rules: Regulatory Reform in Advanced Industrial Countries*. Ithaca, NY: Cornell University Press.

Ward, Andrew. 2009. "Obama Urges Restraint over Bonus Penalties." *Financial Times*, March 24.

Weaver, Karen. 2008. "US Asset-Backed Securities Market: Review and Outlook." In Deutchebank, *Global Securitisation and Structured Finance.* (http://www.globalsecuritisation.com/08).

Wolf, Martin. 2009. "Why a Successful US Bank Rescue Is Still So Far Away." *Financial Times*, March 24.

Working Group on Financial Stability. 2009. "Financial Reform: A Framework for Financial Stability." *Group of Thirty*. Washington DC, January 15.

5

Barack Obama's Election and America's Racial Orders[1]

Rogers M. Smith and Desmond King

BARACK OBAMA'S RISE to the presidency has been accompanied by much debate, in both academia and popular political discourse, over whether his success represents a "postracial" politics or is the harbinger of a postracial era in U.S. politics (e.g., Connerly 2008; Street 2008; Bobo and Dawson 2008, 1; Sinclair-Chapman and Price 2008, 739). Though there is great skepticism, particularly in academia, about whether the United States is genuinely moving beyond a politics shaped by racial divisions, even skeptics accept that Obama ran a postracial, or at least a "race-neutral," campaign (Baiocchi 2008; Sinclair-Chapman and Price 2008, 741). Here we seek not to challenge but to give greater specificity to these contentions by analyzing the 2008 presidential campaign strategies and the prospects for racial equity in the nation's future through the lens of what we have argued to be the basic structure of American racial politics: the continuing clashes between America's rival racial institutional orders (King and Smith 2005; 2008; 2011).

I. Was It a Postracial Election?

To understand if it makes sense to analyze the present and future of U.S. politics in postracial terms, we begin with the question: Should we simply accept that the United States has already entered an era of postracial politics? After all, a major party nominated and elected a presidential candidate commonly seen as black, and neither that candidate nor his opponent focused on race or racial issues during the campaign and in their proposed policy choices facing the country. Surely this silence about race and racial policies is a defining characteristic of a postracial politics.

Though we agree that a postracial politics would display such silence, race may be excluded from discussion for different reasons, as the nineteenth-century gag rule showed. We argue that modern alliances on racial issues, not the absence of racial concerns, moved discussions of race to the margins of both campaigns in 2008. Note that not only was Barack Obama the first non-white candidate ever to be nominated by a major party in the United States for either president or vice president, but also, though all of humanity probably originated in Africa, Obama was the first person of known, modern African descent to be nominated and elected in a country with a European-descended majority population anywhere in the world, including all of North America, South America, Australia, and Asia, as well as Europe. Many of those continents have far from trivial percentages of African-descended populations. It is simply inconceivable that such a broad pattern of political exclusion, dating back for more than six centuries, can be altered without consciousness of race playing a significant part.

It may be said, however, that although Americans grasped the momentous novelty of Obama's candidacy, racial equity in the United States has improved so greatly that it is understandable that neither candidate focused on race or race-related problems. That contention is, if anything, even more of a nonstarter. The familiar, painful litany of the United States' continuing and severe racial gaps in material well-being encompasses virtually every dimension of life, from economic well-being to health to housing to education to the criminal justice system. And though the United States has become a more multiracial nation and is becoming still more so, the sharpest divides remain between blacks and whites. We summarize those gaps because they remain the baseline for any credible analysis of American racial politics.

Economic Well-Being

In 2007, as the current deep recession was just beginning, the poverty rate among African Americans was already 24.5 percent, almost three times what it was for non-Hispanic whites (8.2 percent) (DeNavas-Walt et al. 2008). Among blacks, 11.2 percent were in deep poverty, with incomes less than 50 percent of the official poverty rate, compared with 3.4 percent non-Hispanic whites. And significant inequalities persist above the poverty line: African American median household income in 2007 was 62 percent of the median non-Hispanic white household income (Danzinger and Danzinger 2006, 16, 27). African American family members also had to work for longer hours and more weeks a year to achieve their incomes. Thomas M. Shapiro estimates that in 2000, middle-income black families had to work the equivalent of twelve more weeks per year than white families to earn the same money (Shapiro 2004, 7). And as Melvin Oliver and

Shapiro (2006) have long argued, when we move from income to wealth, the disparities become sharper still. By 2004, the "black-white median net worth ratio" was 0.10, meaning that blacks controlled ten cents of net assets for every dollar of net worth possessed by whites (Oliver and Shapiro 2006, 204).

Health

Blacks today remain nearly twice as likely as whites to lack health insurance, 19.5 percent to 10.4 percent (DeNavas-Walt et al. 2008). The black infant mortality rate is more than twice that of whites—13.7 per 1,000 births versus 5.7 and 5.6, respectively—and life expectancy for black men is six years less than for white men, while for black women it is five years less than for white women (National Center for Health Statistics 2007, 50, 167). Stress-related chronic diseases are a prominent source of these lower life expectancies (Geronimus and Thomson 2004, 249). These worrying statistics arise in part from other inequalities, such as differing labor market opportunities and participation rates. In 2000, roughly 33 percent of black men over 18 years old were not participating in the labor force, compared with 15 percent of white men—a ratio that held for men in their prime earning years, 31 to 50 years of age (Katz et al. 2005, 82).

Housing

There is still a large gap between black household heads who own their own homes (48.4 percent in 2003) and whites who do so (75 percent), and the gap grew between 1990 and 2003, even though home ownership also rose in both groups (Katz et al. 2005, 104; Center for Responsible Lending 2004). That disparate home ownership is not equally stable, either. The Center for Responsible Lending has reported that in 2002, blacks were "3.6 times as likely as whites to receive a home purchase loan from a subprime lender, and 4.1 times as likely as whites to receive a refinance loan from a subprime lender" (Center for Responsible Lending 2004). The higher rates of subprime lending persist even at higher income levels (Fernandez 2007). These circumstances have made it inevitable for blacks to be especially likely to lose their homes during the current foreclosure crisis.

Education

As the Supreme Court has become increasingly reluctant to view patterns of school segregation as constitutional violations, U.S. schools have become still more segregated, as a leading study documents: "The percentage of black students attending majority nonwhite schools increased in all regions from 66 percent in 1991 to 73 percent in 2003–4" (Orfield and Lee 2006, 9). If all students reached comparable levels of educational attainment, that trend might not cause such concern. But in 2000, just 12 percent of black men aged 24–30 years had graduated from college, compared with 30 percent of white men, while black women graduated at the rate of 15 percent, compared with a rate of 33 percent for white women (Katz et al. 2005, 93–94). *Separate* is still too strongly associated with *unequal* in American education as a whole.

Incarceration

Perhaps most notoriously, African Americans have been disproportionately affected by the U.S. explosion in incarceration in the last three decades—the rise of what has become known as the "prison-industrial complex" (Schlosser 1998). By 2005, black men were incarcerated at a rate of 4,682 per 100,000, compared with 709 per 100,000 for white men; and black women were incarcerated at a rate of 347 per 100,000, compared with 88 per 100,000 for white women (Katz et al. 2005, 128). The war on drugs has been decisive to this pattern: rates of drug use among whites and African Americans are not reflected proportionately in arrests (Sentencing Project 2008, 2). Cumulatively, these statistics make it impossible to conclude that there are no longer significant race-related policy issues in the modern United States. To understand why both major candidates shied away from discussions of race and the racial dimensions of policy issues, and what these circumstances portend for the future under President Obama, we must grasp the structure of racial politics in the United States today.

II. Racial Institutional Orders

We contend that the structure of racial politics today, as in the past, is composed of rival *racial institutional orders*. Racial institutional orders are durable alliances of political actors, activist groups, and governing institutions united by their agreement on the central racial issue of their time, which their conflicts help to define. These alliances seek political power to resist or to advance the measures that promote greater material race equality and that are politically pivotal in their time (King and Smith 2005, 2011). So far, there have been three eras of rival racial orders, interspersed with periods of transition. In each of these eras, one order has promoted arrangements thought to advantage those labeled *white*, while a rival order has sought to end many of those advantages.

The three eras thus defined are: the *slavery era*, which spans from 1789 to 1865, when maintaining and extending slavery were the battleground issues; the *Jim Crow era*, which, following a transition period, spans from the mid-1890s to 1954, when maintaining and extending *de jure* segregation and effective black disfranchisement were the central issues; and the modern era of *race-conscious controversies*, which, after a transition period, spans from the mid-1970s and continues today, with its defining battles over whether public policies should be "color-blind" or "race conscious" (King and Smith 2008, 686–688).

During the slavery and Jim Crow eras, the strength of each of the rival racial orders fluctuated over time, but one side eventually achieved a decisive and enduring victory. In the transition periods following these eras, coalitions re-formed in support of or in opposition to different policies, with each side claiming to accept the positions that ultimately prevailed from the previous period. Thus champions of Jim Crow did not seek to restore legal chattel slavery. They instead advocated "separate but equal policies" that antisegregation forces argued, convincingly, were efforts to perpetuate white supremacy, but in different forms and through different means.

Today, proponents of color-blind policies do not seek to restore *de jure* Jim Crow segregation laws. Indeed, both modern advocates of color-blind policies and modern proponents of race-conscious policies see themselves as the true heirs of the triumphant antisegregation civil rights movement, and both criticize their opponents for betraying its aims. For color-blind alliance members, the civil rights movement centered on Martin Luther King Jr.'s famed hope that persons would be judged not by the color of their skin but by the content of their character. They believe that race-conscious measures violate that aspiration and perpetuate racial divisions. For race-conscious alliance members, the civil rights movement's central aim was to reduce entrenched, unjust, material racial inequalities. They see their opponents' rejection of race-targeted policies as perpetuating and even exacerbating pervasive inherited white advantages, whether or not that outcome is intended. We have argued that these two modern racial orders emerged initially over issues of affirmative action in employment, but they also formed in response to legislative and judicial struggles over other issues, including majority-minority districts, census categories, school vouchers, and much more (King and Smith 2008, 700). Table 5.1 summarizes their structure.

Note that some members of the color-blind order, such as white supremacists, clearly support color-blind policies such as affirmative action for strictly tactical, politically potent means to preserve white advantages, while

Table 5.1. America's Institutional Racial Orders

Color-Blind Order, 1978–2009
Most Republican Party officeholders and members after 1976
President, 1981–1993, 2001–2009
Some conservative, neoconservative Democrats
Majority of Supreme Court after 1980
Most lower federal court judges, many state judges after 1980
Some white-owned businesses and business lobbyists
Conservative think tanks advocacy groups (e.g., Center for Individual Rights, Cato Institute)
Fringe white supremacist groups
Christian-Right groups (e.g., Family Research Council)
Conservative media (e.g., Rush Limbaugh)
Conservative foundations (e.g., Bradley Foundation)

Race-Conscious Order, 1978–2009
Most Democratic Party officeholders and members
President (mixed support), 1993–2001
Some liberal, pro-corporate Republicans
Some federal, state judges
Many civil service members of executive agencies
Many large businesses, minority-owned businesses
Most labor unions
Military leadership
Liberal advocacy groups (e.g., ACLU)
Most non-white advocacy groups (e.g., NAACP, National Council of La Raza, Asian American Legal Defense Fund)
Liberal media (e.g., *New York Times*)
Liberal religious groups (e.g., National Council of Churches)
Liberal foundations (e.g., Soros, Ford)

---

other members undoubtedly support these policies sincerely. Though we are unable to judge their proportions or motives, we presume that most proponents of color-blind policies genuinely believe these measures are best for both racial progress and justice. Note also that these modern coalitions cannot be adequately grasped in class terms: the business sector is divided on race-conscious measures, while most unions, formerly frequent opponents of civil rights reforms, now largely support them. But in sharp contrast to the racial alliances of the Jim Crow era, the modern rival racial orders are much more closely identified with the two major political parties. Whereas both parties before 1954 contained segregationists and antisegregationists, today Republicans overwhelmingly favor color-blind policies and the great majority of Democrats favor race-conscious measures, as indicated by their party platforms since 1976 (King and Smith 2008, 691). This partisan polarization on racial issues is consistent with and may indeed be a significant contributor to the heightened partisan polarization documented by many political scientists (e.g., McCarty et al. 2006). And primarily because most U.S. voters are white, and most whites oppose race-conscious policies, the color-blind alliance rose to predominance in the last two decades of the twentieth century along with the GOP, though without ever wholly eclipsing race-conscious proponents, institutions, and policies (King and Smith 2008, 692; 2011, chap. 9).

III. Modern Racial Orders and the 2008 Election

This structure of partisan-allied rival racial orders affected both the McCain and the Obama candidacies. First, Senator McCain, as the champion of the color-blind alliance, could not openly express concern about the race of his opponent: after all, the ideology of his coalition was that race should be treated as politically irrelevant. At the same time, simply because Barack Obama appears black to most Americans, his candidacy undoubtedly raised worries among many in the color-blind order that a President Obama would expand pro-black racial preferences in many ways. But unless Obama provided an opening by strongly advocating such policies, which he was careful not to do, the McCain campaign had the challenge of making those concerns salient to voters without explicitly speaking of race. This may account for the McCain ads asking, "Who is the real Barack Obama?" and claiming that McCain was, in contrast, "the American president Americans have been waiting for" (Kurtz 2008; Raasch 2008). McCain also accused Obama of pursuing a socialist agenda (Curl 2008). And at its close, the McCain campaign spotlighted Joe the Plumber, who repeatedly urged the electorate to "Vote for a real American, John McCain" (Bash 2008). All these tropes represented efforts to raise doubts and to plant fears about Obama, and for at least some of those who favored color-blind policies, those fears must have included concerns that he would champion racial preferences.

Obama faced complementary strategic challenges when campaigning for the presidency as a black American at a time when most voters leaned toward color-blind policies. Press coverage based on interviews with white working-class voters suggest that it would have been enormously difficult for him to speak extensively about race and racial equity issues without triggering widespread anxieties over his support of more expansive race-targeted programs, anxieties that might well have insured his defeat (Wallsten 2008; Simkins 2008). At the same time, his racial identity and his background as a civil rights lawyer meant that many proponents of race-conscious measures were willing to presume he would be far more sympathetic to their concerns than his opponent would, without Obama having to articulate a specifically racial agenda. Even so, Obama would have alienated important segments of his core supporters if he had repudiated race-conscious programs and policies. Hence his best option was to campaign in ways that were largely "race neutral" in the policies he foregrounded, while retaining in the background indications of constrained but continuing support for race-conscious measures such as affirmative action.

Obama made it very clear in his book of policy and campaign positions, *The Audacity of Hope*, that he did indeed favor this strategy for these reasons. In his chapter "Race," Obama offered "a word of caution" about whether "we have arrived at a 'postracial' politics" or "already live in a color-blind society" (Obama 2006, 232). He referred briefly to the sort of statistics on persisting racial inequalities that we have reviewed, as well as to his own personal experiences of racism. Obama then argued, in accord with moderate race-conscious proponents, that "affirmative action programs, when properly structured, can open up opportunities otherwise closed to qualified minorities without diminishing opportunities for white students"; and he added that "where there's strong evidence of prolonged and systematic discrimination by large corporations, trade unions, or branches of municipal government, goals and timetables for minority hiring may be the only meaningful remedy available" (p. 244). But Obama also stressed his understanding of the arguments of those who favor color-blind measures. He advocated an "emphasis on universal, as opposed to race-specific programs" as not only "good policy" but also as "good politics" (p. 247). He concluded: "Proposals that solely benefit minorities and dissect Americans into 'us' and 'them' may generate a few short-term concessions when the costs to whites aren't too high, but they can't serve as the basis for the kinds of sustained, broad-based political coalitions needed to transform America" (p. 248).

In so arguing, in his book and his campaign, Obama sought to build a new, broader coalition that blended those Americans who predominantly favor color-blind policies but who do want to see real material racial progress and can tolerate a few race-conscious measures, with those who think substantial race-conscious measures are needed, but who are willing to see them put on the back burner if progress is indeed being achieved through other means. He did this, for the most part, simply by not talking about race and by minimizing its likely impact on the election, thereby permitting color-blind and race-conscious advocates to interpret his rhetorical emphases on both unity and change in terms congenial to them. But Obama did, of course, feel compelled by the controversy over the racial views of his long-time pastor, Reverend Jeremiah Wright, to address race directly in his speech at the National Constitution Center on March 18, 2008.

There, in contrast to the dominant approach in his campaign, Obama stated, "Race is an issue that I believe this nation cannot afford to ignore right now." He called attention again to persisting material racial "disparities," many of which, he argued, "can be directly traced to inequalities passed on from an earlier generation that suffered under the brutal legacy of slavery and Jim Crow." To the dissatisfaction of some critics, Obama suggested only briefly that "current incidents of discrimination" were also sources of those inequalities. But he did argue, as we have here, that anger "over welfare and affirmative action helped forge the Reagan Coalition," and he contended that conservative politicians and commentators "exploited fears of crime" and built careers "unmasking bogus claims of racism while dismissing legitimate discussions of racial injustice" (Obama 2008a). Nonetheless, Obama counseled against labeling "the resentments of white Americans" as "misguided or even racist." Instead, echoing his arguments in *The Audacity of Hope*, Obama urged "the African-American community" to bind "our particular grievances" with "the larger aspirations of all Americans" by focusing on "investing in our schools and our communities; by enforcing our civil rights laws and ensuring fairness in our criminal justice system; by providing this generation with ladders of opportunity that were unavailable to previous generations." He urged "all Americans to realize that your dreams do not have to come at the expense of my dreams; that investing in the health, welfare and education of black and brown and white children will ultimately help all of America prosper" (Obama 2008a).

In these ways, Obama adroitly restated the central theme of his campaign as embodied in his own life story: the nation must continue to strive to achieve the promise of *e pluribus unum*: "That out of many, we are truly one" (Obama 2008a). He neither minimized the persistence of racial inequalities nor repudiated all race conscious measures, but his emphasis remained on programs, principles, and purposes designed to further the shared values and goals of all Americans.

IV. Beyond the 2008 Election

Aided by a not particularly adept opponent representing a party tied to two long-lasting, increasingly unpopular wars and the worst economic crisis since the Depression, Obama won his historic victory in November 2008. But he also said in his National Convention Center speech, "I have never been so naïve as to believe that we can get beyond our racial divisions in a single election cycle, or with a single candidacy" (Obama 2008a). And so the question remains: If the structuring of American racial politics via struggles between color-blind and race-conscious racial orders helps explain the ways the major party candidates dealt with race in the 2008 campaign, what does the electoral success of Obama's strategy of foregrounding universal programs without repudiating all race-conscious measures mean for whether the Obama administration will move the nation further toward a postracial era?

Again, the starting point for any credible answer must be the long-standing and entrenched material racial inequalities that are present in virtually all spheres of American life. As Obama himself acknowledges, as long as those racial disparities persist, it is a virtual certainty that racial divisions will be visible in American politics as well. And in many ways, the economic recession has deepened the disparities—for example in respect to home ownership and differential levels of unemployment—between African Americans and whites.

The first answer to whether the United States is on its way to a postracial political future, then, is that it depends on whether Obama's combination of "mostly universal/partly race-conscious programs" succeeds in improving many of those patterns of material inequality. At this juncture, it is clear that several programs have been designed to advance this agenda, including the stimulus package (the American Recovery and Reinvestment Act 2009), additional funding for education as part of the stimulus, and most fundamentally, health care reform (the Patient Protection and Affordable Care Act), enacted in the summer of 2010. These are notable achievements. Still, the fact that President Obama's administration seeks to reduce severe material racial gaps while at the same time leading the nation to overcome its worst economic crisis in modern times means that the prospects for dramatic progress in diminishing racial inequalities in the foreseeable future are not good. Nonetheless, the Obama administration's refusal to give up health care reform despite the loss of a Democratic Senate seat in Massachusetts in February 2010 (which led many critics to urge such a change of course) implies a lasting commitment to addressing the United States' entrenched race disparities. If the economy appears at least to be moving in the right direction, Obama may be able to sustain and even broaden his coalition, making a second term and further change possible; though at this writing, the ballooning fiscal deficits and national debt have created a new focus that militates against new policy initiatives. So the notion that Americans will make enough advances in reducing racial inequalities to foster a postracial politics is utopian.

That conclusion will not seem particularly surprising or controversial to most readers. But there is also a second, somewhat less obvious reason that Obama's election and his program do not signify a postracial American political future, much less the achievement of a postracial United States in the present. This reason might be termed the *multicultural challenge*. It is a challenge that goes to the heart of Obama's core promise: to embrace the diversity of Americans and yet to find ways to "bridge our differences and unite in common effort—black, white, Latino, Asian, Native American; Democrat and Republican, young and old, rich and poor, gay and straight, disabled or not," as he put it in his Ohio "closing statement" near the end of the campaign. All Americans are to come to feel and act politically as "one nation, and one people" who will together "once more choose our better history" (Obama 2008b).

One reason that this promise is so challenging is that Americans do not agree on what constitutes their "better history." Some see the spread of religious diversity and considerable secularity, for example, as advances for freedom. Others see those developments as a retreat from the United States' true calling to be a shining "Christian nation." Some believe that their country's "best history" centers on the realization of ideals arising in historically Anglo-American cultural traditions. Others see those cultural traditions as historically responsible for the repression of communities and identities that they regard as most valuable and most their own. Put more broadly, the difficulty is that it may well be impossible to give any specific content to the putative shared, unifying values and purposes of Americans, without appearing to fail to recognize and accommodate adequately the diversity of values and purposes that Americans in fact exhibit.

Obama, of course, presents his own identity as a preeminent example of how unity can be forged from a background encompassing a remarkably broad mix of races, religions, nationalities, geographic residences, educational systems, and economic statuses. But his identity has arguably been forged most of all by his choices to embrace much that characterizes dominant but contested forms of American identity, including Christianity over Islam or secularity, U.S. patriotism over cosmopolitanism or foreign allegiances, and a stress on unity across the races over racial separatism. Among the race-conscious coalition that forms a substantial part of Obama's political base, there are many who favor a more overtly multicultural America. This vision depicts a greater diversity of community identities, both subnational and transnational, which would be not only tolerated but also actively assisted by public systems of political representation, public aid programs, educational curriculum, legally recognized group rights, and many more. Even if by some miracle severe racial inequalities were sharply alleviated during an Obama administration, controversies will likely still remain over whether the kind of unity out of diversity that he offers as a shared national ideal really fulfills the aspirations of all, or even most, of the persons and communities whose differences he seeks to bridge. And because those diverse aspirations include differing visions among members of existing racial groups, it is likely that a United States marked by such controversies will still not be a United States whose politics can credibly be deemed postracial. Nor is it at all clear that it should be: multicultural ideals have force in part because there are good reasons to doubt the propriety of a strongly unified sense of American national identity and purpose.

But even if it is not likely that the United States has entered or stands on the threshold of a postracial political era, and even if there are legitimate debates over whether that goal is desirable, it is also true that the election of 2008 made real a form of racial progress that many thought virtually impossible. Because it did, there are grounds for believing that the Obama administration is working to reduce unjust racial inequalities (such as those related to health) and to foster among Americans a broadly shared sense of common values and purposes that embraces legitimate forms of diversity. Admittedly, the difficulties in making such progress increase every day that the current economic crisis persists; but crises often bring great opportunities as well as great challenges. If that conclusion seems optimistic, we submit that at this historical moment, more than most others, it is permissible to entertain what America's first black president—following Reverend Wright—has appropriately termed *the audacity of hope*.

Note

1. An earlier version of this paper appeared in *Du Bois Review* 6(1) (2009): 9–15. It is used here with the permission of Cambridge University Press. Blame and credit for all our collaborative works should be apportioned equally. The order of the authors' names indicates only which author initiated a particular project. We are grateful to Timothy Weaver for excellent research assistance.

References

Baiocchi, Gianpalo. 2008. "Comments in Panel Discussion: The Social Significance of Barack Obama," Moderated by Doug Harmann. *Contexts* 7(4): 18.

Bash, Dana. 2008. "Joe the Plumber—A No Show!" AC360° Blog, October 30. (http://ac360.blogs.cnn.com/2008/10/30/joe-the-plumber-a-no-show/), accessed March 5, 2009.

Bobo, Lawrence D., and Michael C. Dawson. 2008. "The 'Work' Race Does: Back to the Future." *Du Bois Review* 5(1): 1–4.

Center for Responsible Lending. 2004. *African American Homes at Risk: Predatory Mortgage Lending*. Durham, NC: Center for Responsible Lending.

Connerly, Ward. 2008. "Obama is No 'Post-Racial' Candidate." *Wall Street Journal*, June 13, A15.

Curl, Joseph. 2008. "McCain Decries Obama's 'Socialism.'" *Washington Times*, October 19. (http://www.washingtontimes.com/news/2008/oct/19/), accessed March 5, 2009.

Danzinger, Sheldon, and Sandra K. Danzinger. 2006. "Poverty, Race, and Antipoverty Policy Before and After Hurricane Katrina." *Du Bois Review* 3(1): 23–36.

DeNavas-Walt, Carmen, Bernadette D. Proctor, and Jessica C. Smith (2008). *Income, Poverty, and Health Insurance Coverage in the United States: 2007*. Washington, DC: U.S. Government Printing Office. (http://www.census.gov/prod/2008pubs/p60-235.pdf), accessed March 5, 2009.

Fernandez, Manny. 2007. "Study Finds Disparities in Mortgages by Race." *New York Times*, October 15. (http://www.nytimes.com/2007/10015/nyregion/15subprime.html/), accessed March 5, 2009.

Geronimus, Arline T., and J. Phillip Thomson. 2004. "To Denigrate, Ignore, and/or Disrupt: Racial Inequality in Health and the Impact of Policy-Induced Breakdown of African American Communities." *Du Bois Review* 1(2): 247–279.

Katz, Michael B., Mark J. Stern, and Jamie J. Fader. 2005. "The New African American Inequality." *Journal of American History* 92(1): 75–108.

King, Desmond, and Rogers M. Smith. 2005. "Racial Orders in American Political Development." *American Political Science Review* 99(1): 75–92.

King, Desmond, and Rogers M. Smith. 2008. "Strange Bedfellows? Polarized Politics? The Quest for Racial Equity in Contemporary America." *Political Research Quarterly* 61(4): 686–703.

King, Desmond, and Rogers M. Smith. 2011. *Still a House Divided: Race and Politics in Obama's America*. Princeton, NJ: Princeton University Press.

Kurtz, Howard. 2008. "McCain Spot Asks: 'Who is Barack Obama?'" *Washington Post*, Trail Blog, October 6. (http://voices.washingtonpost.com/the-trail/2008/10/60), accessed March 5, 2009.

McCarty, Nolan, Keith T. Poole, and Howard Rosenthal. 2006. *Polarized America: The Dance of Ideology and Unequal Riches*. Cambridge, MA: MIT Press.

National Center for Health Statistics. 2007. *Health, United States, 2007.* Hyattsville, MD: National Center for Health Statistics. (http://www.cdec.gov/nchs/data/hus/hus07.pdf), accessed March 5, 2009.

Obama, Barack. 2006. *The Audacity of Hope: Thoughts on Reclaiming the American Dream.* New York: Three Rivers.

Obama, Barack. 2008a. "A More Perfect Union: Transcript of Obama's Speech on Race as Prepared for Delivery." *MSNBC.com*, March 18. (http://www.msnbc.msn.com/id/23690567), accessed March 5, 2009.

Obama, Barack. 2008b. "Obama's Speech in Canton, Ohio." *New York Times*, October 27. (http://www.nytimes.com/2008/10027/us/politics/27text-obama.html/), accessed March 5, 2009.

Oliver, Melvin L., and Thomas M. Shapiro. 2006. *Black Wealth/White Wealth: A New Perspective on Racial Inequality*, 2nd ed. New York: Routledge.

Orfield, Gary, and Chungmei Lee. 2006. *Racial Transformation and the Changing Nature of Segregation.* Cambridge, MA: Civil Rights Project at Harvard University.

Raasch, Chuck. 2008. "McCain's 'American' Claim Sparks Critics." *USA Today*, April 3. (http://www.usatoday.com/news/opinion/columnist/raasch/2008-04-03-raasch_N.htm/), accessed March 5, 2009.

Schlosser, Eric. 1998. "The Prison-Industrial Complex." *Atlantic Monthly*, December. (http://www.theatlantic.com/doc/199812/prisons), accessed March 5, 2009.

Sentencing Project. 2008. *Disparity by Geography: The War on Drugs in America's Cities.* Washington, DC: Sentencing Project.

Shapiro, Thomas M. 2004. *The Hidden Cost of Being African American: How Wealth Perpetuates Inequality.* New York: Oxford University Press.

Simkins, Chris. 2008. "US Voters Offer Opinions about Barack Obama, His Race, and Its Impact on the Upcoming Election." *Voice of America News*, October 14. (http://www.voanews.com/english/Africa/2008-10/2008-10-14-voa36.cfm), accessed March 5, 2009.

Sinclair-Chapman, Valeria, and Melanye Price. 2008. "Black Politics, the 2008 Election, and the (Im/Possibility of Race Transcendence." *PS: Political Science and Politics* 61(4): 739–745.

Street, Paul. 2008. "White American Lives in Vicious Racial Denial—Obama Is Making It Worse." *Black Agenda Report*, October 3. (http://www.blackagendareport.com), accessed March 5, 2009.

Wallsten, Peter. 2008. "For Obama, an Uphill Climb in Appalachia." *Los Angeles Times*, October 5, A-1.

PART IV

Obama's Critical Juncture

6

American Renewal and the Politics of the New Middle America

E. J. Dionne Jr.

AMONG THE MANY poll findings explaining the results of the 2010 elections, three were particularly illuminating. First, the age composition of the electorate changed radically. In 2008, 18 percent of voters were under 30, and 16 percent were over 65.[1] In 2010, only 12 percent were under 30, while 21 percent were over 65.[2] Not surprisingly, 2010's older electorate was more conservative. Second, Democrats lost enormous ground among white working-class voters. In 2010, Democrats lost white working-class voters by 30 points.[3] In 2006 and 2008, they had lost these voters by only 10 points.[4] Third, Republicans won control of the House of Representatives because many voters who didn't really like the GOP voted for its candidates anyway. According to the networks' exit polls, 53 percent of November voters had an unfavorable view of the Republican Party; yet 23 percent of this group nonetheless voted for Republican House candidates.[5] These are the quintessential disaffected voters, and they may be the key swing voters of 2012.

I. Retrospective Voters: Dispirited and Disappointed

Combined, these numbers reveal a country and an electorate that was not so much angry as dispirited. True, anger on the Right drove conservative turnout to very high levels. But in core Democratic constituencies and in the middle of the electorate, disappointment more than rage drove decisions, including decisions to stay home.

That disappointment was the mirror image of the hopefulness that inspired Barack Obama's movement in 2008. Even if Obama and the 111th

Congress produced a remarkable legislative record, the president's first two years did not—maybe could not—live up to the dreams and imaginings of the young. The working class was mired in an economic downturn that showed no signs of ending quickly—and this after a long period of income stagnation in supposedly good times.

Thus did so many voters who had little confidence in the Republicans cast grudging protest ballots for the GOP, signaling disappointment with the economic and political performance under a Democratic Congress and White House. These are the voters who cost the Democrats 27 of their 63 House seats in the great belt of states that had once constituted the nation's industrial heartland: New York, New Jersey, Pennsylvania, Ohio, Indiana, Illinois, Michigan, and Wisconsin.[6] Losses in these states alone more than accounted for the difference between majority and minority status for the Democrats in the House. Absent a strategy to recapture the respect of voters in the Greater Midwest— Middle Americans in every sense of the term—Democrats and progressives will find themselves isolated. To these voters, attention must be paid.

For a *Washington Post* column after the election, I interviewed some of the vanquished House members who rode to office on the 2006 or 2008 Democratic waves.[7] Perhaps the most poignant testimony came from Mary Jo Kilroy, who lost her seat centered around Columbus, Ohio. In almost every respect, Kilroy is a Middle American Democrat, in touch with the aspirations of her district and insistent that her role is to represent the poor and the middle class alike. With experience rooted in school board politics, she is grounded in the values no less than the interests of her constituents.

The party's losses among white working-class voters came as no shock to Kilroy. "I watched them in the last four years go from being anxious about the future to being worried, but also hopeful during the 2008 campaign, to being very angry." To explain, she invoked the world as seen by a person "who worked at Siemens for 25 years," a large, global electronics company that had cut employment in her area.

"You have a son who is a high school basketball player and wants to go to college—and then your factory goes off to Mexico," she said. "And you're a man of a certain age and another factory or another employer won't give you a second look. Think of the despair felt by that person."

Voters in this fix, she said, see Washington as "a place where their interests get sold out." What they want is "to feel they're being treated as well as the bankers who get bailed out." Indeed. The exit poll found that 35 percent of the 2010 voters blamed Wall Street rather than either Barack Obama or George W. Bush for the nation's economic problems—and among this group,

Republican House candidates led Democrats, 57 percent to 41 percent.[8] When critics of Wall Street vote overwhelmingly for the Republicans, something is awry in the Democrats' approach.

II. Which "New Majority" and the Limits of Old Arguments

For years, progressives have debated whether they can build a new majority on the basis of well-educated middle- and upper-middle-income white voters, allied with African Americans, Hispanics, and the young. In a view that became increasingly popular after the Democrats' 2006 and 2008 victories, white working-class voters were seen as a shrinking share of the electorate already alienated from liberal candidates by concerns related to religious matters, gun control, and, in some cases, race and immigration.

During the 2008 primary campaign, Obama kicked up immense controversy by seeming to embrace this view. "So it's not surprising then that they get bitter," he told an affluent crowd at a San Francisco fund-raiser, speaking about downscale whites. "They cling to guns or religion or antipathy to people who aren't like them or anti-immigrant sentiment or anti-trade sentiment as a way to explain their frustrations."[9] Later, Obama insisted that he was not out of touch with such voters, but rather understood precisely why they were embittered. "I know what's going on in Indiana, I know what's going on in Illinois," he said. "People are fed up, they're angry, they're frustrated, they're bitter and they want to see a change in Washington."[10] Nonetheless, the controversy resonated because the debate that lay beneath it was very much alive among progressives and Democrats.

It is, in fact, a very old controversy. Following Richard Nixon's 1968 election victory, Fred Dutton, once an aide to Robert F. Kennedy, and a well-known lobbyist, wrote an influential book entitled *Changing Sources of Power: American Politics in the 1970s*. Dutton argued that the progressive future lay with new and younger voters who had been politicized by the movements for civil rights and against the Vietnam War and were more focused on social than economic issues. These voters provided an alternative to the old labor-liberal alliance that had very nearly pushed Hubert Humphrey past Richard Nixon. At the time, Dutton's volume was widely seen as a counterpoint to what was arguably an even more influential book published in 1970, a year before his. In *The Real Majority*, Richard Scammon and Ben Wattenberg contended that the American majority was "unyoung, unpoor and unblack" and that the central figure of American politics was "a 47-year-old housewife from the outskirts of Dayton, Ohio, whose husband is a machinist." (Blue Collar Ohio, it seems, is *always* at the center of discussions of this sort.)

In the world of political sociology, the argument was joined by Ronald Inglehart. His 1977 book, *The Silent Revolution*, argued from extensive survey research that Western societies were moving from old "materialist values" centering on economic and physical security to "post-materialist" values that emphasized personal autonomy and self-expression. Inglehart's thesis anticipated the rise of Green parties in Europe and the growing role of a progressive, educated class in the traditional socialist, social democratic and leftist-liberal parties once rooted in the labor movement. Inglehart's approach was seen by its enthusiasts as transcending Seymour Martin Lipset's argument in *Political Man*, published in 1960, that elections in "every modern democracy" reflected a "democratic translation of the class struggle." Even if many parties renounced "the principle of class conflict or loyalty," Lipset argued, "parties are primarily based on either the lower classes or the middle and upper classes." As a rule, Lipset observed, leftist parties won over less affluent voters by emphasizing "the need for security of income," "the need for satisfying work," and "the need for status, for social recognition of one's value and freedom from degrading discrimination in social relations."

Seen from the perspective of 2011, progressive political parties are still trying to square the insights of Dutton, and Scammon and Wattenberg, with Inglehart and Lipset. Progressives in all the democracies now count on the ballots of well-educated middle-class voters in a way they did not in the 1930s, 1940s, or 1950s. Whether these voters can fairly be called "post-materialist"— post-materialism being an easier disposition in economic booms than in busts—Inglehart was right about the new emphasis on autonomy and self-expression in democratic politics. But Lipset's insight that elections are an expression of a "democratic class struggle" still holds. Indeed, it may be more apt than ever, given the dwindling security of the working middle class and the expanding role of corporate contributions in the electoral world created by the U.S. Supreme Court's *Citizens United v. Federal Election Commission*[11] decision in January 2010, which broke with decades of precedent in declaring that Congress had no right to ban direct corporate spending to influence the outcome of elections.

Yet the results of the 2010 elections at least partially settled the Lipset-Inglehart argument by underscoring the limits of a politics based on an upscale-minority coalition. If the outcomes in 2006 and 2008 showed that progressives and Democrats can split or slightly lose the white working-class vote and still secure a majority, 2010 showed that they simply cannot expect victory when the white working class turns against them by landslide proportions. Again: attention must be paid.

And addressing the aspirations and needs of Middle American voters is essential not only for the pursuit of white working-class voters by liberals and Democrats, but also for their capacity to maintain high levels of support and participation by African Americans and Latino voters as well. For the 2010 election also saw a decline in African American electoral participation and uneven Hispanic participation. As Ruy Teixeira and John Halpin noted in their post-election report for the Center for American Progress, the minority share of the electorate dropped from 26 percent in 2008 to 23 percent in 2010. "This was a sharp drop by recent standards," they wrote. The prospect of the first African American president boosted black voter participation to extraordinary levels in 2008 and raised the Democratic share of the African American presidential vote to an unprecedented (and almost impossible to repeat) 95 percent.[12] But the decline in the minority vote in just two years was a warning sign. Hope needs to be nurtured.

When it comes to both core values and economic interests, African Americans and Latinos are no less "Middle American" than are the white working and middle classes. The aspirations to work for a decent income, to become more affluent over the course of a working lifetime, to open new opportunities for one's children, to see the nation as a whole advance in prosperity and international influence, to have the values of "family, work, and neighborhood" —yes, they are Ronald Reagan's words[13]—reflected in social policy, and to see the religious convictions of those inspired by faith respected: these are commitments that cut across the lines so often perceived as dividing us.

Fear of American decline is the specter haunting our politics, and fear of the decline in the economic stability on which traditional American values rest is the specter haunting our moral debate. Poll findings on this matter were in many cases quite stark. A Fox News/Opinion Dynamics survey released in July 2010, for example, asked voters: "Do you think that the United States is on the rise as a civilization, or is it on the decline?" Among all voters, 62 percent saw the United States as on the decline. Not surprisingly, 76 percent of Republicans felt this way. But so did 64 percent of independents. And Democrats were closely split—43 percent said the United States was on the decline, 41 percent said it was on the rise.[14] Similarly, a Pew Research Center survey in December 2009 found 41 percent of the American public saying that the United States plays "a less important and powerful role as a world leader today," the highest percentage ever to take that view in Pew's surveys, and up from only 20 percent in 2004.[15]

The constituents whom Mary Jo Kilroy described care about their jobs *and* their families, their incomes *and* their country, their autonomy *and* their obligations. Middle Americans are sensibly hybrid beings: communitarian individualists, "tolerant traditionalists" (in William Galston's evocative phrase), and patriotic internationalists.

III. Obama's Difficulties

The difficulties of the first two Obama years heightened the very anxieties that led to his election—and this despite a long list of policy achievements in health care and in financial regulation, and in averting economic catastrophe. One can debate the various choices that Obama made: the original stimulus did need to be bigger; a health plan with a public option would, paradoxically, have been less complicated and easier to explain; his critique of Wall Street excess needed to be stronger and more consistent. Yet his achievements were substantial, and his political luck, so palpable through Election Day 2008, began to run out. Consider the contrast with Franklin Roosevelt, who took power after Herbert Hoover had presided over three of the most miserable years in American economic history. Blame was firmly fixed on Hoover by the time FDR showed up with his jaunty smile and contagious optimism. By contrast, the recent economic downturn may have begun on George W. Bush's watch, but its bitter fruits were harvested only after Obama took office, with month after month of job losses in the hundreds of thousands.

Yet the president himself was responsible for decisions that were within his control, and his central shortcomings were his overlapping failures to forge a clear link between his policies and the values that underlay them; and to offer a consistent and persistent case that his program constituted a straightforward path to renewed American strength and a more secure working and middle class.

The facts on the ground and the strategic failures allowed conservatism, a doctrine that seemed moribund on election night in 2008, to enjoy a far more rapid comeback than all liberals and even most conservatives anticipated. And the new brand of conservatism is far more zealous than the political disposition of either Ronald Reagan or George W. Bush. Barry Goldwater went down to a thunderous defeat in 1964 after he declared that "extremism in the defense of liberty is no vice." That might as well have been the working slogan of the Tea Party movement.

Understanding the Tea Party requires seeing it not only as a revolt against Obama, but also as a reaction to George W. Bush's presidency. In a remarkable essay, the historian Gary Gerstle argued that Bush's unique contribution to conservatism was the embrace of a "multiculturalism of the godly" through which Bush offered "groups of minority voters reason to rethink their traditional hostility to the GOP."[16]

Gerstle noted that on "questions of immigration and diversity, Bush was worlds apart from Patrick Buchanan and the social-conservative wing of the Republican Party" and "was comfortable with diversity, bilingualism and cultural pluralism, as long as members of America's ethnic and racial subcultures shared his patriotism, religious faith and political conservatism."

It was, Gerstle added, that at the "time in which the United States was at war and Europe was exploding with tension and violence over Islam, Bush played a positive role in keeping interethnic and interracial relations in the United States relatively calm."

Christopher Caldwell, a columnist for *The Financial Times*, was one of the first political writers to pick up on the significance of Dr. Gerstle's essay. An American conservative, Caldwell used it to critique Bush's multicultural and compassion agenda and to explain the Tea Party's rise. Intriguingly, he suggested that "many of the Tea Party's gripes about Mr. Obama can also be laid at the door of Mr. Bush."[17]

For example, the main effect of Mr. Bush's faith-based initiative, Caldwell argued, was to funnel "a lot of federal money to urban welfare and substance abuse programs." The No Child Left Behind Act, which "meant to improve educational outcomes for minorities, did so at the price of centralizing authority in Washington." And of course, there was Bush's 2007 immigration reform proposal, "the clearest sign that he was losing the ear of his party."

Whether one agrees or disagrees with Caldwell's views on the substance of the issues in question (I disagree and see the core problem with Bush's domestic compassion agenda as lying in how little money he put behind it), he is absolutely right in seeing that a twin reaction to *both* Bush and Obama helped push American conservatism well to the right of where it had been. The new disposition on the Right was rebellion against some of the more open and tolerant features of the Bush years, and for some, a rebellion against the idea that compassion is a legitimate object of public policy. The rise of this new conservatism helped explain some of the new ferocity in American politics.

In the face of this challenge, there was a dysfunction in the relationship between the White House and its sometimes-friends, sometimes-critics on the Left. The White House often found itself whining about its progressive critics and insisting that whatever the president happened to decide was the *only* sensible and realistic thing to do. For the Left, asking Obama to be bolder in testing the limits of the possible means it was doing its job of pushing the president to do more, and to do it faster.

In the meantime, progressives often spent more time complaining about what wasn't done than in finding ways to build on what had been achieved. It took decades to complete the modern Social Security system and years to move from tepid to robust civil rights laws and from modest to comprehensive environmental regulation. Impatience is indispensable to getting reform started; patience is essential to seeing its promise fulfilled.

And both the liberals and Obama found themselves trapped in the bubbles of legislative and narrowly ideological politics. They lost their capacity to engage the country's moral energies and visionary possibilities. Modern American liberalism, after all, was not some abstract creed. At its best, it had married a practical, get-things-done approach to government with a devotion to fairness, justice, and compassion. These sentiments were grounded in the nation's religious traditions and also in its commitment to community-building that Alexis de Tocqueville so appreciated.

It might be said that if conservatives talked so much about first principles that they seemed to forget how difficult it is to govern effectively, liberals talked so much about specific programs that they forget how much citizens care about the values that undergird those programs and the moral choices that nurture those values.

The contest for the second two years of the Obama's time in office would certainly be shaped most powerfully by the direction of the economy. But to the extent that the parties in the battle had a say in the matter, their battle was destined to be a fight over the definition of the contest itself. Republicans and conservatives set out to make cutting back the size of government and lacerating specific programs the central issue in American politics. They linked this to deficit reduction, but government's reach itself was their central concern. They also attended to reducing the influence of constituencies and organizations sympathetic to the Democratic Party. The most surprising development of 2011 was the war against public employee unions by Governor Scott Walker in Wisconsin and by other Republican chief executives— and the reaction to it in the country. It was a move that, if successful, could undercut the most active and well-financed organizations left on the progressive side of politics. But early polling suggested a surprising backlash against these efforts, particularly among the very white working-class voters who had swung so hard the Republicans' way. The future of American politics hung in part on whether the GOP's efforts against unions would backfire by pushing the voters so prized and carefully studied by Scammon and Wattenberg back to the Democratic Party. If ever there was a case of Lipset's "democratic class struggle," this was it.

But Obama, having been short of narrative in his first two years, seemed to go all-narrative as 2011 opened. Having won what was in effect a $900 billion stimulus package at the end 2010 by capitulating to Republican demands that Bush tax cuts for the wealthy be preserved, Obama used his State of the Union Address in the new year to answer those who feared that America was in decline. "Win the future" was the slogan Obama settled on, and he was to repeat over and over and over again in the coming months. "Our destiny remains our choice," he declared, and he proposed, as Kennedy had before him, to use government to restore American competitiveness, its capacity for innovation and its capacity to lead. It was a speech moderate in tone, and Obama resolutely set about in the weeks after he delivered it to place himself above what he felt that voters saw as the squabbling in Congress. But in the end, a choice would have to be made: between those who saw government as an impediment to American progress, and those who saw it as essential to the country's future. It was a very old American debate, and it would have to be joined again.

IV. A New Politics of Interests and Values

In certain ways, Obama was echoing a call issued in early 2011 by the social scientist Theda Skocpol for a "National Greatness Liberalism."[18] She defined it as "a brawny brand of politics that makes a tough-minded argument about what it will take from our government and democratic politics to regain our national economic strength and rebuild a broad, secure, and innovative middle class." Such a liberalism, she argued, was essential as well for America's standing in the world, for "[o]ur national military and diplomatic strength in a dangerous world depends, too, on our economic renewal as a middle-class capitalist economy."

If this seemed part of the recipe for a restored American liberalism, so, too, was the effort to link Middle American interests to Middle American values. In a powerful 2006 essay, the journalist Garance Franke-Ruta had called for a "remapping" of the cultural debate. Her key insight: "In today's society, traditional values have become aspirational."[19] Why? Because, as she noted, "lower-income individuals simply live in a much more disrupted society, with higher divorce rates, more single moms, more abortions, and more interpersonal and interfamily strife, than do the middle- and upper-middle class people they want to be like." The focus of many "middle-income voters on cultural traditionalism is not entirely separate from their economic aspirations."

She added: "Social solidarity and even simple familial stability have become part of the package of private privileges available to the well-to-do," and "there has been no one on the Democratic side in recent years to defend traditional, sensible middle-class values against the onslaught of the new nihilistic, macho, libertarian lawlessness unleashed by an economy that pits every man against his fellows."

Finding a way to link and resolve concerns over the stagnation of middle-class incomes, the decline in manufacturing employment in the American heartland, the new challenges to America's standing in the world, and the disruption of family and community life was, in fact, a national imperative, not simply a political need. Doing so called for marrying the older quest for security and solidarity with the newer emphasis on autonomy and self-expression. This was the key to reviving an optimism of the American spirit that led a nation to embrace a candidate who campaigned on hope—and that, in truth, has always been at the heart of a successful progressive politics in the United States. There has never been a successful pessimistic progressivism.

In his intuitive way, Franklin D. Roosevelt always understood the need to speak simultaneously to the practical and the aspirational sides of his fellow citizens. "I still believe in ideals," he said in his September 30, 1934, "fireside chat." "I am not for a return to that definition of liberty under which for many years, a free people were being gradually regimented into the service of the privileged few. I prefer, and I am sure you prefer, that broader definition of liberty under which we are moving forward to greater freedom, to greater security for the average man than he has ever known before in the history of America."

Freedom, security, and the American dream: Middle American politics were rooted in these things in 1934. They still are. Obama is, in so many ways, an entirely new sort of American leader. But he is also waging many of the same battles that Roosevelt did, and he is searching still for Roosevelt's political magic, his galvanizing rhetoric, and his capacity to pick and win the right fights.

Notes

1. Edison Research 2008.
2. Edison Research 2010.
3. Teixeira, Ruy, and John Halpin 2010.

4. Ibid.
5. Edison Research 2010.
6. *New York Times* 2010.
7. Dionne, E. J. Jr. 2010.
8. Edison Research 2010.
9. Fowler 2008.
10. Zeleny 2008.
11. *Citizens United v. Federal Election Commission* 2010.
12. Teixeira and Halpin 2010.
13. Reagan 1985.
14. Blanton 2010.
15. *Pew Research Center* 2009.
16. Gerstle 2010.
17. Caldwell 2010.
18. Skocpol 2011.
19. Franke-Ruta 2006.

References

Blanton, Dana. "Fox News Poll: 62 Percent Think U.S. Is on the Decline." *Foxnews.com*, July 30, 2010. (http://www.foxnews.com/us/2010/07/30/fox-news-poll-percent-think-decline/), accessed April 11, 2011.

Caldwell, Christopher. "Bush's Weak Tea for the Right." *The Financial Times*, November 13, 2010, 7.

Citizens United v. Federal Election Commission, 130 U.S. 876 (2010).

Dionne, E. J. Jr. "Can Democrats Step It Up?" *Washington Post*, December 6, 2010, regional ed.: A23.

Edison Research. 2008. National Exit Poll of 2008 U.S. General Election (as reported by CNN). (http://www.cnn.com/ELECTION/2008/results/polls/#USP00p1), accessed April 17, 2011.

Edison Research. 2010. National Exit Poll of 2010 U.S. General Election (as reported by CNN). (http://www.cnn.com/ELECTION/2010/results/polls/#USH00p1), accessed April 17, 2011.

Franke-Ruta, Garance. "Remapping the Culture Debate." *The American Prospect*, February 2006, 38.

Fowler, Mayhill. "Obama: No Surprise That Hard-Pressed Pennsylvanians Turn Bitter."

Gerstle, Gary. "Minorities, Multiculturalism, and the Presidency of George W. Bush." *The Presidency of George W. Bush: A First Historical Assessment*, ed. Julian E. Zelizer. Princeton, NJ: Princeton University Press, 2010, pp. 252–281.

Huffington Post, April 11, 2008. (http://www.huffingtonpost.com/mayhill-fowler/obama-no-surprise-that-ha_b_96188.html), accessed April 11, 2011.

New York Times. 2010. "2010 Midterm Election Results House Big Board." (http://
   elections.nytimes.com/2010/results/house/big-board), accessed April 17, 2010.
Pew Research Center. 2009. "U.S. Seen as Less Important, China as More Powerful."
   December 3. (http://pewresearch.org/pubs/1428/america-seen-less-important-
   china-more-powerful-isolationist-sentiment-surges115), accessed April 17, 2010.
Reagan, Ronald. (1985) "Second Inaugural Address." 1985 Presidential Inaugural. Cap-
   itol Building, Washington, DC, January 20.
Skocpol, Theda. "Time for National Greatness Liberalism." *The American Prospect*,
   March 2011.
Teixeira, Ruy, and John Halpin. 2010. "Election Results Fueled by Job Crisis and Voter
   Apathy Among Progressives." *Center for American Progress*, November 4.
Zeleny, Jeff. "Opponents Call Obama Remarks 'Out of Touch.'" *New York Times*,
   April 12, 2008, late ed.: A15.

7

Barack Obama
and the Angry Left

THE FIGHT FOR PROGRESSIVE REALISM

Lawrence R. Jacobs[1]

BARACK OBAMA IS the most productive liberal president in at least a generation. But his tenure in office has been met with seething disappointment from many liberals and by the slackening of their support for his agenda, and for Democratic Party causes generally.

Conservative commentators and politicians understandably recoiled at the expansion of government; some abandoned principled opposition to embrace rhetorically over-heated charges of government "takeovers" and "death panels." As the conservative outcry is unsurprising, the persistent hostility of liberals to the most liberal president in at least a generation does raise a consequential puzzle about the Obama presidency and contemporary American politics.

The angry Left emerged soon after the 2008 election to savage Obama's selection of his cabinet as posers who would—as William Greider put it— "sustain the failing policies of George W. Bush." Obama's 2009 stimulus and campaigns to pass health and financial reforms elicited incessant complaints about his lack of toughness to face down recalcitrant members of Congress (including Democrats) and well-funded lobbyists, his preoccupation with insider details at the expense of providing sustained passionate public leadership, and his delusional hope in bipartisanship that frittered away valuable time and policy opportunities.[2] Senator Bernie Sanders stirred talk in late 2010 of an extraordinary confrontation with a sitting president—launching a primary challenge after the Democrats' midterm losses when Obama won an extension of long-term unemployment benefits and other Democratic priorities in exchange for accepting Republican demands for a two-year continuation of Bush's tax cuts for the affluent. Attacks from the Left on the most progressive policy shift in generations provoked complaints from the White House—Press Secretary Robert Gibbs sarcastically recommended that leftist critics be "drug tested"[3] while the President searingly lambasted them as "sanctimonious" and as locked into "purist position[s]" that assured that "we will never get anything done."[4]

Accommodation in the service of expanding government services is, of course, not unusual. The most statist health reform by an affluent democracy—the Labour Government's passage of the National Health Service in 1946—acknowledged the vociferous demands of general practitioners and specialists by allowing private practice to continue (albeit on a reduced scale).[5] A similar pattern is apparent in other countries that expanded organized social provision; indeed, it might be described as characteristic.

In Labour's Britain, as in Obama's America, the Left blasted lead government reformers, in part, because the compromises were negotiated with reviled rivals and distrusted moderates. But the American Left's ferocious backlash against Obama's concessions to business, the affluent, and Republicans is different from the dissent seen in other countries or in the past in the United States. The American Left's lack of realism results from the comparatively steep decline in unions and other groups experienced with tactical alliances and from the rising influence of political activists who are guided by hierarchical managerial training rather than federated organizational skills and are primarily animated by moralistic commitments to ideas rather than to advancing the material interests of Middle America and lower-income people.[6] These historic shifts in political organizing have been accentuated by new media and online groups that fan suspicions of betrayal to drive audience shares among targeted demographics and boost membership: MoveOn.org and affiliated blogs and MSNBC's former anchor Keith Olbermann persistently mocked compromises as capitulations and as evidence of treachery[7]

The leftist backlash against Obama expresses an enduring and consequential understanding of U.S. history as defined by bifurcated and unbridgeable conflicts that pit the rich and organized against the often diffuse middle and working strata. Obama's election coincided with the revival of "progressive historiography" that both helpfully reveals the underappreciated advantages of the super-rich and corporate interests and embraces a view of practical politics that treats accommodation of powerful organized interests as inherently flawed and corrupting rather than as a necessary approach to enact policy changes that deliver meaningful (if compromised) benefits to Middle America and initiates new (if contested) progressive paths for future institutional development.

The anger of the Left raises probing questions about the nature of Democratic reforms and the historic significance of the Obama presidency. Do Obama's accommodations to established interests and institutional obstacles on health and finance reform, for instance, corrupt Democratic policy aspirations and manifest the dominance of the ruling clique? Or, do they accomplish immediate progress toward progressive policy goals and open up new avenues for future progress?

This chapter traces the leftist backlash against Obama to the resurgence of progressive historiography. It credits this revival with spotlighting pervasive structural features of American politics that condition and constrain—as this book argues—the actions of any president, including Obama. But, contemporary progressive historiography both over-determines American politics by singling out the super rich and corporate interests, and neglects internal divisions among these interests and countervailing pressures and coalitions that produce significant and, in certain cases, landmark reforms or fends off extreme conservative agendas. The reaction of the angry Left to Obama fundamentally misunderstands the realistic project of politics and stands in stark contrast to the tradition of consequential and cumulative reform stretching back to the New Deal—progressive realism. As the second half of this chapter suggests, generations of lawmakers and policy specialists have expanded economic opportunities and protections against the risk of insecurity by strategically accommodating the inescapable everyday workings of American institutions and politics. The essay argues that Obama's record squarely fits within the tradition of progressive realism. It achieved landmark reforms that have delivered immediate benefits and recast future political possibilities during his first two years in office and then responded to the conservative resurgence by blunting its sharpest attacks during his second two years.

I. Winners and Losers in American History

Writing amidst the Progressive Era, Charles Beard's 1913 account of the U.S. Constitution as designed by and for commercial interests, the landed aristocracy, and the rich inaugurated a reinterpretation of American history as defined by three features (also see Woodward 1951). The first tenet of the progressive account was the unbridgeable differences between classes, economic interests, and the organized groups representing them. Coalitions of diverse groups based on shared policy interests were inconceivable. The second facet was the unavoidable conflict that defined American politics and produced mutually exclusive winners and losers in titanic struggles—robber barons or the people, the rich or the poor. Besieged by mortal struggle, compromise that delivered tangible immediate benefits and opened new future opportunities was inconceivable and possibly betrayed principle. Third, American history presented a sharp morality tale between good and evil—between those who worked to improve social, economic, and political inclusion and those who slavishly advanced narrow economic advantage. Even negotiation with rival factions signaled moral weakness and unreliability.

The most sophisticated recent form of progressive historiography is the aptly titled *Winner Take All Politics*, by Jacob Hacker and Paul Pierson (2010). Its take-off point is the wide and growing income and wealth disparity between the super-rich one percent and the rest of America. With economic inequality defining insuperable differences among income groups and the groups that represent the rich and organized, Obama's compromises with stakeholders—from health care providers, suppliers, and insurers to financial industry advocates—display gullibility and resulted in unnecessary and harmful give-aways to unalterably hostile interests.

Winner Take All Politics attributes the reconcentration of wealth and income to American politics and, specifically, to "organized combat," which supplants the more commonly offered accounts based on the educational premium for higher skilled workers compared to the less-well-educated, technological change, and trade. As unions and other organizations traditionally empowering the less affluent lost sway since the 1970s, the super-rich and corporate businesses used (according to Hacker and Pierson's incisive analysis) campaign contributions, lobbying, and other forms of organizational might to exert "political pressure for less egalitarian policy outcomes" and generate enormous gains. In the latest iteration of America's titanic struggle among economic interests, middle- and working-class America were vanquished by the "organized interests [of business and the affluent who] were highly motivated, mobilized, and involved in [making government policy]."[8] The already advantaged compounded their influence by targeting their organizational and financial resources on institutional structures that routinely block threatening legislation (through presidential vetoes or unprecedented use of the Senate filibuster) even as markets widened inequality. Hacker[9] reports that the overall effect is policy "drift" that boosts the risks of economic insecurity.

Ed Asner spoke for many on the Left when he blasted Obama in February 2011 as "representing corporations more than people." Obama's recurrent accommodations to stakeholders and institutionally empowered legislators produced (in the view of Left critics) an uninterrupted string of capitulations—from the stimulus in early 2009 and health and finance reform during 2010 to the deals with Republicans during the 2010 lame-duck session and in 2011 to extend the debt limit and avert a government shutdown. Rather than ferociously fighting for the public option and independent consumer protection as the respective backbones of health and financial reform, Obama was chastised for handing out sweetheart deals to pharmaceutical and medical device suppliers, surrendering key provisions of financial reform to mitigate opposition from Wall Street and its Democratic congressional allies, and excessively compromising with House Republicans in 2011. For the Left, Obama's policies were abject failures and missed opportunities, demonstrating the unrelenting conservative bias in American politics even under the most propitious political circumstances in decades.

Winner Take All Politics also brims over with the moral outrage that runs through the work of Beard and other progressive-era commentators. The shift in the "balance of organized economic interests in favor of employers and the affluent" allowed greed to triumph over fairness and opportunity for the majority of Americans. The sharp expansion of economic inequality curtailed life circumstances, opportunities for economic security, and the equal voice in a democracy dominated by money and the advantages it buys. By extension, Obama's failure to clearly and uncompromisingly reject Winner Take All Politics was blamed for the disaffection of his initial supporters and their decision to sit out the 2010 election or to vote for Republicans. Tellingly, 6 out of 10 Americans in a May 2010 CBS News poll complained that Wall Street exerted too much influence on the Obama administration, and a third concluded that it was more concerned about the interests of large corporations than those of average Americans.

II. Progressive Realism: Reform Through Accommodation and Institutional Accumulation

Progressive historiography helpfully spotlights the disproportionate gains and influence of the most affluent and best organized, pinpointing a critical source of the enduring conservative bias in American policy discourse and government decisions. One of the valuable contributions of *Winner Take All Politics* is that it properly traces the thrust of Obama's policy decisions to these impersonal forces rather than to often insignificant personalistic traits (from "courage" to timidity) that preoccupy pundits and other commentators, as suggested in the opening chapter of this volume.

But progressive historiography's moralism and teleology of economic conflict blinders its analysis and fuels one of the defining puzzles of contemporary American politics—searing leftist disenchantment with the most significant advancement of progressive domestic policy goals in generations. Clear-eyed analysis challenges progressive fundamentalists on two counts: dominant economic groups are rarely able to "run the show" (as Hacker and Pierson suggest) and, partly as a result, America's diffuse publics and organized progressive forces are able, under certain circumstances, to foster new government initiatives (even if small or incomplete) that immediately expand economic opportunity and initiate future paths of institutional development. Analyzed in terms of concrete, observable policy change, Obama's record to date stitches a tapestry of decidedly progressive—though far from uniform— hues: corporate business and the rich won substantial concessions but also suffered setbacks and outright repudiations as Democrats established new programs or expanded existing ones that advanced progressive objectives (if incompletely) and started new developmental paths.

Sharing the Show

The super-rich and large business enjoy privileged access and disproportionate influence on government, but it takes a leap of logic and faith to conclude that this is tantamount to "run[ning] the show." Uncertainty and divisions regularly split corporate business and the super-rich; the effect is to diminish the ruling block's power as it is unable to provide a singular direction or to prevent strategically astute coalition building that raids its ranks. Indeed, it has long been suggested that the government's main function is to "organize" the dominant economic interests precisely in order to counteract its propensity to splinter.[10]

Although President George W. Bush's tax policies advantaged the super-rich and business, the 2008 election publicly revealed splits over the economic payoff of military adventures abroad and the preeminent focus on tax cuts, helping to fuel Obama's large lead over John McCain in fund-raising on Wall Street. Big moneyed support for Obama illustrates the uncertainty over how particular policies impact the diversity of interests among the most affluent; it exposes the trap of reasoning backward from economic interest—inferring, for instance, from accelerated economic inequality the ruling block's singular preference for continued sharp tax cuts. Another hurdle complicating simple efforts to rule is the imperfection of information, as generations of experience and of research have demonstrated; Lehman Brothers and Bear Stearns supported financial deregulation to advance what seemed like their best interests, only to later discover that it opened a trapdoor to their demise.

The super-rich and corporate America rarely come together as a unitary actor because distinct interests, beliefs, and organization invariably fuel divisions. Private insurers and small businesses tied their interests to defeating health care reform in 2009–2010, while major pharmaceutical and medical device industries and affluent medical providers understood their future prosperity as tied to passing the Affordable Care Act (ACA). Even after private insurers contributed heavily to Republican campaigns in 2010 that promised to repeal ACA, the approaching prospect of huge government subsidies may well prompt a shift in insurer preferences toward opposing the repeal of health reform in order to advance their economic interests.

The Left's fiery criticism of Obama and the Democrats stemmed in part from the financial cost of concessions. But, of course, concessions are instrumental bargains; the proper issue is not simply their cost in the abstract but rather also the value received in return. In the case of ACA, new sources of revenue for providers and insurers were exchanged for support in making historic progress toward achieving a century-long goal of national health insurance: ACA quickly aids tens of millions with medical care access through some of the most redistributive taxes passed in half a century, it begins a process that creates a radically new platform for the next reformist episode, and the initial stakeholder gains are targeted in the future as cost-control mechanisms are implemented.[11]

Conservative reactions to Republican concessions to achieve their policy goals offer an instructive counterpoint—nearly unanimous celebration of Reagan and Bush tax cuts, even though each trimmed their scope and duration in order to secure necessary congressional votes. Conservatives focus on what they achieved; progressives often focus on what was conceded.

The fundamental error of progressive historiography and harsh Obama critics is, first, to equate accommodation to advance legislation with betrayal and, second, to neglect its leverage as a tool for splitting elements of the ruling block and building majority coalitions. *The persistent tendency to link Obama's compromises with failure and betrayal reveals not devotion to principle but an immature understanding of the real workings of politics and an ahistorical conception of progress.* This mind-set leads to the nihilistic conclusion that legislatively necessary and often significant concessions besmirch the New Deal's Social Security and the Great Society's Medicare and Civil Rights legislation, along with Britain's 1945 National Health Service bill and most of the founding laws that started the welfare state in affluent democracies. FDR and his allies won passage of Social Security, for example, by agreeing to severely limit its scope and eligibility in order to secure support from Southern Democratic conservatives; future lawmakers from both parties built on the (incomplete) beginning to overcome the initial limitations and to create the inclusive program of today.

In short, concessions to split stakeholders and broaden coalitions are the leitmotif of the legislative breakthroughs that historically produced the inclusive economic and social welfare policies that American progressives proclaim as their aim.

Operational Liberalism

Obama's vociferous critics from the Left harbor a myopic and simplistic understanding of America's system of governance. They often attribute the failure to enact single-payer health care financing or bank nationalization to weakness in the President's determination, political skill, or devotion to progressive principles. Denouncing Obama as a "coward" for folding to Wall Street on financial regulation, Ralph Nader also attacked the President's resistance to single payer as evidence that "health insurance and drug corporations have a hammerlock on Washington [and on Obama]."[12] In a remarkable display of willful amnesia about the catechism of separate branches competitively sharing powers, Obama was expected to demand and achieve compliance from Congress through fiat, displays of fiery will, or rhetorical flourish that swept away two centuries of deadlock and delay. The reality, known to studious undergraduate students, is that even under the opportune circumstances of unified party government, Obama was unavoidably constrained by the need to secure—without the support of a single Republican and amidst significant Democratic divisions—a majority of the House of Representatives and 60 votes in the Senate to overcome the unprecedented use of the filibuster.

The Left's reaction to Obama stands in stark contrast to the progressive realism that was pioneered by Franklin Roosevelt and Lyndon Johnson and practiced by generations of reformers and devoted technocrats—such as Wilbur Cohen, who helped create Medicare.[13] The pragmatic, institutional approach to reform pursued two general strategies that calibrated legislative initiatives to political realities and the dynamics of institutional development: periods of divided government (including divisive periods of Reagan's presidency) generated careful policies to expand on established inclusive government initiatives like Social Security and Medicare, while periods of unified Democratic government gave rise to policies that focused on promoting new paths of development, even if legislative resistance required limited beginnings.

Progressive realism is consistent with the insights of a growing body of research that studies institutional change over time and the political significance of policy. Rather than politics (voting, lobbying, and other forms of participation) driving policy, established social welfare programs also form the "environment" for politics: policies from old age pensions to Medicare have self-reinforcing political effects that make them durable and prone to expansion—evoking new political collective identities, inspiring a sense of efficacy, and empowering previously marginalized or unengaged groups of citizens.[14] Careful research shows that programs for G.I. benefits and Social Security established in the decades after World War II powerfully impacted the political engagement of their recipients—catapulting them from normal patterns of uneven engagement to aggressive and effective advocates who voted and engaged politically at higher levels than they had previously or that other Americans exhibited.[15]

Institutional development of inclusive social welfare programs not only generated the support and political engagement of beneficiaries but also dovetailed with patterns of general public opinion. Although Americans are uneasy with government in the abstract, majorities in both parties and across income groups do favor concrete government programs that deliver needed help with everyday operations from education to managing the risks of low income in old age, unemployment, and illness. The philosophically conservative side of American culture is supplemented by a sturdy and perhaps expanding predisposition to "operational liberalism"—a pragmatic acceptance of specific government responsibilities in cases of clear need.[16]

Progressive realism has been effective over the past four decades in expanding and protecting established inclusive government initiatives, even as conservative, market-oriented ideas and commitments dominated policy discourse and government decisions on tax policy and other fiscal issues. Focusing on concrete, salient challenges facing everyday constituents, members of Congress, at times from both parties, and with the acquiescence (if not support) of Republican administrations indexed Social Security to the cost of living (under Richard Nixon) to prevent inflation from continuing to immiserate seniors; expanded Medicaid to millions of mothers and children during the Reagan presidency through seemingly technical changes promoted by Democratic Congressman Henry Waxman and child activist Sara Rosenbaum; created and expanded the state health insurance program to cover about 7 million poor children as part of a bipartisan coalition spearheaded by Senators Ted Kennedy and Orrin Hatch; and extended Medicare at Bush's insistence to partially cover the costs of pharmaceutical drugs—a new entitlement that ACA liberalized. Republicans often viewed these efforts in non-controversial, prag-matic terms as necessary, concrete, and focused responses to real-world prob-lems affecting their constituents through no fault of their own.

As impressive, major initiatives by conservative leaders to dismantle the bulwark of America's organized social provisions were repeatedly defeated as even Republican legislators refrained from adding their support. Reagan pro-posed and then backed away from trying to make Social Security voluntary; Bush's vigorous campaign to partially privatize Social Security in 2005 failed to prompt Republican congressional leaders to even give it vote in Com-mittee or on the floor; and Speaker Newt Gingrich's proposal to reduce Medicare and convert it into a voucher program fell flat, but not without re-viving Bill Clinton's political fortunes in 1995.

The expansions and protections of government operations during conser-vative eras were, of course, partial themes in a policy agenda dominated by cutting taxes and reducing government responsibility for counteracting the growth in economic inequality and for assisting the poor, as epitomized by punitive welfare reform. Nonetheless, the steady—if selective—accretion and effective defense of government social welfare operations stand out precisely because of their success in defying the tide of conservatism—a source of intense frustration to conservative activists and commentators who rail at Republican officeholders like George Bush as "impostors."[17] This staying power and defiance of even determined conservatism underscores one of the strengths of progressive realism—its reliance on pragmatic, at times non-con-troversial emendations of existing programs, which cultivate aware and de-voted beneficiaries who are dispersed throughout the country (including in Republican congressional districts). Bush displays the allure of progressive realism—even as he passed historic tax cuts, electoral pragmatism prompted him to substantially expand Medicare and erect part of the institutional lat-ticework for much wider Democratic health reform in 2010.

Progressive realism is most commonly practiced in the obscure work of lawmakers, civil servants, and advocates, but it occasionally bursts into public view, igniting fiery ideological conflict not only with conservatives but with the Left. A core of the Left's dispute with Obama relates to historical institu-tionalism and its insufficient appreciation for consequential, low-salient ex-pansions in the future. Leftist critics are correct that the structure of the beginnings are critical but not more critical than beginning itself—initiating programs that open new developmental paths for later emendation.

Progressive realism's historical institutionalism defines the dispute between Obama's policies and the Left on a host of issues from reform of health care and finance to higher education funding: the Left focuses on the areas of incompletion, imperfection, and compromise in what they see as discrete, fixed-policy products. Obama and his allies focus instead on extending immediate benefits to tens of millions and, as important, on the starting of new (even if partial) programs that they expect to be expanded over time, much as has been the case with Social Security and Medicare.

Leftist critics both undervalue the substantial impact of compromised legislation and overlook the prospective opportunities—indeed, their proposal to expand Medicare from seniors to all Americans as a way to create single-payer financing or public option implicitly acknowledges progressive realism as it demonstrates how an earlier compromised legislative breakthrough (Medicare) prefigures future health reform opportunities. The Affordable Care Act and its invitation to states to start single payer and public option plans may well model new choices for future reformers, as Vermont and other states capitalize on new discretion for liberal ends.

III. What Conservatives Teach

It is telling to compare the Left's knee-jerk criticism of Obama with the institutionally sophisticated reaction of conservatives. While the Left bemoaned what Obama failed to achieve and some even favored repealing ACA in the unrealistic hope of enacting something more liberal, conservatives quickly launched a judicial and electoral countermobilization to retake Washington and to stop health reform as soon as possible. Once implemented, they reasoned, it would become more difficult to to remove new benefits—to seniors for drug coverage, parents for insurance coverage of their children, and subsidies to Middle America for insurance. The political effects of these new benefits may include building program support and creating new constituencies that are available to be mobilized in future elections and policy debates.

The durability of progressive realism's record compares favorably with conservatism over the past three decades. Although some legislators recently elected with Tea Party support challenge Republicans to go further, there is still wide agreement among conservatives on what they achieved. Reagan is credited with inaugurating an unusual period of conservative dominance in which policy prescriptions and government decisions by Republican and certain Democrats focused on making dramatic reductions in taxes and government spending. But, despite a string of conservative presidents and new Republican congressional majorities in the House and resurgences in the Senate, the monumental conservative accomplishment (tax cuts) proved politically vulnerable to reversal, as both Clinton and Obama demonstrated, or to simple expiration, as in the case of Bush's tax cuts, which are on temporary life support—they were initially passed under budget reconciliation rules that stipulated termination after a decade.

As the marginal tax rate and taxes on capital gains have gyrated over the past three decades despite the electoral success of conservatism, progressive realism boasts a record of stability and expansion in critical respects. It defeated counterattacks on Social Security and Medicare, expanded existing programs under conservative governments, and launched major new paths that prepare the way for future reforms of health care, higher education funding, and perhaps finance.

Conservatives are painfully aware of the fragility of their gains and the enduring threat of progressive realism. What remains striking is that the most fervent rhetorical advocates of progressive aims appear unaware of the shifting institutional ground, and their backlash is having consequences. The harsh leftist criticism of the new health law as fatally inadequate contributed, according to Kaiser Family Foundation polls, to support for repeal by about a quarter of Democrats and by 1 out of 7 Americans who have been persuaded that the reform does not go far enough perhaps toward a single-payer system. No wonder the landmark law lacks the vocal and intense support to match the conservative backlash. Contributors to Obama's 2008 campaign are prepared to abstain from giving to his reelection following his deal with Republicans during the lame duck session, according to a Survey-USA survey in December 2010. And, the one-third fall in turnout in 2010 came, in part, from liberals and other Democratic voters in 2008. Anger at the most liberal president in at least half a century may well continue to induce many Democrats to sit out the 2012 presidential elections and contribute to a Republican mandate to roll back the most significant progressive gains in at least a generation.

One of the enduring puzzles of the Obama presidency is the juxtaposition between the Left's ire, on the one hand, and Democratic passage of historic progressive reform and Obama's blunting of the most aggressive conservative onslaught in a generation, on the other hand. The answer lies in Obama's style of leadership, the structural constraints on his actions, and the historic evolution of political organizing and communications. The result may well produce one of the oddest paradoxes in contemporary American politics—Obama's liberalism may give rise to conservative success that is fueled by oddly parallel backlashes by the Left and the Right.

Notes

1. I would like to acknowledge helpful comments from Desmond King, Tom Hamburger, Suzanne Mettler, and Sid Milkis. Responsibility for the views and analyses here are fully mine.
2. Balz 2009; Krugman 2009, 2010.
3. Youngman 2010.
4. Bacon and Wilson 2010.
5. Jacobs 1993.
6. Gottschalk 2000; Berry 1999; Skocpol 2003.
7. Shapiro and Jacobs 2011.
8. Hacker and Pierson 2010, 4, 21, 35–37, 47–49.
9. Hacker 2004.
10. Poulantzas 1978; Lindblom 1977.
11. Jacobs and Skocpol 2010.
12. Nader 2011; Nader 2009.
13. I focus on the tradition of progressive realism that was fashioned by lawmakers and policy specialists. A range of quite distinct scholarly critiques of progressive historiography also developed beginning in the 1940s; limited space does not permit this chapter to rehash this well-known and complicated series of debates (c.g., White 2008).
14. Pierson 2000; Mettler and Soss 2004.
15. Campbell 2003; Mettler 2005.
16. Jacobs and Shapiro 1999; Page and Jacobs 2009.
17. Bartlett 2006.

References

Bacon, Perry, Jr., and Scott Wilson. 2010. "Obama Calls on Liberal Critics to Learn to Compromise." *Washington Post*, December 7.

Balz, Dan. 2009. "Concern, Doubts from the Left on Obama's Health-Care Plan." *Washington Post*, August 23.

Bartlett, Bruce. 2006. *Impostor: How George W. Bush Bankrupted America and Betrayed the Reagan Legacy*. New York: Doubleday.

Beard, Charles. 1913. *An Economic Interpretation of the Constitution of the United States*.

Berry, Jeffrey. 1999. *The New Liberalism: The Rising Power of Citizen Groups*. Washington, DC: Brookings Institution.

Campbell, Andrea. 2003. *How Policies Make Citizens: Senior Political Activism and the American Welfare State*. Princeton, NJ: Princeton University Press.

CBS News Survey. 2010. "Where America Stands." May 20–24. (http://www.cbsnews.com/htdocs/pdf/poll_052510.pdf).

Gottschalk, Marie. 2000. *The Shadow Welfare State: Labor, Business, and the Politics of Health Care in the United States*. Ithaca, NY: Cornell University Press.

Greider, William. 2008. *The Nation*, November 25.

Hacker, Jacobs, and Paul Pierson. 2010. *Winner-Take-All Politics: How Washington Made the Rich Richer—and Turned Its Back on the Middle Class*. New York: Simon & Schuster.

Hacker, Jacob. 2004. "Privatizing Risk Without Privatizing the Welfare State: The Hidden Politics of Social Policy Retrenchment in the United States." *American Political Science Review* 98(2): 243–260.

Jacobs, Lawrence. 1993. *The Health of Nations: Public Opinion and the Making of Health Policy in the U.S. and Britain*. Ithaca, NY: Cornell University Press.

Jacobs, Lawrence, and Robert Y. Shapiro. 1999. "Pragmatic Liberalism Meets Philosophical Conservatism: Americans' Reactions to Managed Care." *Journal of Health Policy, Politics and Law* 24 (Fall): 5–16.

Jacobs, Lawrence, and Theda Skocpol. 2010. *Health Care Reform and American Politics: What Everyone Needs to Know*. New York: Oxford University Press.

Krugman, Paul. 2009. "Not Enough Audacity." *New York Times*, June 25.

Krugman, Paul. 2010. "Freezing Out Hope." *New York Times*, December 2.

Mettler, Suzanne. 2005. *Soldiers to Citizens: The G.I. Bill and the Making of the Greatest Generation*. New York: Oxford University Press.

Mettler, Suzanne, and Joe Soss. 2004. "The Consequences of Public Policy for Democratic Citizenship: Bridging Policy Studies and Mass Politics." *Perspectives on Politics* 2: 55–73.

Nader, Ralph. 2009. "Nader: Obama's Flip-Flop on Single Payer." Single Payer Action. June 17. (http://www.singlepayeraction.org/blog/?p=1011).

Nader, Ralph. 2011. Interview with Amy Goodman, Democracy Now, July 19. (http://www.democracynow.org/2011/7/19/ralph_nader_obama_is_a_political).

Page, Benjamin, and Lawrence Jacobs. 2009. *Class War? What Americans Really Think about Economic Inequality*. Chicago: University of Chicago Press.

Pierson, Paul. 2000. "Increasing Returns, Path Dependence, and the Study of Politics," *American Political Science Review* 94(2): 251–267.

Shapiro, Robert, and Lawrence R. Jacobs, eds, 2011. *The Oxford Handbook of American Public Opinion and the Media*. Oxford: Oxford University Press.

Skocpol, Theda. 2003. *Diminished Democracy: From Membership to Management in American*. Norman: University of Oklahoma Press.

SurveyUSA. December 6, 2010. (http://voices.washingtonpost.com/plum-line/PollMemo_FINAL_120710.pdf).

White, Richard. 2008. "A Commemoration and a Historical Mediation." *Journal of American History* 94: 1073–1081.

Woodward, C. Vann. 1951. *Origins of the New South, 1877–1913*. Baton Rouge: Louisiana State University Press.

Youngman, Sam. 2010. "White House Unloads Anger over Criticism from 'Professional Left.'" *The Hill*, August 10.

Index

Printed in the USA/Agawam, MA
April 18, 2012

565389.026